THE COMEDIES OF
TERENCE

Distinguished as a poet, novelist, essayist, critic, classicist, and historian, Robert Graves has written more than ninety books, among them the popular historical novel *I, Claudius;* his autobiography, *Goodbye to All That,* which has become a modern classic; and *The Anger of Achilles,* a translation of the *Iliad.* His greatest interest lies in poetry, which he has been writing since the age of fifteen. His *Collected Poems* won him both the Gold Medal of the National Poetry Society of America and the Foyle Award in England.

Born in England in 1895, educated at Oxford, Robert Graves served as a captain with the Royal Welch Fusiliers in the First World War, and for a time occupied the Chair of English Literature at the Royal University, Cairo, Egypt. Since 1929, he has been living in Majorca, Spain, with his wife and children, in a stone house overlooking the sea.

Recently he has been elected Professor of Poetry at Oxford University.

THE COMEDIES OF
TERENCE

Edited, with a Foreword, by

ROBERT GRAVES

ANCHOR BOOKS

DOUBLEDAY & COMPANY, INC.

GARDEN CITY, NEW YORK

1962

Library of Congress Catalog Card Number 62–10465
Copyright © 1962 by Roturman S.A.
All Rights Reserved
Printed in the United States of America
First Edition

CONTENTS

FOREWORD

'Terence' (Publius Terentius Afer), born in 185 B.C. and probably a Berber, was bought as a boy at the Carthaginian slave market by a Roman Senator, one Terentius Lucanus, who seems to have fallen in love with his slim, dark beauty and keen intelligence. Lucanus educated him well at Rome; and eventually freed him. Terence's talents and good looks soon attracted the notice of Scipio Africanus the Younger, Gaius Laelius and Furius Philus, who were his close contemporaries and the wealthiest men of the day. With their encouragement he began to translate Classical Greek comedies and adapt them to the Roman stage, as Plautus, Caecilius and others had done before him. Terence's *Fair Andrian,* a combination of Menander's two plays *Andria* and *Perinthia,* was successfully staged at the Megalensian Games of 166 B.C.; and in 161 B.C., his *Eunuch,* based on Menander's play of the same title, made the greatest hit in Roman theatrical history by winning an immediate *encore*—and earned him the record fee of 8000 sesterces, or eighty gold pieces.

His aristocratic friends presently let it be rumoured that, though their high rank forbade any association with the writing trade, they were the real authors of his plays; and Terence was in no position to contradict this. They seem, however, to have soon tired of him; and at the age of twenty-five he sailed for Greece, ostensibly to improve his education. He died at Arcadian Stymphalus in 159 B.C.; his health undermined by news that the ship in which he had sent his advance baggage, containing a number of new plays, was lost at sea.

Terence, like Plautus, wrote a pure Latin, and closely followed the rule of the Dramatic Unities first framed by Aristotle, and since accepted both in Greece and Rome. These comprised unity of action, meaning that sub-plots must materially assist the development of the main plot; unity of time, which restricted all action to the period of a single day; and the unity of place, which allowed no shifting of scene. Moreover, because the Roman audience was slow-witted, each new character had to announce his business or be announced by some other character as soon as he entered: thus everyone knew not only his name and position, but what part of the plot he had to fulfil, why he came, from where, and with what purpose, and all that went on in his mind. This convention made performances even more artificial.

We cannot tell precisely what liberties Terence took with his Romanization of Menander, whose reputation had for two centuries stood as high as Homer's: because *The Dour Man*, the single complete play still extant, is not one from which Terence borrowed. We can only compare him with Plautus, who handled farcical situations in a livelier way, was less careful of the Unities, and had a greater command of language. Terence set himself a standard of literary perfection and artistic restraint which so commended him to scholars and grammarians that his collected plays were used as a text-book in Roman schools and, like Virgil's poems, remained part of the curriculum even when the Christian Church reformed national education. It is regrettable that the very terseness of his Latin makes an accurate modern English rendering read drily and flatly; as I have found to my disappointment. Nor can we blame Terence for this. He knew his trade, being a master of the dramatic surprise, and though the turnings and twistings of the plot provide admirable theatre, the Romans, unlike (say) the Elizabethans, preferred penny plain to twopence coloured in dramatic entertainment. His plays continued to be staged before appreciative audiences for three hundred years.

A revival of Terence in English must, I believe, be based

on the translation made in 1689, with fascinating vigour, by a young Cambridge student Laurence Echard (1670–1730)— later Dr Echard, Prebendary of Lincoln, Archdeacon of Stow, and author of a well-known *History of England*. Echard firmly held to the Aristotelian Unities, which had been revived by the French dramatists of his day, and frowned on the wild, un-Classical English drama. 'The non-observance of dramatic rules,' he observes in his Preface, 'has occasioned the miscarriage of so many excellent geniuses of ours, particularly that of the Immortal Shakespeare.' Yet he saw that Terence's plays could be made vastly more readable if dressed up in the language of Restoration Comedy. He wrote that Terence's bluntness of speech was unsuited to the manners and gallantry of his own times, but that he had taken it upon himself to correct this defect and, in some places, had lent a scene greater humour than it originally contained—'but all the while we have kept so nigh to our author's sense and design that we hope our additions can never be justly called a fault.' Even so he despaired of getting the popular London theatres to stage the plays, 'because,' he wrote,

> of the difference betwixt the Romans and ourselves in customs, humours, manners and theatres. The Roman plots were too often founded on the exposing of new-born children and their unexpected rescue, or on the buying of mistresses and music-girls. The spectators were pleased to see a covetous old father cheated of a round sum by his slave; to watch the young spark, his son, miserably in want of cash, join with the slave in the intrigue, so that he might get something to stop the mouth of his mistress whom he keeps without the father's knowledge; to find a bragging soldier wheedled or abused by a cunning parasite; to hear a glutton talk of nothing but his belly, and the like. Our plots nowadays turn chiefly upon variety of love intrigues between married couples, ladies very dexterously cuckolding their husbands, gallants in danger upon the same account, with their escape either by witty excuses or hiding themselves in dark holes or closets. We are all for gallantry in conversation and

shouldn't endure the chief lady in the play to be a mute, as Terence makes her. Our amorous sparks love to hear the pretty rogues prate, snap up their gallants and repartee them on all sides. We shouldn't like to have a lady married without knowing whether she gives her consent or no—a custom among the Romans—but would be for hearing all the rare and fine things that lovers can say to each other in the way of courtship.

The fact was that since freedom of speech had been curtailed at Athens even before the death of Aristophanes, Menander's courageous predecessor, and no topical reference could thereafter be safely made to any contemporary event or character, the theatre had been reduced to plots involving certain stock bourgeois types. The debauched young spark, the grave old father, the distressed mother, the confirmed bachelor, the good-natured, expensive courtesan, the parasite, the boastful soldier, the greedy bawd-master, the scheming slave, and an occasional sour old woman . . . All parts were played, as on the Elizabethan stage, by men or boys; but because public morality banned tender love between members of the same sex, Terence could not supply his heroine with a speaking part, even when the plot hinged on the hero's love for her. And the scene (without props or curtain) must always be a street in front of three houses where the principal characters lived.

Difficulties caused by the need for introducing actors who, though visible to the audience, were supposedly invisible to one another, were overcome it seems by use of a *siparium*, or folding screen, which could be interposed between them and which let hidden characters deliver audible asides. Terence, by the way, never allowed the 'stage to grow cold' between Acts, for fear his audience might drift away during intermissions and come struggling back late; or even, as they had done at the *première* of *The Mother-in-Law*, visit the neighbouring Circus to watch a tight-rope act and never come back at all. The division into Acts can therefore be disregarded, though intermissions may have been marked by songs to flute accompaniment, as the title pages suggest.

I have followed Echard's example in not translating Terence's prologues, which are concerned either with begging the audience to behave decently, or with dramatic squabbles which would be of historical interest only if Terence had mentioned names, which he refrained from doing.

Under the early Roman Empire, an enormous increase in the size of the unroofed theatres, and a lack of any contrivance to magnify the sound of actors' voices, or any control on the audience's hubbub, put an unbearable strain on the cast. Only people seated close to the orchestra could follow the turns of an intrigue; those behind had either to know each stock play by heart, or guess what was happening from the actors' miming. To distinguish one character from another, each wore a different-coloured dress: white for an old man, multi-coloured for a young spark, yellow for a courtesan, purple for the rich, red for the poor, a short tunic for a slave, and so on . . . But this was not enough: by the second century A.D., the rival attractions of chariot racing, gladiatorial shows and opera, had killed comedy altogether.

Nevertheless, I can see no reason why *The Eunuch,* for instance, could not be recast as a modern musical—though, of course, by a breach of Terence's cherished Unities—with great success. Meanwhile, let me repeat, if any of his plays are performed in the original, this should be done by gentlemen in periwigs, ladies in jewelled stomachers, and lacqueys of the period fixed by Echard's translation. I follow his English pretty faithfully—the seventh edition (1729), 'revised and corrected by Dr Echard, Sir R. L'Estrange and others'—but whenever he uses contemporary slang now obsolete, and words that no longer preserve their seventeenth-century meaning have substituted clearer language of the same date. Sometimes, also, where he has missed the sense of the Latin, or worked from a corrupt text, I make the necessary amendment.

It is extraordinary that Terence was praised so long by educated Christians for his moral values. How could they have swallowed the heartless, vicious rape of virgins—by the heroes of *The Mother-in-Law* and *The Eunuch*—condoned as pardonable whims of youth? Or (in *The Mother-in-Law* again) the cruelty of a husband who forces his wife to expose her infant daughter, condoned as economic prudence? Or, in *The Eunuch,* the sympathy demanded from the audience for two well-bred young sparks who plan to maintain a courtesan at the expense of a rich soldier whom she cheats?

It was a fascination with the strange forms that popular entertainment takes in different civilizations, which made me choose this editorial task. A close reading of Terence is a fine corrective to any idea that may still be current, about the glory that was Greece and grandeur that was Rome during the Hellenistic period; and an assurance that, in some respects at least, this age is not so morally depraved after all.

R. G.

Deyá, Majorca, Spain.

THE COMEDIES OF
TERENCE

THE FAIR ANDRIAN

A comedy acted at the Feast of Cybele, when M. Fulvius
and M. Glabrio *were Curule Ediles, by the Company of*
L. Ambivius Turpio *and* L. Attilius Prenestae.

Flaccus, *a freedman of* Claudius, *composed the music, which
was performed upon two equal flutes, the one right-handed,
and the other left-handed.*

*It was taken wholly from the Greek, and acted under the
Consulship of* M. Marcellus *and* C. Sulpicius.

A.U.C.587   Before Christ 166

DRAMATIS PERSONAE

SIMO, *an old rich merchant of Athens, very kind and indulgent to his son, but otherwise of a sour disposition*

CHREMES, *his easy-tempered friend and neighbour, father to Philumena*

PAMPHILUS, *Simo's son; very courteous and obedient, but passionately in love with Glycerie, the Fair Andrian*

CHARINUS, *a young gentleman, his friend; in love with Chremes' daughter Philumena*

SOSIA, *Simo's steward*

DROMO, *his footman*

DAVUS, *servant to Pamphilus; a saucy, cunning, intriguer; always helping his master out in his amours, and playing tricks upon Simo*

BYRRHIA, *servant to Charinus*

CRITO, *a stranger from the Isle of Andros; an honest, downright countryman*

GLYCERIE, *the Fair Andrian, mistress to Pamphilus*

MYSIS, *her maid, faithful and careful*

LESBIA, *an old drunken midwife*

NON-SPEAKING PARTS:

ARCHILLIS, *Glycerie's nurse*

SERVANTS

ACT ONE

SCENE: *The street before* SIMO's *door*
TIME: *Morning*

Enter SIMO, SOSIA, *and* SIMO'S SERVANTS, *with provisions brought from the market*

SIMO, *to the* SERVANTS. Lay down your burdens, and begone. But stay, Sosia; I have something to tell you.

Exeunt SERVANTS.

SOSIA. I understand ye, Sir; you'd have me take care of these things, I suppose?

SIMO. Quite another business.

SOSIA. Can my poor skill be further serviceable to you?

SIMO. Nay, there's no need of that skill of yours in the case: only be as faithful and secret as ye have always been, and the business is done.

SOSIA. I wait your pleasure, Sir.

SIMO. I'm sure you can't but know what a fair and easy master I have been to ye, ever since I bought ye as a child. At last, indeed, in requital of your good services, I gave ye your freedom; the most that I could do for ye.

SOSIA. Sir, I'm not forgetful of it.

SIMO. Nor do I repent it.

SOSIA. I'm very glad, Sir, to find ye pleased with any thing I ever did, or can do; and am much obliged to ye for your good opinion. But, with all respect, Sir, this somewhat troubles me; for such a reminding a man of benefit seems to hint that he may be insensible of it. . . . But, in one word, Sir, how can I be of service?

SIMO. I'll tell you: in the first place you are to understand that the business of the wedding is all sham.

SOSIA. Is it so indeed? Then why do ye make so public a pretence of its honesty?

SIMO. I'll tell ye the whole mystery of it, and thereby throw such a light on my son's character and my designs, that you'll immediately see what part you are to act in this business. . . . When I first took him from school, Sosia, I left him a little to himself, to try which way his genius would lead him; which had been hard to know for certain, or indeed to make a fair guess at, whilst he was still under the awe of a master's rod.

SOSIA. Right, Sir.

SIMO. You know how common a thing it is for most young men to give up themselves wholly either to horses, hounds, books, or the like. Now he was not over-fond of any of these, though he took part at all. This I liked well.

SOSIA. Ye had reason, Sir; for not to be too much addicted to any one thing, I take to be the most excellent rule of life.

SIMO. Then for his behaviour, Sosia. He was never ill at ease upon any occasion; nor yet ill-mannered, but took people at their own valuation, never offending them, nor showing himself presumptuous. And I think this was the way to get reputation and friends without envy.

SOSIA. He took a wise course. For as the world goes now, civility is current coin; downrightness buys nothing.

SIMO. Meanwhile, from Andros, about three years ago, comes a woman who takes lodgings in our neighbourhood, forced hither by the scantiness of her own fortune and the neglect of her relations. But a fine woman indeed, and in the very flower of her age.

SOSIA. Ah, Sir! I fear this same fine woman bodes us no good.

SIMO. At first indeed she lived a very honest, thrifty, and laborious sort of life; earning her bread as a sempstress. But afterwards, when the love-business came on, bringing golden promises from this man and t'other (as most people prefer their pleasures to their work), she accepted their offers, and immediately set up in trade. Some of her gallants, as ill luck would have it, carried my boy along with them for company's sake. Then said I to myself, 'The Fool's noosed, he's smitten with her.' At that time I made it my business, every morning, to watch the lads going and coming, and would ask one of them now and then, 'Hark ye, ye little rogue, tell me to whose turn fell Chrysis last night?' For, you must know, that was the woman's name.

SOSIA. Very well, Sir.

SIMO. They'd tell me that Phaedrus, Clinias, or Niceratus perhaps had been the lucky man (for those were all her lovers). 'Ay, but my good lads,' I'd say, 'what of Pamphilus?' 'O he!' they'd cry, 'Why, as usual, he only ate with them and paid his club fee.' This pleased me to the very soul. So I continued to pump 'em from time to time, but heard not one word that Pamphilus had ever been dabbling in folly. This I thought a sufficient trial and proof of his virtue: for when a lad has to do with such sort of cattle, and comes off clear, you may safely trust him with his own management. When others saw how I relished it, they agreed with me, one and all, and said a hundred fine things, I warrant ye, what a blessed father I was, to have such a promising son. . . . In one word, Pamphilus' reputation so wrought upon my neighbour Chremes, that nothing would suit him but a match between my son and his daughter, with a good portion over and above, too. The proposal made, we both agreed upon it and this was to have been the wedding-day.

SOSIA. Very good: and what's the obstruction now?

SIMO. I'll tell ye . . . A very few days ago, Madam Chrysis dies . . .

SOSIA. In a good hour, Sir! All is well then. To be frank with ye, I did not like this same Chrysis.

SIMO. Hear me out! My son, and his club-fellows, together took care of her funeral. He was really sad, and now and then dropped a tear, which I did not dislike; for, thought I, since he is so much moved, though it is clear that she was not at any time his mistress, how lamentably he would take on if I should die! All this I judged to be the effects of good nature and a sweet temper . . . Therefore, to show him my esteem, I went to the funeral myself, without suspecting anything.

SOSIA, *anxiously.* How, Sir! And what then?

SIMO. I'll tell ye . . . The body is brought out, the procession moves off, and amongst the women it was my fortune to cast my eye upon a girl with a face . . .

SOSIA. Good enough, perhaps?

SIMO. Ay, Sosia, and an air so modest, so pretty, nothing could have been more charming . . . Now, finding this girl so much more concerned than the rest and her behaviour so much more genteel and graceful than any there, I asked the servants in a whisper who she was. They told me: 'The dead woman's sister.' That struck me to the very heart. 'Well, well,' thought I, 'the whole business is unravelled. My son's tears are no longer a mystery.'

SOSIA. I'm in such a fright to know how this story will end . . .

SIMO. Well; on marches the funeral, we follow, come to the place where the body is to be buried, lay it on the pyre, and give her a tear. Meantime the sister runs like a madwoman toward the fire, and truly almost into it. At which Pamphilus in a great terror reveals that love which he had so well dissembled and hidden before; runs to the girl, takes her in his arms: 'My dear Glycerie,' says he, 'what are you at? Would ye destroy yourself?' With that, all in tears, she flings herself upon him, and with so much tenderness, too, that you might easily perceive it wasn't the first time in their acquaintance.

SOSIA, *in amaze.* Ah! How's this, Sir!

SIMO. Away go I very moody and dissatisfied, but with not enough grounds to make a quarrel of it. For if I had reproached him, he'd have said: 'Pray, Sir, what have I done? What have I deserved? What's my fault, Sir? A foolish woman would have burnt herself, I hindered her, and saved her life it may be.' This were a plea I could hardly have rejected.

SOSIA. You've reason, Sir. For had you blamed him for saving her from the flames, what would ye have done if, instead, he had thrown her in?

SIMO. Next day comes my neighbour Chremes, storming like a madman. He said that there was roguery in the case, and that most certainly Pamphilus was entangled with this woman. I denied it, he affirmed it and, in fine, went away in a huff, threatening to break off the match with his daughter.

SOSIA. And did ye not then read your son a lecture?

SIMO. No, no; the grounds were still insufficient for a quarrel.

SOSIA. How so, I beseech ye?

SIMO. He might have said: 'Sir, would you put a stop to all my pleasure of this nature? Shortly I must be married, and consult my wife's pleasure; meantime, pray, Sir, let me live merrily a while longer.'

SOSIA. Well, Sir! if this won't do, what exception can you possibly take to his behaviour?

SIMO. Why, if he refuses to marry upon the account of his miss, that business must be laid home to him first. Now, my design is to find a just cause of being angry, should he not agree to this mock-wedding. And if the rogue Davus has any tricks in his head, let him play them now while there's no danger in him—though I know he'll be at it tooth and nail; and more to plague me, perhaps, than to please my son.

SOSIA. What makes ye think so?

SIMO. D'ye ask the question? 'Tis always thus: What's bred in the bone will ne'er quit the flesh. But if I find him tampering, I'll . . . In short, let us suppose that Pamphilus doesn't boggle (as I heartily wish he won't) then there's only Chremes to be sweetened, and I hope that can be done. Now the part you're to act is to countenance the marriage, terrify Davus, watch over my son, and spy upon their plottings.

SOSIA. Enough, Sir, I'll take care of all . . . Now I suppose we may retire, Sir.

SIMO. Go, I'll follow ye presently.

Exit SOSIA.

SIMO *walks about studying.*

SIMO. I'll stake my life on it: Pamphilus has no stomach for this marriage. For if he had, Davus wouldn't have been so startled at the talk of it . . . But hold, yonder he comes!

Enter DAVUS *at another part of the stage, not seeing* SIMO.

DAVUS, *to himself.* I should have wondered greatly if this business had gone off well for us; I couldn't trust Simo's pretended sweetness: when he heard the match was broken off, he stood with his finger in his mouth, and never so much as grumbled at it . . .

SIMO, *overhearing.* But Sirrah! now he will, you shall see, and make ye smart for it too.

DAVUS, *to himself.* I'll warrant ye his business was to coax us into a fool's paradise, and in the midst of all our hopes to have caught us napping, before we could take thought and spoil the job. A cunning old fellow!

SIMO, *listening.* This rogue! What says he?

DAVUS, *aside, discovering* SIMO. God's Life, my master's at the back of me, and I never dreamt of it.

SIMO. Davus!

DAVUS, *feigning not to know him.* Umph! What's that?

SIMO. Here, Sir. Come here to me.

DAVUS, *muttering.* What does this old fellow want?

SIMO, *partly hearing.* D'ye mutter, Sirrah?

DAVUS. Who I, Sir?

SIMO. And ask questions too? . . . Sirrah, 'tis the town-talk that my son keeps a miss.

DAVUS. Ay, the town's much concerned, I warrant, for what young Mr Pamphilus does.

SIMO, *angrily.* Rascal! d'ye heed what I say or no?

DAVUS. O yes, Sir, very much.

SIMO. I should be looked upon as a hard father, I know, for peeping into his intrigues. . . . For what is gone and past I care little. He had liberty enough, so long as 'twas fitting for me to give it, or for him to take it. But now the case is altered. New circumstances call for new measures and manners. Therefore I require you, and if it were decent, I should even entreat ye, good Davus, to see that my son mends his ways.

DAVUS. Sir, I'm in the dark all this while.

SIMO. Young wenchers, you know, turn pale when they hear the word 'marriage.'

DAVUS. Ay, Sir, so indeed it is said.

SIMO. . . . Then if any such young *wencher* has a tutor who thinks as he does, why he'll be sure to take his advice and oppose whatever match is offered him.

DAVUS. Really, Sir, I don't understand ye.

SIMO. No! that is strange.

DAVUS, *angrily.* Why, Sir, I'm plain Davus still, not a gazer in the crystal.

SIMO. Then you would hear the rest in plain words?

DAVUS. Yes, Sir, I should prefer it.

SIMO. Look ye, Sirrah! if I catch ye in any of your roguy legerdemain tricks to hinder this match, or find that ye have a mind to show how shrewd you are at plotting, I'll have you sent to Bridewell, with your skin stripped over your ears, Sirrah! there to lie and rot—upon this sole condition, that whenever I take you out, I'll be ready to take your place at the treadmill . . . What! does your Rogueship understand me now? Have not I spoke plain enough yet?

DAVUS. Ay, well enough. It is the very thing itself, without concealment.

SIMO. Well, Sirrah! Take heed! If there is one matter in which I will not be tricked, it is this!

DAVUS, *jeeringly.* Gently, gently, Sir, I beseech ye.

SIMO. Rascal, dare ye laugh at me too? But I know ye well enough. Therefore remember what I tell ye; do not put

mischief before common sense and afterwards pretend ye
had not fair play shown ye . . . Take this for a warning.
Exit SIMO.

DAVUS, *alone.* Why, seriously, poor Davy, 'tis high time to bestir thy stumps, and to leave off dozing, at least if we may
guess at the old man's meaning by his ill temper. If thy
brains do not help us out, there's trouble in store either
for my master Pamphilus or for thee . . . And hang me
for a dog, if I know which side to take, whether to help
my young master, or play fair with his father . . . If I
leave Pamphilus, the poor rogue may hang himself, for
aught I know; but if I help him, I dread that old fox
whom the Devil can't out-wit . . . In the first place he
has certainly smelt out his son's haunts, then he suspects
me and keeps a deadly close eye on my goings and com-
ings lest I should deceive him once again. If he catches
me, there's an end of poor Davy; or if the whim take him,
right or wrong, he'll find an occasion to cast me into
Bridewell without delay . . . Besides all this, here's another piece of damned luck, this same Andrian girl
(whether she be his wife or his miss I can't tell) is un-
doubtedly with child by my master. And, troth, it is the
pleasantest thing in the world, to hear them tell of their
adventure; for they seem to have lost their heads as well
as their hearts. Whatsoever God sends them, he has resolved to recognize and bring it up. And they are trying
to foist the mother upon the world as a citizen of Athens.
Once upon a time, they say, a certain old man, a merchant
of our town, was cast away on the Isle of Andros with
an infant daughter and presently died. Chrysis's father did
there take this young orphan, and bring her up in his
home. It is all stuff, or at least, upon my conscience, so
it sounds, though the story takes hugely with 'em . . .

MYSIS *appears at* GLYCERIE'S *door.*

But hold! here comes her girl Mysis . . . I'll go to the
'Change and hunt up my master Pamphilus; I would not
have his father surprise him without warning from me.
Exit DAVUS.

As MYSIS *enters upon the stage,* ARCHILLIS *comes to the door.*

MYSIS, *to* ARCHILLIS. Yes, yes: I understand ye, Archillis, without all this noise. You'd have me fetch the midwife in any case. Upon my word, Lesbia's a true toper, and a giddy-brained creature, not fit to be trusted with a woman's first labour: nevertheless, I'll have to bring her here, I suppose.

ARCHILLIS *retires and* MYSIS *turns to the spectators.*

MYSIS. Didn't ye see how eager that old trot was to have her crony come, so that they might fuddle their noses together? . . . Well! Heavens grant my poor mistress a good delivery, and that any other woman may miscarry under her hands rather than she . . .

Enter PAMPHILUS *at a distance.*

MYSIS. But what is this? Mr Pamphilus seems strangely disordered? . . . It makes me tremble to think what should be the matter . . . There's mischief a-brewing, and I'll stay a little to see what comes of it.

She retires to one side of the stage.

PAMPHILUS, *to himself.* Was ever so cruel a thing yet done or thought of by man? Is this the part of a father?

MYSIS, *aside.* What mischief's in the wind now?

PAMPHILUS, *to himself.* If this be not cruelty, before God and man, there's no such thing in nature! . . . My father, it seems, designs to marry me today. One would have thought I might have known about this before, or at least have had some notice of my own wedding.

MYSIS, *aside.* Alas! What do I hear?

PAMPHILUS, *to himself.* What means this Chremes too, who but lately declared against the match? Has he changed his own mind, because he saw I would not change mine? Is he so resolutely bent to rend me from my dearest Glycerie? Once it comes to that, I'm ruined beyond redemption . . . Was there ever such an awkward and unlucky fellow upon earth as I? . . . O heavens! Is there no way to shuffle off the alliance with this Chremes? How grossly have I been abused and trampled on? Both parties signed and sealed the annulment. Then, of a sudden, the same contract is on again. But why—unless there's some damnable roguery at the bottom of it, which I'm very suspicious of.

Scornfully.

Now because this dowdy wench lies upon her father's hands, and nobody else will marry her, it seems that I must.

MYSIS. I vow these words make my poor heart go pit-a-pat.

PAMPHILUS, *to himself.* But what shall I say of my father all this while? Alas for him! That he should so heedlessly conceal a thing of such great consequence . . . He told me upon the 'Change, as he went by me five minutes ago: 'Pamphilus, you are to be married today, go home, and make yourself ready.' Which sounded to me as if he said: 'Go home now, and hang yourself.' It so stunned me that I found no word to answer, nor the least colour of excuse, however foolish, false, or extravagant. In short, I was tongue-tied . . . But if anybody should ask me now: 'What would ye have said, supposing you had had timely notice of it?' Why, sure I would have found something to say or do . . . But as the case now stands, where shall I begin first? So many difficulties cumber and distract my soul at once. On this side stand love and pity for my dearest Glycerie, besides resentment at being so rudely forced into wedlock with another; on that side, stands the reverence that I owe my father, who has hitherto indulged me in all that heart could wish. Shall I turn rebel at last? . . . I'm very unhappy, and which side to take I know not.

MYSIS, *aside, coming nearer.* Alas! How I dread to learn which side he'll take! But now 'tis absolutely necessary either for him to speak with her, or for me to tell him something about her. For when a mind hangs in the balance, the least thing in the world may turn the scale.

PAMPHILUS. What voice is that? . . . Is it you, Mysis? Well met!

MYSIS. O Mr Pamphilus, well met indeed!

PAMPHILUS. How fares your mistress?

MYSIS. How think ye, Sir! Why, she's just now in her labour!

And it goes harder with the poor creature, now that she hears this is your wedding-day and fears lest you should leave her at last.

PAMPHILUS. O hideous! How could I entertain such a thought? Shall I suffer an unfortunate gentlewoman to be ruined for my convenience, when she has put her life and honour into my hands—one whom I have loved with the tenderness of a husband? Shall I expose so much modesty and virtue to the shameful need that will be forced upon her by my desertion? No, no; it must never be.

MYSIS. That is to say, never if you can help it: but I fear you won't stand the brunt of your father.

PAMPHILUS. But do ye think me such a scoundrel, so ungrateful, so inhumane, nay, and so brutal too, that neither friendship, love, nor honour can make or keep me honest?

MYSIS. This I can assure ye, Sir; you will do her great wrong if you forget her.

PAMPHILUS. Forget her, say ye? . . . O Mysis, Mysis, what Chrysis spake to me about her sister is engraven on my heart. She was just dying, I remember, when she called for me: I went to her, you all withdrew, leaving the three of us alone. She thus began: 'Mr Pamphilus, you see the youth and beauty of this poor girl; I needn't tell ye how little these avail to secure either her virtue or her fortune. . . . Now, by this hand of yours, and your natural goodness, I beg of ye, I adjure ye by the faith you have given my Glycerie, and by her solitary condition, to be true to her, and never forsake her. . . . If you have ever been as a brother to me, if you are the man in the world whom she most esteems, if she has never denied ye any thing that she could grant ye; why, then I now bequeath ye to her for a husband, a friend, a guardian, and father too. I leave ye also master of my fortune, to do with it as ye please.' . . . With these words she joined Glycerie's hand with mine, and in the very action died. So I received Glycerie, and am resolved to keep her.

MYSIS. Indeed, Sir, I hope so.

PAMPHILUS. But why go from your mistress at this time?

MYSIS. To fetch her a midwife.

PAMPHILUS. Prithee, make haste then.

As she is going off.

But hark ye, not a word of the wedding to her, for fear it should make her the worse.

MYSIS. I understand ye.

Exeunt severally.

End of the First Act

ACT TWO

CHARINUS, *attended by his slave* BYRRHIA

CHARINUS, *as they enter*. How's this, Byrrhia? Is she to be married to Mr Pamphilus today? Hah!

BYRRHIA. The truth is neither better nor worse.

CHARINUS. How know ye that?

BYRRHIA. I had it from Davus at the 'Change.

CHARINUS. Unlucky creature that I am! There's some life in a man as long as he lies hovering betwixt hope and fear, but once he comes to despond, he sinks amain, and his heart grows heavy as a lump of lead . . .

BYRRHIA. For goodness sake, Sir, be at least so much of a philosopher, as to content yourself with what you have if ye can't have what ye want.

CHARINUS. Nay, there's nothing that I want, but only my dear Philumena.

BYRRHIA. Ah, Sir, were it not better to try whether ye can put that love out of your head, than to indulge your passion thus? Here you stand blowing at the red hot coals, and to no purpose neither.

CHARINUS. 'Tis easier to give counsel than to take it, and if you had my sickness you'd agree to that.

BYRRHIA. Well, well, Sir! I'll not argue further.

Enter PAMPHILUS *at a distance*.

CHARINUS. But stay a little, I see Mr Pamphilus yonder. Since my life is at stake, I'm resolved on a last throw.

BYRRHIA. What whim takes my master now?

CHARINUS. Why, I'll go down on my knees to him, and pour out such a dismal story of love, that my tears may persuade him to put off the wedding for two or three days. Meantime something may happen.

BYRRHIA, *aside*. And that something is just nothing at all.

CHARINUS. What think ye, Byrrhia, had I best go to him or no?

BYRRHIA. By all means, Sir, though only to make him believe you'll cuckold him, if he marries her.

CHARINUS. Go hang yourself, ye suspicious cur.

PAMPHILUS, *coming nearer*. O here is Mr Charinus. . . . Your servant, Sir.

CHARINUS. Oh, Sir, the very man I wanted! . . . For if you don't help me to keep up my heart, if you don't protect, assist, and advise me, I'm utterly undone.

PAMPHILUS. Troth, Sir, you've found me in a poor condition either to assist or advise ye. But, pray, Sir, tell me what you'd have me do.

CHARINUS. Aren't you to be married this very day, Sir?

PAMPHILUS. 'Tis so reported.

CHARINUS. If ye do, Sir, you've seen your last of me.

PAMPHILUS. Why so, Sir?

CHARINUS. Alas, Sir, I dare not tell ye. . . . Prithee, Byrrhia, you tell him.

BYRRHIA. I will, Sir.

PAMPHILUS, *to* BYRRHIA. Well, what's the business?

BYRRHIA. He's in love with your bride, there's no more to it than that, Sir.

PAMPHILUS. Truly, Sir, your feelings differ from my own . . . But, pray be plain with me, is there no nearer engagement between you and her?

CHARINUS. Ah, Sir, none at all.

PAMPHILUS, *aside*. Oh, my soul, I wish there were.

CHARINUS. Now, if you have any love or friendship for me, I adjure you not to marry her . . .

PAMPHILUS. Sir, I'll do the best I can for you.

CHARINUS.   . . . But if you can't avoid it, or if the wedding be so close to your heart's desire . . .

PAMPHILUS, *angrily*. My heart's desire!

CHARINUS.   . . . At least put it off a day or two longer, that I may get out of the way.

PAMPHILUS. But hear me a little, Mr Charinus! This is all to the tune of 'I thank you for nothing'; for let me assure ye, I am even more against a match with Philumena than you are for one.

CHARINUS. Your words bring me to life again.

PAMPHILUS. Now if there be anything that you and Byrrhia can do between you, fall to work upon it; lie, contrive; so order the matter that she may be yours, and let me take care that she shall never be mine.

CHARINUS. Enough, Sir.

PAMPHILUS, *seeing* DAVUS *far off*. But yonder comes Davus in the lucky minute, I rely on his advice.

CHARINUS. Ah, Davus . . .

To Byrrhia.

As for you, Sirrah, you're good for nothing but to give me counsel which I shall never be the better for. . . . In short, out of my sight!

BYRRHIA. With all my heart, Sir.

BYRRHIA *runs out.*

Enter DAVUS *at a distance, looking about him.*

DAVUS, *to himself.* In the name of goodness! What a world of joy do I bring my master! . . . But where's he now? For I've news—ha, ha!—which will rid him of his present fears, and make his heart leap in his belly.

CHARINUS. There's something pleases Davus, if one only knew what it was.

PAMPHILUS. There's nothing in it; the fellow hasn't heard the full story of my misfortunes.

DAVUS, *to himself*. . . . I'll warrant, did he but know he was to be married today . . .

CHARINUS. D'ye hear him, Sir?

DAVUS, *to himself*. He'd run about the town after me, post-haste, in a pitiful condition. . . . But where shall I find him?

CHARINUS. What! Have you no word for your man?

DAVUS, *to himself, going off*. Well, I'll be marching.

PAMPHILUS. Soho, Davus, stay!

DAVUS, *not knowing him*. Who's the fellow that interrupts . . . ?
Turning about.
O Lord! my master Pamphilus! the man I looked for. . . . And hey-day! here is Mr Charinus too! rarely well met, for I've business with you both.

PAMPHILUS. Ah, Davus! quite ruined.

DAVUS, *interrupting*. But hear me first.

PAMPHILUS. I'm a lost man . . .

DAVUS, *hastily*. I know your grief.

CHARINUS. And my life is at stake . . .

DAVUS, *turning to* CHARINUS. That I know too.

PAMPHILUS. I'm to be married . . .

DAVUS, *angrily*. As if I did not know that too.

CHARINUS. But today, Davus!

DAVUS. Zookers! You both make me mad, the one and the other. I know all . . .
To PAMPHILUS.
You're afraid ye must marry her, and—
To CHARINUS.
—you're afraid you may not.

CHARINUS, PAMPHILUS *together*. Thou hast nicked the mark.

DAVUS. Both fears are needless, Sirs, you can trust me.

PAMPHILUS. Prithee, good boy, without any more ado, rid me of mine.

DAVUS. So I will, Sir, in a trice. *Imprimis*, Mr Chremes gives away no daughter today.

PAMPHILUS. How d'ye know that?

DAVUS. I know't well enough, Sir, . . . Your father just now took me aside, and told me: 'My son must be married to-day,' with a long story at the tail of it, not worth a second telling. Upon this I ran full speed to the 'Change, to acquaint you with the news, where, when I found ye not, I climb up to a height, and thence stare me round about, but still no Pamphilus appears. By chance I espied Byrrhia, asked him if he had seen ye, but got no tidings: which fretted me to the very guts. To work goes my noddle, to know what I should do. Meanwhile, on my return, I began to smell the whole business out: 'Ah, ha!' I thought, 'there's no sign of a wedding feast being prepared in our house, and the old man is out of sorts too. A sudden marriage, and nobody informed! These things don't hang well together.

PAMPHILUS. Well, what of all this?

DAVUS. Away marched I to the house of neighbour Chremes. When I reached his door I found not a creature stirring, which made me laugh in my sleeve.

CHARINUS. That's good news.

PAMPHILUS. On with your story.

DAVUS. There I lingered awhile, but the Devil a person saw I going out or in; not even an old governess; nor the least preparation or bustle in the whole courtyard.

PAMPHILUS. A good sign, I confess.

DAVUS. Does this look like a wedding?

PAMPHILUS. Indeed, Davus, I think not.

DAVUS. Enough of your 'think nots' . . . Ye know nothing, I see. Why, 'tis plain as a pike-staff. As I was beating the hoof homeward, whom should I meet but Mr Chremes' boy coming back from the market with a bunch of herbs and three ha'porth of little fishes, for the old man's supper.

CHARINUS. God-a-mercy, Davus. This day hast thou set me upon my legs again.

DAVUS. Be not too sure of that, Sir!

CHARINUS. Why so? Your master is not likely to have her.

DAVUS. Call you that logic? As if there were never another man in the world, but yourself and my master! Unless you look about ye, pay court to the old gentleman's friends and ply the old gentleman himself briskly, you'll soon be back in the dumps again.

CHARINUS. Your counsel's good, I'll follow it. Though in truth my hopes have often jilted me. And so farewell!

Exit CHARINUS.

PAMPHILUS. Prithee, Davus what has my father in mind? Why does he walk these devious ways?

DAVUS. I'll tell ye, Sir. If he is now vexed that Mr Chremes won't part with his daughter, he can rightly blame none but himself for it, until he finds how the prospect of the marriage affects you. For if you kick against it, he'll lay the blame for his disappointment at your door; and there will be the devil to pay then.

PAMPHILUS. What! Shall I truckle to him?

DAVUS. Why, Sir, he's your father, and you have a hard task with him. Besides your mistress has no friend to stand by her; given the least occasion, he'll quickly make the town too hot for her.

PAMPHILUS, *angrily and scornfully*. Too hot for her!

DAVUS. It will be a moment's work to send her packing, Sir.

PAMPHILUS. Prithee, honest Davus, what shall I do in this case?

DAVUS. Why tell him you'll marry whom he pleases.

PAMPHILUS. Oh!

DAVUS. Why that sigh now?

PAMPHILUS. How can I tell him a thing so far from my heart?

DAVUS. Why not, I pray?

PAMPHILUS. O Davus, never, never. . . .

DAVUS. Don't say that, man!

PAMPHILUS. Would you persuade me to break my oath?

DAVUS. Consider well what will happen if you do.

PAMPHILUS. I have. It will reconcile me with my father, but break my mistress' heart.

DAVUS. No, no, you're wide off the mark. . . . Now, I fancy that your father will say some such thing as this: 'Come, son, I must needs have ye marry today!' 'With all my heart,' say you. . . . Well; and what can he quarrel at now? Your dutiful reply will ruin all his designs, and leave you as free as ever you were. For 'tis certain as certainty itself, that Mr Chremes won't give ye his daughter; so your father will not ask you to alter your present habits, in case he may alter his mind. All you need do is to tell your father you'll marry, and if he can find it in his heart to be angry, let him. But do not flatter yourself that nobody else will part with his daughter to a man in your circumstances. For I tell ye that, rather than let ye continue as a carefree bachelor, your father will forgo a dowry and marry you to some beggar-wench. . . . Look ye, if he find ye indifferent to one match, he'll sleep on it, and find ye out another . . . nobody knows when. In the meantime, something may happen on our side.

PAMPHILUS. Think ye so?

DAVUS. No doubt of it, I'll warrant ye.

PAMPHILUS. Have a care where thou leadest me.

DAVUS. What, will ye never have done?

PAMPHILUS. Well, I'll say just as you'd have me say. But take special care it don't come to my father's ear that I've a child, and that I'm in for a maintenance.

DAVUS. O confident devil!

PAMPHILUS. Why, she bound me upon my oath to take care of it, as a token that I would never forsake her.

DAVUS. Well, we'll take care of it, never fear!

Enter SIMO *at a great distance.*

Yonder comes your father, put on your pleasant face, quick.

SIMO, *to himself.* These wretches are comparing notes; I've a mind to see what they are at.

DAVUS. The good old man takes it for granted that you'll refuse to marry. He comes from some corner or another with a speech well prepared. He questions not but that it will put ye to a confounded nonplus . . . Be sure to have all your brains about ye.

PAMPHILUS. I'll do what I can, Davus.

DAVUS. Come, Sir, say no more than that you'll marry her; and if ever he opens his mouth to ye again upon that business, never trust Davus!

Enter BYRRHIA *at another part of the stage, watching them.*

BYRRHIA, *to audience.* Mr Charinus has excused me awhile from all other services, to let me spy upon Mr Pamphilus's designs about this wedding: for this purpose have I dogged the heels of his greybeard father Simo . . . O, and now they are all together . . . Faith, I'll play at Bopeep here.

Withdraws to one side of the stage.

SIMO, *coming nearer.* O here are the gentlemen I want.

DAVUS. Psst! Mind your cue.

SIMO. Pamphilus!

DAVUS, *softly.* Turn quick, as though you had not seen him.

PAMPHILUS, *turning hastily about.* Hah, my dear father!

DAVUS, *aside to* PAMPHILUS. Excellent, in faith.

SIMO. I must have ye marry today, as I told ye.

BYRRHIA, *aside.* Now I'm plaguily afraid how he will answer.

PAMPHILUS. Sir, I shall be ready to obey ye in this, and all other commands.

BYRRHIA, *aside.* Say ye so!

DAVUS, *aside.* That has stopped the old man's mouth.

BYRRHIA, *aside.* What did he answer?

SIMO, *in confusion.* Why, this is like a son, when ye cheerfully do as your father would have ye.

DAVUS, *aside to* PAMPHILUS. Will ye believe me another time?

BYRRHIA, *aside.* Alas, now it seems, after all, that my poor master must go whistle for a wife.

SIMO. Go in, Pamphilus, that you may be at hand when you're wanted.

PAMPHILUS. I'm going, Sir.

Exit PAMPHILUS.

BYRRHIA, *coming out from his covert*. Is there no faith in man? Well, I find the old saying stands good, 'Every man for himself.' I remember, once I had a glimpse of this lass; 'Sbobs, a charming creature! And Mr Pamphilus is in the right, if he had rather lie with such a beauty himself, than that my master should: . . . I'll go tell him all; and even a few hard words with a little hard news.

Exit BYRRHIA.

DAVUS, *aside*. Now the old man suspects me of some notable intrigue—concludes that I planted myself here upon the same account.

SIMO. What says Davus to the world?

DAVUS. There's no news stirring, Sir.

SIMO, *angrily*. None, say ye?

DAVUS. None at all, Sir.

SIMO. Truly but I hoped for something.

DAVUS, *aside*. He has lost his aim, I perceive; and that nettles him.

SIMO. Sirrah, can ye speak without a lie in your mouth?

DAVUS. Most fluently, Sir.

SIMO. Come, does not this marriage stick in my son's stomach, because of his entanglement with that Andrian?

DAVUS. Why truly, Sir, no . . . or if so, that uneasiness would pass in a day or two's time (d'ye understand me, Sir?) and all would be well again. But now he has fairly taken the point by the right handle.

SIMO. I commend him for it.

DAVUS. Indeed when you winked at his sportiveness, and the hot blood of youth excused him, he did wench a little; but secretly, and, like a man of honour, taking care it should be no blot on his escutcheon. . . . Now 'tis time to look out for a wife, his thoughts fly wholly upon matrimony.

SIMO. Yet methought he looked a little down in the mouth.

DAVUS. That was not because you have chosen him a bride. There's something else he didn't take so well at your hands.

SIMO. What's that, pray?

DAVUS. A mere trifle, Sir.

SIMO. What sort of trifle?

DAVUS. Nay, nothing at all of consequence.

SIMO. Well, well, I must know what it is.

DAVUS. He says that you're too sparing of your purse.

SIMO, *angrily*. Who, I?

DAVUS. Yes, you Sir. '. . . For,' says he, 'my father has laid out but ten groats for a supper, and is that to be my wedding-feast, forsooth? Which of my companions can I invite to such entertainment as this?' And under the rose, Sir, I think you're a little close-fisted; I could wish it were otherwise.

SIMO. Leave your prating, Sirrah.

DAVUS, *aside*. I've stung him, I see.

SIMO. Leave me alone and all will be well . . .

Exit DAVUS.

SIMO, *alone*. What's the meaning of all this? . . . What would this old schemer be at? . . . If there be any piece of roguery here on foot, I'll lay my life he is chief actor in it.

End of the Second Act

ACT THREE

Enter MYSIS *and* LESBIA *on one part of the stage;*
on another SIMO *and* DAVUS *observing them*

MYSIS. Truly, Lesbia, you're much in the right there. A faithful lover is a very great rarity.

SIMO. This maid belongs to the Andrian?

DAVUS. Yes, Sir.

MYSIS, *to* LESBIA. But this Mr Pamphilus . . .

SIMO. What says she?

MYSIS. . . . Has signed and sealed over again . . .

SIMO. So, so!

DAVUS. Would that either the old man's ears were stopped, or her tongue cut out.

MYSIS. . . . For whate'er God sends her, he has ordered it to be brought up.

SIMO. Confusion! What do I hear? If what she says be true, all's past recovery.

LESBIA. A sweet-natured young gentleman, I'll warrant ye.

MYSIS. Oh, a most sweet-natured . . . But come along, for you'll be too late else.

LESBIA. Well, let's in, then.

Exit MYSIS *and* LESBIA.

DAVUS. How shall we recover ourselves out of this relapse?

SIMO, *softly, walking aside.* What means all this? . . . Is my son so madly in love then, and with a foreign woman too? But hold! now I see which way the hare goes . . . I couldn't spy it before, like a senseless sot as I was.

DAVUS, *partly overhearing.* What's that he thinks to have found out?

SIMO, *aside.* Oh! here begin the rogues' tricks; they pretend the girl is with child, to frighten off Mr Chremes from the match.

GLYCERIE, *within.* Oh! . . . Oh! . . . Help, kind heavens! Free me from my pains, I beseech ye. Oh . . . .

SIMO, *softly, to* DAVUS. Ha, ha, ha . . . so nimble! A very good jest! After she hears of my being at the door, she falls in labour forsooth. . . . Your farce wasn't well timed, Mr Rogue.

DAVUS. Meaning me, Sir?

SIMO. Ah, Sirrah, did your actors lack a prompter?

DAVUS. I don't understand you, Sir, in the least.

SIMO. If this rascal had served me so in a real wedding, here would have been fine work with a vengeance; but now he makes a rod for his own back. For my part, I'm safe enough.

Enter LESBIA *from* GLYCERIE'S *house, not seeing* SIMO *and* DAVUS.

LESBIA, *to* ARCHILLIS *at the door.* For what has been done, Archillis, and for a woman in her condition, everything is as well as a body could wish. In the first place, let her be well bathed and then let her take the dose I prescribed her to drink, and just the quantity; I shall be back again in a minute . . .

ARCHILLIS *retires,* LESBIA *speaks to herself.*

Heart of my body! Pamphilus has got a very pretty boy; I hope in heaven he'll live to make as good a man as his father, who scorned to wrong this innocent creature.

Exit LESBIA.

SIMO. What man alive that knew thee, wouldn't swear that this was one of thy rogue's tricks?

DAVUS. What rogue's tricks, Sir?

SIMO. Within doors the midwife gives no orders about the woman and her child; but when she is once out, she bawls from the street to those indoors, that the whole town rings with it. . . . Why, Davus, what dost thou see in my face, to think of making so palpable an ass of me? Had this scene been more artfully played, it would not have so insulted my five wits.

DAVUS, *aside*. Faith, the old fool cheats himself, not I.

SIMO. Didn't I charge ye strictly? Nay, didn't I threaten ye too? But what cared you? 'Tis all but so much breath lost. Can ye think me so doltish as to believe this woman's brought to bed?

DAVUS, *aside*. Oh, have I found out his blind side? I know my cue then.

SIMO. Have ye never a tongue in your head, Sirrah?

DAVUS. As if you believed it? As if you hadn't news of this beforehand!

SIMO. Who should have given me such news?

DAVUS, *jeeringly*. Strange! Did you find out this imposture, and all by yourself?

SIMO. Very fine! So you mock me now?

DAVUS. I'm sure someone told ye, Sir. How should ye suspect it else?

SIMO. How? Because I know thee for a rogue.

DAVUS. As much as to say that I put this scene upon the stage?

SIMO. Nothing more certain. I know it.

DAVUS. Sir, you're mightily mistaken in your man.

SIMO. Mistaken in my man!

DAVUS. For if ever I open my mouth, you think at once that I lie.

SIMO. Who is the liar: you or I?

DAVUS. Truth, at this rate I dare scarce move my lips.

SIMO. This I'm certain of, that there has been no child born here.

DAVUS. Are ye so certain of it? Yet for all that, you'll have one laid at your door before the day is out. This, Sir, will certainly be, and remember now that I told ye so, that if there should happen any roguery in the case, it mightn't be laid to Davus's charge. I would fain have ye believe better things of Davus.

SIMO. But how d'ye know they'll trick a child upon us?

DAVUS. I heard it, and believe it too. And there are a thousand circumstances which persuade me so. For, first, the gentlewoman cried out that she was with child by your son, which is found to be a mere sham. Then, as soon as she heard of a wedding on foot, her maid forsooth was sent away for the midwife, and the midwife could smuggle in another bastard child. . . . But if you should chance to disregard the child at your door, the wedding may go on.

SIMO. How's this? . . . As soon as ye heard of these plots, pray why couldn't ye have acquainted Pamphilus with all?

DAVUS. And who was it d'ye think but I parted them? For the whole town knew that he was up to the ears in love. Now he has his mind upon marriage. As for the business of the child, let me alone with that. Go on with the wedding as you've begun. Heaven prosper it, I say.

SIMO. Very well! . . . Now ye may go in, and wait there till I come, and get ready what's wanting.

Exit DAVUS.

SIMO, *alone*. This fellow wasn't very urgent to force his stories upon me; and maybe all he said wasn't true, neither. Be it this way or that, I care not a straw: the main thing I stand upon is my son's promise. . . . Well, I'll go see for my neighbour Chremes, and beg his daughter; then if I get her, I'll have a wedding today in spite of all. I don't question my son's promise. If he draws back, I can fairly force him to obedience now . . .

Enter CHREMES.

Here comes the man in as good time as a body could wish. . . . A good day to ye, neighbour Chremes.

CHREMES. O Sir, you're the man I looked for.

SIMO. And I for you.

CHREMES. You're well met, Sir . . . There are those who told me they heard from your own mouth that this day your son and my daughter were to be married. Now I'm come to see whether you or they are of sound wits.

SIMO. Have a little patience, and you'll hear my desires, and an answer to your question too.

CHREMES. Well, neighbour, let's have it then.

SIMO. I beg of ye, for Heaven's sake, by our friendship, begun with our childhood, and increased with our years— by your dear daughter, and my only son (whose welfare depends wholly upon you)—to assist me in this weighty point, and let the match still go on, as we formerly designed.

CHREMES. Pray, Sir, no such entreaties. As though I couldn't grant it without all this begging. D'ye think I am not the same man as when I first made the offer? If the match be for their good, let them be sent for without a moment's delay. But if more harm than good be like to come of it, I'd have ye consider matters impartially, as though she were your daughter, and Pamphilus my son.

SIMO. It is upon such conditions that I desire it, and press it forward so hard. Nor should I have been so urgent, had not the matter required it.

CHREMES. But how, I beseech ye?

SIMO. O Sir, my son and his mistress have fallen out.

CHREMES. Mere tales!

SIMO. Believe me, neighbour, it is true.

CHREMES. Yes, faith, just as I told ye, Love is a mere caterwaul, where scratching begets kissing.

SIMO. Say ye so, Sir? Pray then let us prevent the worst now that we have fair opportunity, the edge of his appetite being taken off by affronts and ill-usage. Let us give him a wife before this wheedling miss, by her tricks and false tears, can soften his love-sick mind to pity. I hope, Sir, when he is once reclaimed by the pleasant conversation of a virtuous wife, he will easily wind himself out of these mischiefs.

CHREMES. You are of this opinion, but I am not. They will never endure to be together, and I shall be as uneasy under it as I ever was.

SIMO. But how can ye know, till you have experienced it?

CHREMES. It would be ill to buy experience at the expense of my daughter.

SIMO. Why, let the worst come to the worst, if such a thing should happen (which Heaven forbid!) they can but part. But should he once mend his ways, consider how many advantages will happen. First, I shall have my son well settled, you an honest son-in-law, and your daughter a good husband.

CHREMES. What's all this ado for? If you're fully persuaded that all will prove for the best, God forbid I should be your hindrance in the least.

SIMO. Indeed, Sir, I have always had a high esteem for ye.

CHREMES. But to the purpose.

SIMO. Well, Sir?

CHREMES. How come ye to know that your son and his mistress are fallen out?

SIMO. Why, Sir, Davus, a privy-counsellor of theirs, told me so and urged me to strike up the match with all speed. And d'ye think he would have done it, hadn't he known my son was willing too? . . . Now I think of it, you shall hear it from his own mouth.

To SERVANTS *within.*

Soho! Within there, bid Davus come hither . . .

Enter DAVUS *to them.*

But see! Here he comes himself.

DAVUS, *to* SIMO. I was just coming to you, Sir.

SIMO. Well, what's the matter?

DAVUS, *fawningly.* Why don't ye send for the bride, Sir? It grows late.

SIMO, *to* CHREMES. Look ye there now, d'ye hear him?

To DAVUS.

Well, Davus, servants are slippery, and I had a fancy once that you would as lief serve your master a foul trick as another man, especially in the case of my son's amours.

DAVUS. Lord, Sir! I do such a thing!

SIMO. I was once of that opinion; and for fear of the worst, kept something to myself which now I'll reveal to ye.

DAVUS. And what may that be, I pray, Sir?

SIMO. I'll tell ye, since I can now find it in my heart to trust thee.

DAVUS. So you're satisfied in my fidelity at last?

SIMO. In short, there was nothing of marriage in the case.

DAVUS. How, Sir, no marriage?

SIMO. No, no, it was but a mere contrivance to feel your pulse.

DAVUS. Can ye tell me so in truth?

SIMO. Even just so, Davus.

DAVUS. Why, look ye Sir, I could never comprehend this. Bless me! there's a clever scheme for you.

SIMO. But hear me now. . . . No sooner had I sent you in, whom should I meet but my neighbour here, in the very nick.

DAVUS, *softly*. 'Sdeath, is it come to this then?

SIMO. . . . I begged him to part with his daughter, and with much ado I prevailed . . .

DAVUS, *softly*. Undone, undone!

SIMO, *partly hearing*. How! What say ye?

DAVUS. I said it was excellently well done.

SIMO. As for Mr Chremes, he's ready.

CHREMES. Well, I'll just step home, and bid my daughter make ready; then I'll come back, and tell ye how she took it.

Exit CHREMES.

DAVUS *looks simply at* SIMO.

SIMO. Now, prithee, Davus, seeing this is a match wholly of thy making . . .

DAVUS, *aside*. 'Twas wholly of my making, with a pox on it.

SIMO. . . . I'd have ye take my son in hand, and help to reclaim him.

DAVUS, *coldly*. Yes, Sir, I'll do my best.

SIMO. That's easily done, now he's at odds with his miss.

DAVUS. Well, Sir, set your heart at rest.

SIMO. Do it then; but where's he now?

DAVUS. Ten to one he's at home.

SIMO. Well, I'll step in, and tell him just what I told you. *Exit* SIMO.

DAVUS, *alone*. So! I shall be hanged . . . I've no more to do, but straight to prison goes poor Davus with a vengeance . . . there's no crying *Peccavi* in the case. I've turned all topsy-turvy, imposed upon the old man, noosed his son into matrimony, and brought a business about that the one never dreamt of, and the other feared like the gates of Hell . . . This comes of super-subtlety! Had I sat still, and not tampered, all had been well enough.

Enter PAMPHILUS *at a distance.*

But look now (as my evil genius would have it) yonder he comes. . . . I'm a lost man already. . . . What would I not give for a convenient precipice to dash my brains out?

PAMPHILUS, *to himself*. Where's the villain that has undone me?

DAVUS, *aside*. Heavens! What will become of me?

PAMPHILUS, *to himself*. I must confess I'm well enough served, like the senseless short-sighted fop I was. What, venture my life and soul to the secrecy of this prating fool! I shall pay dear for being a blockhead; but, as I live, that dog shan't avoid my wrath.

DAVUS, *aside*. If I 'scape hanging this bout, I'll be sworn the gallows will never have me.

PAMPHILUS, *to himself*. What excuse shall I make to my fa-

ther? How break the match off, when but just now I engaged myself to it. . . . How shall I dare face his displeasure? . . . I'm at my wit's end.

DAVUS, *aside, listening.* And so am I, in good faith, but
though I am on tenterhooks, yet I must pretend I've a
scheme in my head will fetch him off again though 'twere
only to postpone this plaguey business a little longer.

PAMPHILUS, *seeing* DAVUS. Hah! Are ye there?

DAVUS, *softly, hanging his head.* 'Sdeath, he sees me.

PAMPHILUS, *angrily.* Pray come hither, good Mr Rogue!
What excuse now? . . . Don't ye see, you rascal, what a
miserable condition your damned contrivances have
brought me into.

DAVUS. But I'll soon bring ye off again.

PAMPHILUS. You bring me off again!

DAVUS. Yes Sir, without doubt.

PAMPHILUS, *scornfully.* Without doubt, as ye did before.

DAVUS. I hope, Sir, a little better this time.

PAMPHILUS. How can I credit such a villain? Can you set
to rights again a matter entirely lost and desperate? . . .
Very fine! What a rare fellow have I relied upon, who this
day amidst a calm has raised a storm, and forced an
odious match upon me against my conscience too? . . .
Didn't I tell you how it would be, you rascal?

DAVUS. You did so, Sir.

PAMPHILUS. What do ye deserve for your pains?

DAVUS. A halter, I must confess. . . . But, pray Sir, reprieve
me, until I've recovered my senses a little. I'll soon see
what's to be done in the case.

PAMPHILUS. I'm sorry I have not time to give you your deserts. I have scarce enough to care for myself, much less
to punish you.

Exeunt Ambo.

End of the Third Act

ACT FOUR

Enter CHARINUS *by himself*

CHARINUS. Did ever anybody know, or even read of people so horribly base as to take pleasure in the miseries of others, and out of their ruins to build their own fortunes? . . . Ah! is this true or no? Yes, yes! it is true with a vengeance. There is an evil sort of men that scruple to make a downright refusal, until forced to what they are. They draw the mask aside with trembling hands and, being past all shame, they cry: 'Pray who are you, Sir? What are you to me, Sir? Shall I resign my mistress to you, Sir? Oh Sir, I'd have ye know charity always begins at home.' If ye charge them with breach of honour, they are not ashamed as they should be; yet they can blush when there is no reason for it. . . . What measures shall I take? . . . Shall I go to him and call him to account for this affront? . . . I'll give him ill language enough . . . 'Hold, Sir,' some may say, 'you will be never the better for it.' . . . Oh, but I will, much: I shall certainly plague him to some purpose, and so ease my mind a little that way.

He goes towards SIMO'S *door, where he is met by* PAMPHILUS *and* DAVUS.

PAMPHILUS. Ah, dear Sir, I have most inconsiderately ruined you and myself too, except Heaven help us.

CHARINUS, *scornfully*. How! 'Inconsiderately' do ye call it?

Are ye now fumbling for an excuse? You're a fine man of your word, indeed.

PAMPHILUS. How so, Sir?

CHARINUS. D'ye think to catch me a second time with your cheats?

PAMPHILUS. What do ye mean, Sir?

CHARINUS. No sooner had I told ye of my passion for Madam Philumena, than you were strangely smitten with her. . . . What a wretch was I, to judge of another's generosity by my own!

PAMPHILUS. You are still under a mistake, Sir.

CHARINUS, *very angrily.* Were not your joys complete enough before, without duping my poor heart, and driving me on with fantastic hopes? . . . But there, take her, for all I care.

PAMPHILUS. I take her! . . . Ah Sir, you can't conceive what troubles I lie under, and to what a miserable pass this rascal of mine has brought me by his damned projects.

CHARINUS. What wonder, since he took you for his pattern?

PAMPHILUS. I'm sure ye wouldn't talk at this rate, if ye knew either me or my circumstances.

CHARINUS, *jeeringly.* Yes, yes: I know very well some words have passed between your father and you, and that's the reason he is angry with ye; yet he couldn't force ye to marry today.

PAMPHILUS. Nay, Sir, to let you see how little ye know my trouble, there was no wedding to be today, nor any wife designed for me.

CHARINUS. Yes, Sir, I know it was a voluntary compulsion . . .

PAMPHILUS. But hold, Sir, ye don't know the business yet.

CHARINUS. Is it not enough to know, that you're set upon having her?

PAMPHILUS. Why d'ye rack me thus? Do but hear . . . He never gave over urging me to tell my father I'd marry her. Nay, he lay pressing and begging of me till I could hold out no longer.

CHARINUS. What 'he' d'ye mean?

PAMPHILUS. Why, Davus, that's who.

CHARINUS. Who, Davus?

PAMPHILUS. 'Tis Davus all over.

CHARINUS. How so?

PAMPHILUS. Indeed I can't tell, I know no more than that the angry Gods have punished me for listening to that rascal.

CHARINUS, *to* DAVUS. Is this true, Sirrah?

DAVUS. Ay, too true.

CHARINUS. What say ye, villain, hah! . . . The gallows reward ye for it. . . . Now answer me; if all the devils in hell were mustered together, to force a match upon your master, what advice could they have given more proper to their design than yours?

DAVUS. I confess, Sir, I have been a little outwitted, but yet I don't despair.

CHARINUS, *jeeringly.* Very likely.

DAVUS. The last nail would not serve, but we'll drive one in that shall—unless you fancy that a bad beginning always makes a bad end.

PAMPHILUS, *jeeringly to* DAVUS. Right, boy; I know that if only you'll set your wits to work, you'll provide me with two weddings instead of one.

DAVUS. Sir, as your servant I'm bound to trudge for ye night and day, with might and main, even to venture my neck, as long as I can do you any good. For what falls out badly I deserve your pardon. Though my measures were crossed, yet I did my best. If you can find how to do better, yourself, I'll leave you to it.

PAMPHILUS. With all my heart . . . but first put me back in the conditions you found me.

DAVUS. I'll do it, Sir.

PAMPHILUS. But without a moment's delay!

DAVUS. Hold! Did you hear the creak? . . . Glycerie's door has opened.

PAMPHILUS. What's that to do with you?

DAVUS. I have a notion . . .

PAMPHILUS. A notion at last? Hah!

DAVUS. Egad, yes, now I've hit on it! You shall hear all presently.

Enter MYSIS *from* GLYCERIE'S *house.*

MYSIS, *to* GLYCERIE *within.* Well this Mr Pamphilus of yours, I'll go hunt him up, and bring him along with me. Wherever he may be. . . . But, my dear, don't you lie fretting yourself in the meantime.

She comes from the door.

PAMPHILUS. O Mysis!

MYSIS. Who spoke?

Turning about.

O Mr Pamphilus, you're well met.

PAMPHILUS. Why, what's the matter?

MYSIS. I am to charge you from my mistress, that if you have any love for her, you'd come to her at once; she says she longs strangely to see ye.

PAMPHILUS. Alas, unhappy man! . . . My misfortunes come one upon the neck of another . . .

To DAVUS.

Must Mr Charinus and I both be plagued on your account? I'm sent for because she heard of the wedding.

CHARINUS, *pointing to* DAVUS. Hadn't this gentleman tampered with our affairs, how well and quiet might all have been!

DAVUS, *aside to* CHARINUS. Have done, Sir! Isn't my master mad enough himself, but you must make him worse?

MYSIS, *to* PAMPHILUS. Ay truly, Sir, 'tis indeed that which makes my poor mistress take on so.

PAMPHILUS. Mysis! I swear to thee, by all that's sacred, I'll never leave this creature, though I should lose all the friends I have in the whole world for it. 'Tis she I longed for, and my longings are granted; our natures agree together. He that offers to divide us, I'll bid him farewell; for Death, and nothing but Death, can do the same.

MYSIS. I'm revived by your words.

PAMPHILUS. The Delphic oracle never pronounced a greater truth! If the breaking off this match could seem to be done by anybody else but me, I should be glad of it for my father's sake. But if that can't be, I'll even be bold, and tell him how the land lies.

To CHARINUS.

. . . What think ye of me?

CHARINUS. Just as deep in the dirt as I am in the mire.

DAVUS. My brains are at work.

CHARINUS, *jeeringly, to* DAVUS. Thou'rt a bold Trojan.

PAMPHILUS. I knew what ye'd be at.

DAVUS. Depend on me, I'll arrange this business to your liking.

PAMPHILUS. It must be speedily, then.

DAVUS. I have it in my head, Sir! I have it!

CHARINUS. What is it, I prithee?

DAVUS. Your pardon, Sir, I'm working for my master, not for you; therefore don't mistake me.

CHARINUS. Well, I'll be content with that.

PAMPHILUS. Tell me, Davus, what will you do now?

DAVUS. Come, come, I am pressed for time, and must not spend it in prating. To speak plainly with ye, pray go: the two of you hinder me.

Pushing them.

I had rather have your room than your company.

PAMPHILUS. Very well, I'll go greet my mistress.

Exit PAMPHILUS.

DAVUS, *staring at* CHARINUS. Still on the same spot? Have you no business elsewhere?

CHARINUS. Shall I tell ye the very truth?

DAVUS, *interrupting him.* Yes, yes; why not? . . . here begins a long, long tale . . .

CHARINUS. Prithee, what shall poor I do?

DAVUS. There speaks ingratitude! Are ye not content that I

have put off the wedding, and reprieved ye for one short day?

CHARINUS, *shaking his head.* But yet, Davus . . .

DAVUS, *interrupting.* But yet what?

CHARINUS. I still hope to marry her.

DAVUS. A ridiculous hope.

CHARINUS. See that you come to my house yonder, if possible. *Pointing to his house.*

DAVUS. What should I come for? I've no business with ye.

CHARINUS. But if something should happen . . .

DAVUS, *interrupting.* Very well, I'll come.

CHARINUS. And you'll find me at home, for certain.

Exit CHARINUS.

DAVUS. Mysis, I must go out a little; do but you stay till I come back.

MYSIS. What for?

DAVUS. For a certain reason of my own.

MYSIS. Prithee, be quick then.

DAVUS. I'll be back in a trice.

Exit DAVUS.

MYSIS, *alone.* Is there nothing in this world that a man can call his own? . . . Blessed Heaven! I took this Mr Pamphilus to be the very heart and soul of my mistress, a friend, a lover, and in effect a husband, and all in one, and ready to serve her upon every occasion; and yet, after all, what miseries does this unfortunate woman endure for his sake? And how much greater is her present trouble than all her former satisfaction!

Enter DAVUS with GLYCERIE's child in his arms.

O here comes Davus again . . . Prithee, good boy, what have we here?

Discovers the child.

Where do ye carry that child?

DAVUS. Now, Mysis, we need but one cast of thy skill and cunning.

MYSIS. What plot is this, Davus?

DAVUS. Here, take the child quickly, and lay it at our door.

MYSIS. Prithee, what? On the cold ground?

DAVUS. Can't ye take some of those herbs from the altar, and strew them under it?

MYSIS. Why can't you do it yourself?

DAVUS. Why? Because if my master engages me to swear whether I laid it there or no, I hope to swear with a safe conscience.

MYSIS. I understand ye. . . . But pray how came this sudden qualm of conscience upon you? . . . Give the child to me then.

She takes the child and moves towards SIMO's *door.*

DAVUS. Prithee, hasten and be back again in a moment, that I may teach ye your lesson.

CHREMES *appears at a great distance.*

But, oh the devil!

MYSIS, *starting back.* What's the matter now?

DAVUS, *aside.* Here comes the bride's father, and I must even go another way to work now.

MYSIS. I can't imagine what's in your mind.

DAVUS. I'll make as if I had just come from that street there on the right-hand. . . . Be sure to put in a word or two, as the occasion calls, to make our stories hang together.

MYSIS. On my conscience, I understand your designs no more than does a post. But if I can do you any service (which you know better than I) I'll stay where I am, without hindering your business.

As CHREMES *comes towards* MYSIS, DAVUS *sneaks to the other side.*

CHREMES, *to himself.* Everything's ready now for my dear Philumena's wedding, and we've nothing to do more but invite the guests. . . .

Seeing the child at the door.

But what have we here, in the name of goodness?

Goes nearer and uncovers the child's face.

A child, upon my life!

To MYSIS.

Hark ye, gossip! Did you lay this child here?

MYSIS, *aside, looking fearfully about*. Hah! What's become of him?

CHREMES. What! Are ye tongue-tied?

MYSIS, *aside*. Alas! he's not to be seen. . . . O dear heart, the fellow has left me, and is vanished.

DAVUS *appears seemingly out of breath, pretending not to see* CHREMES, *and bawls as loud as he can*.

DAVUS. Bless me! what a bustle's yonder in the market! . . . There's squabbling and arguing indeed . . . Ay, corn is confoundedly dear.

Aside, to audience.

. . . Troth, what else can I say?

MYSIS, *aside, to* DAVUS. Prithee, why must I be left alone here?

DAVUS, *looking upon the child*. Hey-day! What farce is this?

Turning to MYSIS.

Oh, ho! Whence came this bantling? Pray who brought it hither?

He winks at her.

MYSIS, *not understanding*. Are you a fool that ye ask me such a question?

DAVUS. Whom should I ask but you? There's nobody else here to ask.

CHREMES, *aside*. I wonder whence it came?

DAVUS, *angrily, with an elbow in her ribs*. Come, will ye give me an answer or no?

MYSIS. O, O!

DAVUS, *softly to her*. To the right-hand a little.

MYSIS, *softly to him*. Are you out of your wits? Wasn't it yourself? . . .

DAVUS, *softly*. If ye speak one word save what is to the point, beware lest . . .

Aloud.

D'ye threaten me? Whence came this child? . . .

Softly.

Speak out boldly, wench!

MYSIS. From our house.

DAVUS, *aloud.* Ha, ha, ha! . . . 'tis no wonder that a strumpet should be so impudent.

CHREMES, *aside.* I'm much mistaken if this woman be not the Andrian's maid.

DAVUS. Can ye find nobody else to make sport with? Are we such simpletons in your eyes?

CHREMES, *aside.* I came at the very critical minute.

DAVUS. You'd best make haste, and be off with the child from the door. . . .

As she is about to lift it up, he speaks softly.

Nay, stay awhile; see that ye don't budge from this place.

Holding up his finger.

MYSIS, *softly.* Shame on ye, ye do so fright me!

DAVUS, *aloud.* Do I speak to you, or do I not?

MYSIS. Why, what would the man have?

DAVUS. A pox on your seeming innocence! Come, tell me whose child you've laid there! Once for all, tell me.

MYSIS. You don't know, I warrant ye.

DAVUS. A fig for what I know! Tell me what I ask!

MYSIS. 'Tis yours: from your house.

DAVUS, *aloud.* Which of ours? All of us didn't beget it.

MYSIS. Why, 'tis Mr Pamphilus's.

DAVUS, *very angrily.* Zookers! What, my master Pamphilus's?

CHREMES, *aside.* I was in the right to be against this match.

DAVUS, *very loud.* This is a roguery deserves the lash.

MYSIS. Why d'ye bawl so?

DAVUS. Didn't I see this very child brought to your house last night?

MYSIS. Oh, thou brazen face!

DAVUS. I'm sure I saw Gammer Lesbia, that old wine jar, waddling along with something hid under her skirts.

MYSIS. 'Twas a blessing that many honest women were present at my mistress's labour; they can bear witness to the truth.

DAVUS. I'm sure she did not know for what sort of a man she designed this trick. 'I warrant you,' said your honest woman, 'that when Chremes sees the child, he'll not part with his daughter.' But in faith, he'll do it the sooner for that imposture.

CHREMES, *aside*. I' faith, but he won't, though.

DAVUS. Now therefore, in plain English, if ye don't take away the bastard, I'll kick it into the middle of the street, and take ye and set your arse in the kennel.

MYSIS. You're either drunk or mad, for sure.

DAVUS. How one piece of roguery brings out another! Now they begin to buzz it about that this Glycerie is a citizen of Athens . . .

CHREMES. How?

DAVUS. . . . So that the law will compel him to marry her in spite of all.

MYSIS. By your leave, sweet sir, is she not in truth a citizen?

CHREMES, *aside*. How nearly was I fooled! Why, I had almost put my head in the noose!

DAVUS. Now, who told you that, I prithee?

Turning about to CHREMES.

O Sir, you're come in the luckiest time that could be. . . . Pray, Sir, hear me . . .

CHREMES. I've heard all.

DAVUS. How all?

CHREMES. Why all from the beginning.

DAVUS. You've heard it then? . . . Fine rogueries are on foot! Now shouldn't this same jade be publicly carted?

To MYSIS.

Don't think that poor Davus is the man you play these tricks upon. Here's the gentleman himself.

Pointing to CHREMES.

MYSIS. Ah dear! Indeed, Sir, if it please your worship, I haven't spoke one word of a lie.

CHREMES. I know the whole business. . . . But is my neighbour Simo within?

DAVUS. I think so, Sir.

Exit CHREMES.

DAVUS *attempts to fondle* MYSIS.

MYSIS. Hands off, varlet! If I don't do all that lies in your power to relieve my mistress, never trust me.

DAVUS. Oh thou silly soul, thou dost not know how the case stands.

MYSIS. How should I?

DAVUS. Why this is the bride's father, and without all this talk between us, he couldn't have known what we wished him to know.

MYSIS. Couldn't ye have honestly told me what part I should play?

DAVUS. Pshaw! As if there were no difference between what you said *impromptu*, forced by nature, and what you would have dully rehearsed under my direction!

Enter at a distance CRITO *in country clothes.*

CRITO, *to himself*. Why, I am told that our Chrysis lived somewhere down this lane, where she found there was more to be got by whoredom in the town, than by virtue in the country. But now that she's dead, I'm heir-at-law to her goods. Where shall I ask about her? . . . O, there are folks . . .

Goes up to them.

By your leave, I pray.

MYSIS. By my soul, who's that? Isn't it old Crito, poor Mrs Chrysis's kinsman? . . . It is: the very same.

CRITO. O Mysis! I'm glad to see thee.

MYSIS. No gladder than I to see you, good Crito.

CRITO, *sorrowfully*. And is it true what they tell me of poor Chrysis, hah?

MYSIS, *sighing.* Yes, indeed; she has left us to our sorrows.

CRITO. Pray, how do you fare, lass? . . . How goes the world? Pretty hoddy, hah?

MYSIS. I should not say hoddy. . . . They that can't do as they would, must even do as they must, as the saying is.

CRITO. What of young Glycerie? Has she found her relations here?

MYSIS. Ah, would that she had!

CRITO. What, not yet! . . . Then I have brought my hogs to an ill market. 'Sblud, if I had known so much beforehand, the Devil a foot would I have stirred out of my house. For she passed everywhere for Chrysis's sister, and now she will have got possession of what was left. And for me, who know nobody at Athens, to entangle myself in law-suits, why, there are examples enough in the world to keep me from burning my fingers. And, now I think of it, she may get some spruce gallant to plead her cause, for she was in the 'teens, let me tell ye, when she went from us. The judges will cry out: 'This is a base rascal, that sets up only a forged title to be the heir.' And who would find it in his conscience to make the poor girl a beggar?

MYSIS. Go thy ways, honest Crito; in truth thou art the same Crito still.

CRITO. Come, bring me to her, however; since I'm come so far, let me see the poor rogue.

MYSIS. With all my heart.

Exit CRITO *and* MYSIS *with the child.*

DAVUS, *looking carefully about.* I'll follow 'em, but not for the world would I have the old man see me go.

Exit after them.

End of the Fourth Act

ACT FIVE

CHREMES *and* SIMO

CHREMES, *entering*. Come, Mr Simo, you've had proof enough
in all conscience of my friendship to ye; and I've run risk
enough for ye, therefore pray let us have no more of these
importunities. I have complied with ye now so long that
I was within a very little of ruining my daughter.

SIMO. Nay, Sir, I must more and more entreat and adjure ye
to stand by your word, and let your actions show the
world the sincerity of your promises.

CHREMES. But pray see, Sir, how unreasonable your passion
makes ye; for as long as you can obtain your own ends,
you don't regard common civility, nor well consider what
you'd have yourself. If you did, I am sure you wouldn't
desire to serve me in this manner.

SIMO. In what manner, pray?

CHREMES. Ah, Sir, do ye ask that question? You've tricked me
into offering my daughter to a wild spark of the town
that's already engaged, and a marriage-hater, too—so I shall
have 'em always wrangling, and forced to part in a fort-
night's time—my daughter's to be mortified, and your son
to have the benefit of it. I promised ye, and began to
make my promise good, whilst the case seemed convenient
to my interests; but since 'tis so no longer, ye must have
patience. His mistress, they say, is a free citizen, and there's

a child got between 'em; therefore pray don't offer us any
further disturbance.

SIMO. For goodness sake, Sir, don't trouble your head with
such idle stories. I tell ye, it is their chief interest to paint
him in as bad colours as they can; 'tis a trick from one end
to the other, to break off the match. Now, if you but take
away the cause, the effect will cease of itself.

CHREMES. You're wrong indeed, Sir, for just now I saw her
maid and Davus quarrelling about this very thing.

SIMO. I know the trick.

CHREMES. Nay, they were in earnest, for they little thought
I should see them.

SIMO. That I believe too, for I had an inkling of this stratagem from Davus, and I thought to have given you a hint
of it—but something put it out of my head.

Enter DAVUS, *just appearing at* GLYCERIE'S *door.*

DAVUS, *to them within.* . . . May Heaven grant that no
grief come within these walls today!

CHREMES. Look ye, yonder's your man, Davus.

SIMO, *in a fret.* Whence comes the rogue?

DAVUS, *to them within.* Let her rely upon this honest stranger
and myself.

SIMO, *aside, listening.* What new mischief is a-brewing?

DAVUS, *aside.* Well, the man came in the nick of time. Never
could anything have passed so pat to our purpose.

SIMO, *aside, partly overhearing.* Ah damned rogue! Whom
does he commend so?

DAVUS, *to himself.* Now Devil do thy worst, we are as safe
as a thief in a mill!

SIMO, *aside.* Why don't I speak to him?

DAVUS, *softly, perceiving* SIMO. 'Sdeath! here's my old master.
What had I best do?

SIMO, *scornfully, to* DAVUS. Oh, how is it with my fine gentleman?

DAVUS, *very briskly.* Oh, my good masters, Simo and Chremes
both! Why, all things are ready within for the wedding.

SIMO, *jeeringly*. You have taken a world of pains I don't doubt.

DAVUS, *leeringly*. Now, Sir, send for the bride as soon as you please.

SIMO. Very well! . . . there's nothing wanting but that. . . . But, good Sir, let me ask ye one question: what business had you at that house, Sirrah?

Pointing to GLYCERIE'S *door.*

DAVUS. Who—I, Sir?

SIMO. Ay—you, Sir.

DAVUS. Mean ye me, Sir?

SIMO. Yes, you, Sir, if ye must be told so often.

DAVUS. Why, Sir, 'twas not three minutes since I went in . . .

SIMO, *angrily*. Sirrah, do I ask ye how long since?

DAVUS. . . . With my master Pamphilus.

SIMO, *hastily*. And is he there then? . . . O, my torture! . . . Ye hang-dog, didn't ye tell me that their affections were broken all to pieces?

DAVUS. So they are, Sir.

SIMO, *hastily*. What should he be doing there then?

CHREMES, *jeeringly*. What d'ye think, Sir? . . . Only enjoying another brush of quarrel with her.

DAVUS. Ah, Mr Chremes, there's more in the wind; I'll tell ye perhaps one of the foulest stories you ever heard.

Pointing to GLYCERIE'S house.

Here's a certain old man just come to town, whence the Lord knows, a shrewd wary fellow, I'll warrant him; if ye did but see him, you'd say he's no ordinary personage, for he looks as grave as an alderman, and talks like a judge.

SIMO, *hastily*. What news from him, pray?

DAVUS. Nay, none to speak of . . . Only I remember he was a-saying . . .

SIMO. Well, but what was he a-saying?

DAVUS. . . . That he certainly knows Glycerie to be a citizen of Athens.

SIMO, *in a fury.* Soho! Dromo, Dromo!

DAVUS, *aside.* What's to do now?

SIMO, *louder.* Dromo, I say!

DAVUS, *in a fright.* But hear me, Sir!

SIMO. Dog! speak but another word . . .

> *Louder yet.*

Why, Dromo! Dromo!

DAVUS, *upon his knees.* I beseech ye, Sir, hear me!

> *Enter* DROMO.

DROMO, *to* SIMO. Your pleasure, Sir.

SIMO. Take this rascal into the house, and truss him up immediately.

DROMO. Whom do ye mean, Sir?

SIMO. Davus here.

DAVUS. Why, good Sir, why?

SIMO. 'Tis my pleasure . . .

> *To* DROMO.

Take him away, I say.

DAVUS. Why, what have I done, Sir?

SIMO, *to* DROMO. Away with him.

DAVUS. If you catch me in a lie, cut my throat!

SIMO, *stopping his ears.* I'll not hear a word . . . I'll settle your business for you, i' faith!

DAVUS. Notwithstanding my news be true?

SIMO. Notwithstanding . . . do you—

> *To* DROMO.

—take him and fetter him: And, d'ye hear, let him be tied neck and heels, like the beast that he is. . . . Away!

> *Exit* DROMO *leading* DAVUS.

SIMO, *walking about in a great passion.* Odsdeath, Sirrah, I'll teach ye this day what 'tis for a servant to put tricks upon his master, and for a son to make sport with his father!

CHREMES. For heaven's sake, Sir, moderate your anger.

SIMO. Ah, Sir! Where the duty of a son is concerned, that's

a tender point. Don't ye pity me? . . . That I should take so much pains for such an ungrateful wretch!

Weeps, looking towards GLYCERIE'S *house.*

Soho! Pamphilus! Come, Pamphilus . . . leave your fulsom nest . . . Have ye no shame left?

Enter PAMPHILUS.

PAMPHILUS. Who calls there? . . .

Seeing SIMO.

Oh, 'tis my father. I'm a dead man!

SIMO, *very angrily.* What say'st thou, the most ungrateful . . .

CHREMES. O fie, Sir, have done with this ill language, and argue the case calmly!

SIMO. As though the worst language wasn't too good for him.

To PAMPHILUS.

And d'ye say now that Glycerie is a citizen?

PAMPHILUS. 'Tis so reported, Sir.

SIMO. Reported, Jackanapes! . . . O, prodigious impudence! was ever such a credulous coxcomb? And does he repent of anything he has done? Nay, has he the grace so much as to blush at it? . . . Is he so little master of himself as to have set his heart upon such an infamous woman, without regard either to the laws of Athens, or to the will and pleasure of his father?

PAMPHILUS, *sighing.* Ah me!

SIMO. O Pamphilus! are ye at last convinced? . . . then, then indeed you should have thought of this, when first you took your swig of all that's base—then you should have cried, 'Ah me!'

Walks about in a rage.

But what do I mean? Why should I plague and torment myself in my old age for a mad hot-headed fool? Shall he play the puppy, and must I suffer for it? . . . even let them kennel together, and he shall make his best of her!

PAMPHILUS, *in a soft tone.* Dear Father! . . .

SIMO, *interrupting.* Why 'dear Father'? As though you stood in need of such a father. . . . You've got your house, your wife and child, and the dear Father never the wiser; you've even brought your cheating stranger to prove her a citizen. . . . You've won the day, and much good may it do ye!

PAMPHILUS. Pray hear me one word, Sir.

SIMO, *turning away.* What can you say for yourself?

CHREMES. Good Sir, give him a hearing.

SIMO. I hear him! Pray why should I hear him, Mr Chremes?

CHREMES. At least give him leave to speak, though you are deaf to the matter.

SIMO. Let him speak then, who hinders him?

PAMPHILUS, *in a soft tone.* Sir, I confess I loved, and if to love be a sin, I confess that too. . . . But now, dear Sir, I'm at your disposal, and submit to whatsoever you shall think fit or command. Would ye have me marry one woman and part with another? Then I must bear both ills as well as I can. Only thus much let me beg of ye, that you won't believe that I suborned this old man; let me but clear myself of that charge, and bring him face to face with ye.

SIMO. Bring him?

PAMPHILUS. Pray, Sir, let me!

CHREMES. 'Tis nothing unreasonable, pray let him!

PAMPHILUS. Sir, I beseech ye don't deny me!

SIMO. Well, let it be so, then.

Exit PAMPHILUS.

You see, Sir, I'm content with anything, as long as I be not grossly imposed upon.

CHREMES. Between father and son, a small punishment suffices for a great fault.

Re-enter PAMPHILUS *with* CRITO.

CRITO, *entering.* . . . Well, without wasting more words—for three reasons are as good as three thousand—I'll do it either for your own sake, or for truth's sake, or for the sake of poor Glycerie for whom I've a kindness.

CHREMES. Why, upon my word, is that not old Crito of

Andros? . . . the very same . . . Troth, Crito, I'm glad to see thee: what wind blew thee to Athens?

CRITO. A chance one. . . . Is this Mr Simo?

CHREMES. Yes.

SIMO. D'ye ask for me? . . . Hark ye, friend, have you the face to say Glycerie is a citizen of Athens?

CRITO, *bristling.* And you, Sir, have you the face to call me liar?

SIMO. You've learned your lesson by rote, I perceive.

CRITO, *angrily.* What's that, pray?

SIMO. Would ye know? . . . Don't ye deserve to be laid by the heels for this? Are ye come here to cheat and inveigle raw young gentlemen, and to feed their minds with fine foolish and gay promises?

CRITO. Is the man mad?

SIMO. Then ye make matches 'twixt them and their whores.
CRITO *stares in wonder at him.*

PAMPHILUS, *aside.* Alas! how do I tremble for fear lest old Crito should not stand his ground!

CHREMES, *to* SIMO. If ye knew this man as well as I, you'd be of another mind. Why, he's as honest a man as e'er broke bread.

SIMO. He honest! . . . to come just in the nick on the wedding-day, to offer himself as witness though he was never here before in his whole life! Well, should his testimony be regarded?

PAMPHILUS, *aside.* If I weren't afraid of my father, I've a word at the tip of my tongue would help old Crito out.

SIMO. False evidence is this pedlar's stock-in-trade!

CRITO. What does he call me?
Walks about in a huff.

CHREMES. 'Tis his way, you'd better let him be.

CRITO. Let him mind his manners. If he thinks he can say whatever he has a mind to, I'll make him hear something that he has no mind to.
To SIMO.

Pish! Do I hinder or care a fart for your wedding? Why can't ye bear your misfortunes like a man? . . . Whether I spoke true or false you'll know immediately.

Turning to CHREMES.

Once upon a time, d'ye see, there was a vessel wrecked at Andros, and every soul perished but a certain Athenian merchant and the little girl with him. This man being in want, he applied himself as it happened to Chrysis's father. . . .

SIMO, *interrupting.* Now he begins a fine tale!

CHREMES. Pray let him go on.

CRITO, *angrily.* Why does he put me out by his interruptions?

CHREMES. On with your story!

CRITO. Well, now this same Chrysis's father (d'ye remember?) was my kinsman. And at his house did I hear the man himself say that he was a merchant of Athens. In short, there he died soon after.

CHREMES. His name?

CRITO. His name! . . . Let me see: ah yes, his name was Phania.

CHREMES, *aside.* Bless me! I'm in a cold sweat.

CRITO. Why, truly, Sir, I think they called him so. However, this I'm sure of, he said he was from Rhamnus here.

CHREMES. O heavens!

CRITO. . . . And a world of people in Andros heard as much as I.

CHREMES, *aside.* Would that the truth were as I heartily hope it to be.

Aloud.

. . . But prithee, Crito, tell me what said he about this girl? Did he say she was his own?

CRITO. No, Sir.

CHREMES. Whose then, pray?

CRITO. His brother's, I think.

CHREMES. On my soul, she's mine then!

CRITO. What d'ye say, Sir?

SIMO, *hastily*. How's this? What say ye?

PAMPHILUS, *aside*. Courage, Pamphilus, courage!

SIMO. What makes ye believe it so readily?

CHREMES. Why, this Phania was my brother.

SIMO. I know it; I was well acquainted with him.

CHREMES. In the time of the late wars he fled to where I was in Asia, and brought my daughter off in the ship with him. Now, Sir, this is the first news I've since heard of either; I had long mourned them both for dead.

PAMPHILUS, *aside*. Methinks I'm in another world; my mind's distracted 'twixt fear and hope, joy and wonder at such a sudden blessing.

SIMO. I'm glad upon several accounts she's found to be your daughter.

PAMPHILUS. I can well believe that, Sir!

CHREMES. But hark ye, Crito, there's one scruple yet that makes me uneasy.

PAMPHILUS. To the Devil with you and your scruples! This is like hunting for a knot in a bulrush.

CRITO. What's that, Sir?

CHREMES. My daughter was no Glycerie. The name won't do.

CRITO. Truly she had another when she was a little one.

CHREMES. Prithee, what was it? Don't ye remember?

CRITO. I'm hammering at it.

He studies upon it.

PAMPHILUS, *aside*. Shall I suffer his poor memory to impede the current of my joys, when I can cure all with a word? No, I'll not suffer it.

Aloud.

D'ye hear, Mr Chremes? Passibula's the name you want.

CRITO, CHREMES, *together*. Ay, that's it, that's it! The very same!

PAMPHILUS. I had it from her mouth a thousand times.

SIMO, *to* CHREMES. Truly this is good news for all of us, and I hope you think so too.

CHEMES. As I hope to be saved, 'tis true.

PAMPHILUS, *to* SIMO. And what's to be done next, Sir?

SIMO. Why, now we are all friends again.

PAMPHILUS. The best of fathers! . . . I suppose Mr Chremes will allow us to remain in *statu quo*.

CHREMES. For every reason in the world, unless your father's against it.

PAMPHILUS, SIMO, *together*. I'm sure he's not. I agree, I agree.

CHREMES. Mr Pamphilus, you shall have two thousand pounds for a marriage portion.

PAMPHILUS. I'm satisfied, Sir.

CHREMES. Well, I'll go at once to my poor girl. Friend Crito, come along with me, for I doubt she'll remember who I am.

Exeunt CRITO *and* CHREMES.

SIMO. And hadn't ye better send for her now?

PAMPHILUS. I think 'twere better, but that shall be Davus's business.

SIMO. Nay, that can't be.

PAMPHILUS. Why so, Sir?

SIMO. Because he's a little engaged.

PAMPHILUS. And how, Sir?

SIMO. Why, i' faith, he's bound neck and heels.

PAMPHILUS. Ah, Sir, that wasn't well done.

SIMO, *merrily*. I'm sure I ordered it to be well done.

PAMPHILUS. Pray, Sir, let it be undone then.

SIMO. Well, so it may be, I think.

PAMPHILUS. But immediately, Sir, if you please.

SIMO. I'll go in and see about it.

PAMPHILUS. A blessed and happy day's work!

Exit SIMO.

Enter CHARINUS *at a distance*.

CHARINUS, *to himself*. Well, I'll go see how affairs go with Mr Pamphilus.

He observes him.

Oh, yonder he is.

PAMPHILUS. Some may be apt to think my heart is far
  From what my lips do utter, yet I declare
  The Gods themselves would not immortal be,
  Were there not joys immortal as they are.
  And now methinks I'm all encircled round
  With heavenly bliss, if no left-handed God
  Come in between, and spoil my sweets with sour . . .
  Oh! for a friend, to whom I might relate
  This blessed change, to make it more complete.

CHARINUS. What's the meaning of these raptures?
  Enter DAVUS *at a distance.*

PAMPHILUS. Oh, yonder's Davus, the one man of the whole
earth I could have wished for; for I'm sure there's not a soul
else can more heartily relish my change of fortune.

DAVUS, *to himself.* Where should I light upon my master now?

PAMPHILUS. Oh Davus!

DAVUS, *not seeing him.* Who called?

PAMPHILUS. 'Tis I, old rock!

DAVUS, *turning about.* What, you, Sir?

PAMPHILUS. Ay, ye don't know yet what good fortune has
overtaken me.

DAVUS, *shrugging.* No, faith; but I know, to my sorrow, what
ill fortune has been mine.

PAMPHILUS. Ay, boy, that I know too.

DAVUS. And no wonder: in this world bad news always flies
faster than good.

PAMPHILUS. My dearest Glycerie has found her parents.

DAVUS, *merrily.* Brave tidings, by George!

CHARINUS, *aside, listening.* Bless me!

PAMPHILUS. And her father is a great crony of my father's.

DAVUS. Who's that, pray?

PAMPHILUS. None other than Mr Chremes.

DAVUS. Spoken like a cherubim!

PAMPHILUS. I've now nothing to do but to marry her, and . . .

CHARINUS, *aside.* Alas, fond man! He lies in a day-dream!

PAMPHILUS. Then for the child, Davus . . .

DAVUS. Ye need say no more of him; I'll warrant ye he'll grow to be an hero at last.

CHARINUS, *aside, going to them*. I'm a made man, if all this be true. . . . I'll e'en speak with 'em.

PAMPHILUS. Who goes there? . . . Oh, dear Charinus, you're come at the luckiest time that could be.

CHARINUS. I'm very well pleased . . .

PAMPHILUS. How! have ye heard the news then?

CHARINUS. Every syllable. . . . Well I hope you won't forget your old friend on your wedding-day. Mr Chremes is now so bound to you, that if you'll but say the word, I'm sure he'll give Philumena to me.

PAMPHILUS. I warrant I'll not forget ye. . . . But 'twould be too long to wait Mr Chremes's coming. Let us even go to my mistress, where we shall be sure to find him. . . . Davus, do you go off, and fetch a company to escort her to our house. . . . What makes ye stand like a post? . . . Why don't ye move?

DAVUS. I'm going, Sir.

Exeunt PAMPHILUS *and* CHARINUS.

DAVUS *turns to the spectators.*

DAVUS. Gallants, you must not expect their return, for the match and everything else will be made up within doors. . . . One clap, good gentlemen!

End of THE FAIR ANDRIAN

THE MOTHER-IN-LAW

A Comedy acted at the Roman Sports when C. Julius Caesar *and* Cn. Cornelius Dolabella *were Curule Ediles. At that time it was not acted quite through.*

Flaccus, *a freedman of* Claudius, *composed the music, which was performed on two unequal flutes.*

It was taken wholly from the Greek of Apollodorus.

Acted first under the Consulship of Cn. Octavius *and* T. Manlius, *it was acted a second time at a Funeral Solemnity, and a third time, when* Q. Fulvius *and* L. Murcio *were Curule Ediles.*

A.U.C.588   Before Christ 165

DRAMATIS PERSONAE

LACHES, *an old gentleman of Athens, very honest and true-hearted, lately retired into the country*

PHIDIPPUS, *another old citizen of Athens, his neighbour and friend, indulgent to his family, angry when stirred*

PAMPHILUS, *Laches's son, a genteel, civil, good natured young gentleman, a respecter of his parents, though formerly somewhat debauched*

PARMENO, *servant to Pamphilus, and his confidant; a trusty, merry, inquisitive fellow*

SOCIA, *another servant of Pamphilus's*

SOSTRATA, *the Mother-in-law, wife to Laches, a submissive, peaceable, kind old gentlewoman*

MYRRHINA, *wife to Phidippus, easy-going and timorous*

BACCHIS, *a noted courtesan, formerly mistress to Pamphilus, very honest and generous, considering her circumstances*

PHILOTIS, *another courtesan, of a merry, gentle, sweet nature*

SYRA, *an old woman of the same trade, peevish, revengeful and ill-natured*

NON-SPEAKING PARTS:

PHILUMENA, *wife to Pamphilus and daughter to Phidippus*

SCIRTUS, *a boy of Laches's*

THE NURSE

TWO SERVANTS *of Bacchis's*

PORTERS

WAITING-MAIDS

ACT ONE

SCENE: *The street in front of* PHIDIPPUS'S *and* LACHES'S *door*

TIME: *The morning*

Enter PHILOTIS *and* SYRA

PHILOTIS. Faith, old Syra, there's not one in forty of these young fellows who keeps faith with a mistress. . . . Why, here's Mr Pamphilus now, how many thousand oaths did he swear to Bacchis (solemnly and credibly, too) that he'd never marry while she lived? Very good, yet my gentleman's married for all that.

SYRA. For that reason, girl, let me advise and conjure you as a friend, to pity none of the male sex, but fleece them, maul them, pick the very bones of every creature of them whom you get in your clutches.

PHILOTIS, *sighing*. What, all without exception?

SYRA. Ay, every mother's son of them! . . . Take this from an old woman; that none of these sparks who are so sweet upon ye, has any other design than to have his will of ye at as cheap a rate as he can. And prithee, child, shouldn't thou in justice countermine them?

PHILOTIS. But to serve all alike is too cruel, I vow.

SYRA. Cruel to be revenged on one's enemies, or to catch cheats in their own traps! Ah, what pity it is that I have not your youth and beauty, or you my experience in these matters.

Enter PARMENO *at a distance.*

PARMENO, *to* SCIRTUS *within.* If the old gentleman should ask for me, tell him I'm just gone to the water-side, to enquire when Mr Pamphilus comes home. Do ye hear, boy? If he asks for me you may tell him so; if not, say nothing; then this excuse will serve for another time.

He comes from the door.

But is that Philly there? . . . Whence comes she, I wonder?

Goes up to them.

Philotis, I'm heartily glad to see ye.

PHILOTIS. And I you, honest Parmeno.

SYRA. Cods-buddikins, Parmeno, how dost thou do, my lad?

PARMENO. Uds-fish, Granny, how dost thou?

Exit SYRA.

PARMENO. But prithee, Miss Philly, where have you been diverting yourself this live-long while?

PHILOTIS. I have enjoyed but little diversion, Heaven knows, ever since I marched off to Corinth with the Captain—the veriest brute upon earth—where I led a dog's life for two whole years together.

PARMENO. Ay, faith! I warrant ye, you often sighed for old Athens again, and could have wished yourself hanged for undertaking the journey.

PHILOTIS. 'Tis impossible to tell you how eager I was to be rid of my spark and come home, where I might have liberty to see ye all once more and to enjoy my friends and merry-meetings as formerly. For there I couldn't utter a word but what was put into my mouth by that rascally Captain.

PARMENO. Such cutting ye short of your tattle must needs have gone against the grain, I fancy.

PHILOTIS. Indeed, it did. But what a tale is this that Bacchis has just now been telling me! I could never have imagined Pamphilus would find it in his heart to marry so long as she lived.

PARMENO, *angrily.* 'Marry,' says she?

PHILOTIS. Hey-day! Why, isn't he married?

PARMENO. Married indeed he is! But I have a notion that this marriage won't hold long.

PHILOTIS. Pray Heaven it may end, and to Bacchis's advantage! . . . But how shall I be certain of the truth? Good boy, satisfy me in this particular.

PARMENO. That's no proper question to ask; pray don't be so inquisitive.

PHILOTIS. You're afraid, I warrant, that I should blaze it abroad? But let me perish if I ask with any such thought in my head. 'Tis but for my own private satisfaction.

PARMENO. All your fine wheedling shall never make me trust to your discretion; I value a whole skin.

PHILOTIS, *in a jaunty way*. Well, don't then; who cares? As if now you weren't even more eager to tell me, than I to know!

PARMENO, *aside*. Edad, she's in the right there. She has hit upon my greatest weakness. . . . Well, Madam, promise secrecy upon your honour, and I'll tell you all.

PHILOTIS. So! Now you're come to yourself again! Upon my honour, I promise then; fire away with the tale.

PARMENO. Listen with care.

PHILOTIS. Well?

PARMENO. Mr Pamphilus was in the very height of his passion for Madam Bacchis, when Mr Laches, his father, began earnestly to prod him towards marriage. He offered the usual arguments of all fathers in like circumstances: namely, that he was an old man with but an only child, and feared to be left destitute of support in his old age. At first Mr Pamphilus rejected the proposal; but when his father came to press him more zealously than before, he was brought to such straits that he couldn't tell which to prefer, whether love or duty. At last the old man, by whining and teasing at his son's heart, screwed him up to such a pitch that he consented to marry Philumena, his neighbour's daughter. Pamphilus didn't take it so ill until his wedding-day drew on. But when he saw that all things were ready, and that marry he must, without more ado, he sorrowed so deeply, that I swear if Bacchis herself had seen him in that plight, she couldn't but have pitied him. For whenever he had any spare time for being by himself, he'd call me aside and cry: 'Ah, Parmeno. I'm a lost man! What have I done? To what a dismal condition have I brought myself? I am unable to bear the weight of it. Oh, 'twill break my heart!'

PHILOTIS. The Devil and his dam take this Mr Laches for a nasty old cur!

PARMENO. To cut short my story, the bride was brought home. The first night he did not touch her; nor the following night neither . . .

PHILOTIS. The Deuce take ye! What, a young fellow to have his bride in bed with him on the wedding-night, and pretty tipsy too, I warrant ye, and not . . . A likely business, in truth! Come, this sounds like a lie!

PARMENO. I know you can't believe me, because no man comes to you, unless he comes sharp set with passion. But alas, our young gentleman had no appetite at all for his woman.

PHILOTIS. Well, what then?

PARMENO. A few days after, he takes me aside, and tells me that Philumena was still as honest a virgin as ever, for all that they had shared a bridal bed—though until he married, he had hoped a wife might have served his turn pretty well. 'But now,' said he, 'I'm resolved to part with her before long. 'Twould be a baseness in me, and much to the poor gentlewoman's prejudice if I did not return her to her friends as whole as when she came to me.'

PHILOTIS. That was spoken like a gentleman of honest principles.

PARMENO. 'But then,' continued he, 'it won't be safe to publish my intentions; and for me to send her back with no least complaint against her would be somewhat too peremptory. My one hope is that when she finds there's no living together of her and me, she'll be gone of her own accord.'

PHILOTIS. But meanwhile did he continue his visits to Bacchis?

PARMENO. As regularly as the sun in his course! But (as 'tis usual for women) when she saw him pledged to another, she became more peevish and demanding than formerly.

PHILOTIS. I' faith, and well she might!

PARMENO. And this, indeed, was the chief cause of their parting. For by this time he had recollected himself, and seriously considered first his mistress's character and then his wife's and their behaviours; Philumena, he found, was a sweet-natured gentlewoman, virtuous and modest, patient under a husband's affronts and incivilities and willing to wink at his faults. Therefore, partly touched with remorse for having so ill-used his wife, and partly tired with his whore's insolence, he at last gave Bacchis the slip, and settled his affections upon Philumena, whose humour he found so agreeable to his own. . . . In the meantime, an old kinsman of our master dies at Imbros, and makes him his heir; and most unwillingly our love-sick Pamphilus is posted away by his father to collect the money left him. He leaves Philumena with his mother; for the old gentleman lives retired in the country, and seldom visits Athens.

PHILOTIS. But where's the flaw in the match? As I thought, there was perfect love between the two of them?

PARMENO. I'm going to tell ye. At first, for a few days or so, the mother and the daughter-in-law agreed mighty well together. Then, all of a sudden, the young woman began to hate the old one most mortally, without any quarrel or complaint on either side.

PHILOTIS. How came it about then?

PARMENO. If at any time my old Lady Sostrata came to have a little chat with Philumena, she'd fly at the sight of her. But when she could avoid her company no longer, she'd pretend her mother had sent for her upon some business of religion; and away she went. After she had been away a while, my Lady Sostrata sends a message desiring her company at home; but is returned a lame excuse about I know not what. She sends a second time, but no daughter-in-law comes. At last, after many messages, they pretend she is sick. Thereupon my Lady steps over herself, to pay her a visit, but can get no admittance. Yesterday, when the matter came to my old master's ears, he left the country upon this very account, and discoursed with her father about it. I can't learn as yet what passed between them; but I'm in a peck of troubles to know what will come of it. . . . Now you've got the long and short of my story. . . . I must be off to the place I designed.

PHILOTIS. And so must I, too. I've made an assignation with a country squire for much about this time.

PARMENO. I'll throw an old shoe after ye, and wish ye good luck!

PHILOTIS. Farewell, Parmeno.

PARMENO. And farewell to thee, my little Philly!

Exeunt severally.

End of the First Act

ACT TWO

Enter LACHES, *and* SOSTRATA *after him*

LACHES, *entering*. Bless my soul! The female sex makes me
mad! What a confounded conspiracy is this, that all women
should take the same bias, and follow the same plaguey
course in all they do or baulk at doing? When did you see
a mother-in-law who did not hate her daughter-in-law?
The endeavours of wives to oppose their husbands are the
same, and their cross-grained stubbornness is the same. I
fancy they are all trained up for mischief in the same
school, of which damned place of education (if there be
any such) I'll be sworn my own dame is the school-
mistress.

Walks about in a huff.

SOSTRATA. 'Tis hard that I should be accused of a business
of which I know nothing.

LACHES. You know nothing of this, then?

SOSTRATA. As I hope for mercy, I don't! And as I hope (my
dear Laches!) that we may live long together, so also I
don't!

LACHES. Heaven forbid that the years be many! say I.

SOSTRATA. That I'm wrongfully accused, time will show.

LACHES, *jeering*. Yes, yes; you are wrongfully accused. . . .
Can any words be evil enough to expose ye in your true

colours? You who have disgraced me, yourself and our family, and are laying up sufficient wrath to torment your son? Then you've provoked our new friends and relations to hate us, those who were pleased to honour our son with their alliance. And you, forsooth, must now start to confound all by your ill-conditioned whims and ways.

SOSTRATA. Who, I?

LACHES. Woman, I say you! You must take me for a block, not a man! Think ye that because I have retired to the country I know nothing of your pranks and transactions in town? But let me tell ye, I know much better what's done here than what's done at my own residence; and this is because my reputation abroad depends upon your behaviour at home. I heard long ago, indeed, that Philumena could not endure ye, nor did I wonder at it, considering that it would have been a greater miracle if she could. But I little thought she would have learned to hate the whole family upon your account. Had I been aware of that, I should have bid her stay, and packed you off instead, i' faith. . . . Pray see, wife, how little reason ye have to vex me thus! I retired to the country, gave way to ye, allowed ye enough both for your necessities and your pleasures. And that my estate might the better be enabled to afford this, I've toiled and wearied myself more than is convenient for my age. Couldn't ye, after all this, have taken care that nothing disturbed my repose?

SOSTRATA. By all that's good, what has happened has not been brought about by any fault of mine!

LACHES. Nay, but it was so! For you're sole mistress here, and must take the sole blame. Surely you might have managed things better in your own house, since I've taken all other cares off your hands. An old woman to stand squabbling with a girl? Fie, fie! You won't lay the blame upon her, will ye?

SOSTRATA. No! Dear husband, I lay no blame upon her.

LACHES. On my soul, I'm glad of that, for the poor girl's sake. But as for you, do the worst ye can, for I can't think any less of ye than I do already.

SOSTRATA. But, good husband, how do ye know that she may not be only pretending displeasure against me, so as to be the longer at home with her mother?

LACHES. Never tell me that! Wasn't yesterday's shutting the door in your face sufficient proof of her hatred?

SOSTRATA. They told me that she was very faint and weak; therefore it wasn't convenient to disturb her.

LACHES. She's sick, I fancy, of your ill humour more than of anything else. And no wonder, in truth; for there's not a mother in this city but would have her sons marry. And whoever is the person that pleases her, that one they must have. Ay, ye are all alike! For no sooner do the lads marry in order to comply with your whims, then, to comply with your whims again, they must turn their wives out of doors!

PHIDIPPUS *appears at his door.*

PHIDIPPUS, *to* PHILUMENA *within.* Though 'tis clear that I've authority to force you into obedience, yet my fatherly affection persuades me rather to give way, and not oppose ye in your stubborn mood.

LACHES. Oh! here's my Brother Phidippus come in good time. I shall learn all from him.

They meet one another.

I confess Brother, I'm as indulgent to all my family as is any man; yet I do not allow my kindness to corrupt their morals. If you were also so careful, I believe it would be to your advantage, as well as ours. But now I find ye let them ride ye as they please.

PHIDIPPUS, *aside.* Look ye there, now!

LACHES. Yesterday I called upon ye to speak about your daughter. You sent me away no wiser than I came. But let me tell ye, you are ill-advised to conceal the cause of your anger, if you wish for a lasting alliance between us. Have any of us offended ye? Then pray, let us know; so that, either by disproving or justifying what we are said to have done, you may be given ample satisfaction. If sickness be the cause of keeping your daughter at home, let me tell ye, Brother, the suggestion that she wouldn't have proper attendance at my house reflects unkindly upon us. As I hope to be saved, though you are her father, you could not outdo me in this respect. Nor can you be more solicitous of her health than I am, and that for my poor boy's sake; for I perceive he loves her more than his life, and I'm confident he will highly resent this slight upon his parents when he comes to hear of it. Therefore, pray let's have her home before he returns from his voyage.

PHIDIPPUS. I'm satisfied, Brother, of your extraordinary care and affection for my daughter, and am apt to believe every word you've said. But then I'd have ye believe me too, when I say that 'tis my hearty desire to bring Philumena to your house, if I could prevail upon her by any means.

LACHES. Why, what hinders ye?

Softly.

Hark ye, does she consider herself injured in anything by her husband?

PHIDIPPUS. Nay, not in the least degree! For when I strongly urged her to return, and made as though I'd force her, she vowed by all the gods that she couldn't endure your house while her Pamphilus was away. Everyone has his failings; mine is to be so soft-hearted that I can't cross and thwart my own flesh and blood.

LACHES, *aside to* SOSTRATA. Do ye hear that, Mistress?

SOSTRATA, *aside.* Ay, to my sorrow.

LACHES. Is that your resolution then, Brother?

PHIDIPPUS. As the case stands, 'tis so . . . But have ye anything else to say? For a small business calls me in haste to the Piazza.

LACHES. I'll bear ye company, if ye please!

Exeunt PHIDIPPUS *and* LACHES.

SOSTRATA, *alone.* In good faith, we poor wives have earned a very ill name with our husbands, because of a few bad creatures who make the world judge hardly of us all. For, as I hope for Heaven, I'm as innocent as a sucking infant of what my husband charges against me. Yet 'tis almost impossible for me to be believed, there's such a common scandal sticks to the name of mother-in-law. But let me die if I'm one that deserves it! For I've been as tender to this creature as if she'd been a daughter of my own. I can't imagine why this misfortune should light upon my head! Therefore, upon this and many other accounts, I'm extremely desirous of my son's return.

Exit SOSTRATA.

End of the Second Act

ACT THREE

Enter PAMPHILUS *and* PARMENO, *at the farther part of the stage*

PAMPHILUS. Was ever man so perplexed in his love as I? Unhappy wretch! On my life, have I been so bad a husband as to deserve this?—was it this which made me so desirous of returning home? Far better to have spent my days anywhere in the world, than to come back and find myself so unhappy. For whenever misfortune befalls a man, the more time that glides by before he knows it means so many days of happiness clearly gained.

PARMENO. However, Sir, your return will enable you to repair matters the sooner. Had you stayed longer, the breach would have grown far wider. Now, Sir, I'm confident that your presence will have a great influence upon them all. You'll learn about the whole business, rectify misunderstandings, and restore a general friendship. These dreadful apprehensions of yours are in themselves but very slight things.

PAMPHILUS. Why do ye try to comfort me, knowing that I'm the greatest wretch alive? Before I married this woman, my heart was engaged elsewhere; how much I suffered upon that account may be easily guessed without my telling. And yet I never dared to refuse the match that my father arranged for me. I had no sooner weaned my affec-

tions from Bacchis, and fixed my love upon Philumena
than, alas, a new business forced me to leave her for awhile.
And for the trouble that has divided our house, I fear I
shall find either her or my mother to blame. And, if either,
the consequences will make me more miserable still. For,
hark ye Parmeno, filial duty bids me bear with my mother's
failings; and as for my wife, I'm a thousand ways bound to
her, in gratitude not only for her meekly bearing with my
ill humour, but for concealing from all the world my unkind usage of her. Certainly, Parmeno, some extraordinary
thing must have happened, to occasion the quarrel which
has now lasted so long.

PARMENO. Some frivolous thing or other, I'll warrant ye, Sir!
For upon close study you'll find that the greatest quarrels
haven't always had the greatest occasions. 'Tis frequent,
Sir, to find that a certain offence makes one man stark mad,
and your mortal enemy forever, when the same thing
doesn't move another in the least. How do children bite
and scratch for the smallest trifles! And why? Marry, because their understandings are weak and unable to direct
them. And your women can be as easily moved as children. One chance word, perhaps, has been the cause of all
this disturbance.

PAMPHILUS. Well! go in, Parmeno, and let them know I'm
here.

PARMENO, *going off, hears a noise and stops short.*

PARMENO. Hah! What happens here?

PAMPHILUS, *listens.* 'S't!

PARMENO. Here's a sad bustle! They run up and down like
Bedlamites . . . Pray, Sir, come a little this way . . .

PAMPHILUS *goes towards him.*

A little closer yet . . .

They both listen at PHIDIPPUS's *door.*

Hah! Do ye hear, Sir?

PAMPHILUS. Hold your prating!

Sound of shrieking within.

Bless me! I hear somebody shriek.

PARMENO. So, you enjoin me silence, and talk yourself!

MYRRHINA, *within doors*. Prithee, dear child, as little noise as may be.

PAMPHILUS. That's like Philumena's mother's voice. . . . Ruined!

PARMENO. Why so?

PAMPHILUS. Undone!

PARMENO. Wherefore?

PAMPHILUS. Ah, Parmeno, some more than ordinary mischief has happened, which they conceal from me.

PARMENO. They said indeed that your lady was not in good health. Whether that be it or no, I can't tell.

PAMPHILUS. I'm a lost man.

Angrily.

Why didn't ye tell me this before?

PARMENO. I couldn't tell ye everything at once.

PAMPHILUS. What's her sickness?

PARMENO. That I can't tell, either.

PAMPHILUS. How? Has nobody gone for a doctor?

PARMENO. I can't tell that, neither.

PAMPHILUS. But why don't I go in myself, and learn for certain what's the business? . . . Ah, my dear Philumena, in what condition shall I now find thee? Should thy life be in danger, I shall certainly die with thee.

Exit PAMPHILUS.

PARMENO, *alone*. I don't think it convenient to venture in after him! For I very well know that they don't care for any of our family. Yesterday they shut the door against my Lady Sostrata herself. If Madam Philumena should chance to grow worse (which, in truth, I wouldn't have happen for my poor master's sake) they'll soon pretend that one of Madam Sostrata's servants entered, brought the Devil along with him, and that thereupon she grew worse immediately. So my mistress will be blamed; but I shall have the worst of it. A plague on them all!

The noise increases within.

Enter SOSTRATA *on the other side.*

SOSTRATA, *to herself.* Alas, I think I've heard a strange sort of bustle in my sister's house, and for some time too. I vow, I'm extremely afraid poor Philumena's sickness grows worse and worse. But Heaven forbid! Now I'll pay her a visit.

She is going in.

PARMENO. Hark ye, Madam!

SOSTRATA. Hah!

PARMENO. You'll meet with another repulse, Madam.

SOSTRATA, *turning about.* Ha, Parmeno! are you there? . . . Alas, poor wretch! What shall I do? Shan't I go see my son's wife, when she lies sick no farther off than next door?

PARMENO. If you'd be ruled by me, Madam, you'll neither see her, nor send to see her! For to have affection for one who utterly hates you, seems a double piece of folly. You'll bestow your labour to no purpose, and be troublesome besides. . . . Besides, Madam, your son went in to see how she fared, as soon as he came to town.

SOSTRATA. How! My son Pamphilus is ashore?

PARMENO. Yes, Madam.

SOSTRATA. Heavens be praised! . . . That news has revived me, and set my heart at rest.

PARMENO. 'Tis upon this account especially that I wouldn't have ye go in. For if her pains be a little abated I'm confident, now that they're together, she'll up and tell him all that has passed; and how the difference between you two first began. . . . But see where he comes! He seems very melancholy.

Enter PAMPHILUS.

SOSTRATA, *embracing him.* Ah, my dear, dear child!

PAMPHILUS. Your blessing, Madam!

SOSTRATA. Welcome home heartily! . . . But how is it with your wife?

PAMPHILUS, *wiping his eyes.* Why, she's on the mend.

SOSTRATA. Heavens continue it so! . . . But why in tears, son? Why thus melancholy?

PAMPHILUS. Nothing at all, Madam.

SOSTRATA. What was that bustle? Tell me: was she taken with a sudden fit?

PAMPHILUS. Yes, Madam.

SOSTRATA. What's her sickness?

PAMPHILUS. An ague.

SOSTRATA. A quotidian ague?

PAMPHILUS. So they tell me. . . . Pray, Madam, walk in! I'll follow immediately.

SOSTRATA. So I will.

Exit SOSTRATA.

PAMPHILUS. Parmeno, do you run to meet my servants and help them home with their luggage.

PARMENO, *grumbling*. What the deuce! Can't they find their way home without a guide?

PAMPHILUS. You'll be gone, won't ye?

Exit PARMENO.

PAMPHILUS, *alone, walking about discontentedly*. Where shall I now begin to give an account of those many surprising misfortunes that have befallen me, part of which I heard, and another part of which I saw with these very eyes—so that I ran out of the house, half distracted? . . . For when I hastily went in just now, in great concern for my wife, thinking to find her suffering from another sort of sickness than what, alas! she has—the maids, being surprised at first sight and all of them overjoyed, cried out: 'He's come!' But immediately after, I saw that they changed countenance, because I happened to come at such an unlucky minute. Meantime one of them ran upstairs, to give Philumena notice of my arrival; and I, eager to see my wife, followed close behind. No sooner had I arrived, but I perceived her ailment at once (unhappy creature that I was!); for they had no time in the world to conceal the business, and her cryings-out did sufficiently reveal her condition. When I

saw this, 'Base and unworthy!' cried I! and with that flung
out of the room all in tears, struck with horror at such an
unheard-of, dismal accident. Her mother, poor soul, followed me close, caught me at the door, and flung herself at
my feet, melting into tears, so that I couldn't help but pity
her. And truly I'm of the opinion that, as a man's fortune
rises or falls, so he too is up or down. She thus addressed
me: 'My dear Pamphilus, you're an eye-witness now of the
cause that made this unhappy creature leave your house.
She was raped on the street some time ago by an unknown
villain, and has fled hither to hide her shame from you and
the world.'

He wipes his eyes.

Alas! the very remembrance of her earnest entreaties makes
me weep afresh. . . . 'Whatsoever chance or fortune,'
continued she, 'has brought you hither at this juncture, we
both implore ye (if we may in equity and justice presume
so far) to conceal this mischance from the eye of the world.
If ever (dear Pamphilus), if ever you were aware that she
felt any tenderness for ye, she begs ye in return not to think
this small favour too much to grant her. As for taking her
again, use your own discretion! You're the only person who
knows either of her lying-in, or that the child is none of
yours. For, they say, you would have nothing to do with
her for the first two months; and 'tis now no more than
seven since you changed your way. Your behaviour shows
what your thoughts are about it. Now, if it be possible
(my dear) I wish for nothing more than that her lying-in
may be concealed from her father, and from every other
soul besides. But should it come out, let it pass for the
honest effect of marriage; for I'm sure none will think otherwise than what is most probable, namely that you are the
child's father. The same child shall immediately be exposed, and you shall be none the worse; and by this means
you will not only suffer no inconvenience, but protect your
unlucky wife's reputation besides.' I gave the mother my
word, and am resolved to keep it. But as for taking her
again, I cannot think that it accords with my honour; nor
will I do it, though her love and conversation have a great

influence over me . . . I can't refrain from tears, to think what a melancholy life I must lead for the future.

Weeps.

O fortune, fortune! What a changeable thing thou art! But my former love for Bacchis has inured me to this usage. I conquered that by the exercise of reason, and here I must endeavour to do the like . . .

Enter PARMENO, SOCIA, *and* PORTERS, *at a great distance, with trunks, portmanteaux, etc.*

. . . But yonder comes Parmeno with the rest! I do not desire him to be hereabouts at this time; for he's the only person I made privy to my neglect of Philumena, when we first married. I fear lest he should hear her frequent shrieks, and know thereby that she's in labour. I must e'en send him on some errand or other until all's over.

PARMENO, *to* SOCIA. Say ye so? Had ye such a wretched voyage?

SOCIA. In sober sadness, Parmeno, I cannot tell thee what a dismal thing it is to be at sea.

PARMENO. Indeed!

SOCIA. Truth, thou art a happy fellow. Little dost thou know what dangers thou escapest by staying always on dry ground. I omit other hardships—but hearken only to this: thirty long days and nights or more was I on shipboard, expecting every minute to be soused to the bottom of the sea, 'twas such plaguey stormy weather all the time, and the wind against us.

PARMENO. Abominable!

SOCIA. So indeed I found it. In short, if I knew that I must go back, upon my soul I'd show them a light pair of heels before I'd do it.

PARMENO. Ay, old boy, thou hast been ready for flight upon far slighter occasions than this. . . . But hold, yonder's my master Pamphilus before that door . . . Go in, all of you, and I'll step up to see if he has any business with me.

Exeunt SOCIA *and* PORTERS.

PARMENO *goes to* PAMPHILUS.

PARMENO. Are you here still, Sir?

PAMPHILUS. Yes, I have waited for you.

PARMENO. What's your pleasure?

PAMPHILUS. You must run as far as the Tower.

PARMENO. Who must?

PAMPHILUS. You must.

PARMENO. As far as the Tower! For what pray, Sir?

PAMPHILUS. To find out Callidemides, my Myconian landlord, who came over in the same vessel with me.

PARMENO, *aside.* 'Sdeath! I'll be sworn this master of mine
has made a vow, that if ever he got ashore, he'd make me
run my heart out!

PAMPHILUS. Why don't ye stir?

PARMENO. Must I say anything to him, or must I only find
him?

PAMPHILUS. Tell Mr Callidemides I can't meet him today as
we appointed; so that he need not await me to no purpose.
Fly!

PARMENO. But, Sir, I don't know what manner of man he is.

PAMPHILUS. I'll tell ye how to know him . . . He's a huge,
fiery-faced, frizzle-crowned fat fellow, with wall-eyes, and
looks as if he'd eat ye.

PARMENO. Plague on him for a son of a whore!

Going off, turns back.

But suppose he be not there, must I stay till night for him?

PAMPHILUS. Ay, ay! Run, Sirrah!

PARMENO. I beg your pardon if I cannot do that; I'm quite
foundered already.

Exit PARMENO, *hobbling.*

PAMPHILUS, *alone.* He's gone . . . Now, what course shall
poor I take? I'm at a strange loss how to conceal Philumena's
labour, as her mother desired me to do. I swear I can't
but pity the poor woman. I'll do what I can, but still I'll

discharge my duty to my parents, for love must give way to obedience.

Enter LACHES *and* PHIDIPPUS, *at some distance.*

But lack-a-day, there's my father and Mr Phidippus together . . . They are coming this way, too! I can't imagine what to tell them.

LACHES, *to* PHIDIPPUS. Didn't ye inform me just now that your daughter had no other complaint, but that she longed for my son's home-coming?

PHIDIPPUS. Yes.

LACHES. I hear he's landed. Let her be brought home, then.

PAMPHILUS, *to himself*. What excuse can I devise for not taking her home again?

LACHES, *overhearing*. Whose voice is that?

PAMPHILUS, *to himself*. Yet I'm fully resolved to maintain my first design.

LACHES. O here's the man we were talking of!

PAMPHILUS. Your blessing, Sir.

LACHES. I'm glad to see thee!

PHIDIPPUS. Welcome home, Pamphilus, I'm also glad to see ye so sound and lusty after your voyage.

PAMPHILUS. I'm obliged to ye, Sir.

LACHES. Are ye but just landed, Son?

PAMPHILUS. Just now, Sir.

LACHES. Well! and what has our kinsman Phanius left us? Hah!

PAMPHILUS. Why really, Sir, he was a man much given up to pleasure in his lifetime. Such as he seldom leave much to their heirs; however, they leave this behind them: that as long as they lived, they lived like gentlemen.

LACHES. Then thou hast brought nothing home save that pretty sentence? No inheritance, hah?

PAMPHILUS. What little he left, may do us some little good.

LACHES. Let it be none at all! . . . I wish heartily he were alive, and in health again.

PAMPHILUS. You may safely wish that! He's past wishing for. I dare swear I know how you would choose, else.

LACHES, *to* PAMPHILUS. Yesterday my brother here invited his daughter to stay at his house.

Aside to PHIDIPPUS, *thrusting him with his elbow.*

Say you did!

PHIDIPPUS, *softly to* LACHES. Don't punch me so . . .

Aloud to PAMPHILUS.

So I did.

LACHES. But now he'll send her home again.

PHIDIPPUS. So I will.

PAMPHILUS. Sir, I know the whole business, how everything has been managed since I went. I heard the whole story as soon as ever I arrived.

LACHES, *in a passion.* Hang those envious Devils who were so officious as to tell it ye!

PAMPHILUS. I'm sure I took all possible care to avoid giving any of ye the least offence. And had I a mind to it, I could tell you how faithful, loving, and kind I've been to her. But I should prefer that ye should hear it from her own mouth. You'll the sooner believe my good nature, when the story comes from her who is now so unkind to me. Heaven's my witness, I had no hand at all in this difference; but since she thinks herself too good to bear with my mother, when modesty might have taught her to pardon an occasional ill humour. And since there's no other way of settling the difference, I must even part with either one or the other. And so, Mr Phidippus, filial duty obliges me to take my mother's part before my wife's.

LACHES. I am not displeased, Pamphilus, to find ye so ready to sacrifice all to the interests of your parents. But take care you don't press this quarrel too far.

PAMPHILUS. How can I quarrel with Philumena, who never ill-treated me in any way, but on the contrary has proved the best of wives? I love her, honour her, and still desire with all my soul to keep her. Ay, I've always found Philumena wonderfully sweet tempered towards me; and now I wish with all my heart that she may spend the remainder of her life with a more fortunate husband than I am—since mere necessity tears her from me.

PHIDIPPUS. 'Tis in your own power to hinder that.

LACHES, *angrily.* Take her home again, if you be wise.

PAMPHILUS. That's not my intention, Sir. I must consult my mother's interest.

Exit PAMPHILUS.

LACHES. Whither now? Stay, stay, I say! Where are ye going?

PHIDIPPUS, *surlily.* What whim's this?

LACHES. I told ye, Brother, how highly he'd resent this! That was why I begged ye to send home your daughter in time.

PHIDIPPUS, *in a huff.* 'Sblud, I never thought he would prove to be such a churl. Does he think I'll go cringing to him with cap in hand? If he's disposed to take his wife home, well and good; if not, let him refund her portion, pack off, and a fart for him!

LACHES. Look ye now, you're in as great a fume as he!

PHIDIPPUS. Pamphilus has grown mighty difficult to control methinks, since his voyage . . .

LACHES. His anger will soon pass, though, indeed, he had some cause for it.

PHIDIPPUS. Because, forsooth, you've got a small bequest fallen to ye, you puff yourself up finely!

LACHES. What! Would ye fall out with me, too?

PHIDIPPUS. Let him consider well, and bring me the answer today, whether he'll have her or no; so that if he won't, another may.

Exit PHIDIPPUS *in a huff.*

LACHES, *alone.* Stay, Brother, hear me but one word! . . . He's gone. But what's this to me? In short, let them order matters how they please for all I care. Since neither my brother nor my son will listen to reason, nor heed one word of mine, I'll direct all my forces against my wife, the cause of all this mischief, and discharge upon her all that sticks in my stomach.

Exit LACHES.

End of the Third Act

ACT FOUR

Enter MYRRHINA, *in disorder*

MYRRHINA. I'm ruined! What shall I do? Which way shall I turn? Alas! What answer can I give my husband? I'm sure he heard the child cry, which was what made him run so hastily into my daughter's chamber, without a word to me. Should he find out that she's been in labour, I vow I can't conjure up the least excuse for concealing the matter . . . The door opens! I'm afraid he's hot upon the scent, and coming after me. . . . I'm a dead creature!

Enter PHIDIPPUS.

PHIDIPPUS, *entering.* As soon as my wife saw that I was going into my daughter's chamber, away she slunk out of doors. But here she is, though . . . How now, wife?

She seems not to see him.

Hark ye, 'tis you I address!

MYRRHINA. Meaning me, my dear husband?

PHIDIPPUS. I, your husband! Do ye regard me as a husband, or even as a man? For had ye esteemed me as either one or t'other (gentlewoman!) you would never have dared put me to such public scorn by your baseness!

MYRRHINA. By what baseness?

PHIDIPPUS. By what? . . . Isn't your daughter brought to

bed? Hah! are ye tongue-tied now? . . . Who's the father, pray?

MYRRHINA. Is that a question for a grandfather to ask? . . . Dear heart, who do ye think should be the father but her own husband?

PHIDIPPUS. I believe it, nor is it for me to think otherwise. But I'm amazed that ye should have kept the business in such secrecy and hugger-mugger, especially when she was delivered fully nine months after marriage, and all things were as they should be. Could ye be so damnably malicious as to wish death for the poor child—which, if it lived, would be the pledge of lasting friendship between us all —rather than allow your daughter to live happily with a husband whom you loathe? . . . I took it to be wholly their fault, but now I find 'tis all yours.

MYRRHINA. I'm a miserable creature.

PHIDIPPUS. Would I were sure of that. . . . It now comes fresh into my mind: what you formerly said on this subject when the match was first made. You professed, forsooth, that you couldn't abide a son-in-law who kept wenches, and slept away from home whole nights together.

MYRRHINA, *aside*. I had rather he should suspect anything in the world than guess at the true cause.

PHIDIPPUS. I knew that he kept a mistress long before you did (Madam Wife!), but I never counted that such a mighty fault in a young man. For 'tis what we are all born with, though the time will quickly come when he'll hate himself for it. But you, I see, are still the same, and could never be at ease until you had parted them and annulled the marriage, because it was of my making. Now 'tis plain that you resolved from the start to wreck the match.

MYRRHINA. If this match had been to our advantage, do ye think I could have treated my own flesh and blood so cruelly?

PHIDIPPUS. Pish! You able to foresee or judge what's to our advantage? Maybe somebody informed you that they saw him going to, or coming from, his mistress; and what of all that, if he did it privately and seldom? Isn't it more handsome for us to wink at such failings, than blaze them abroad and win ourselves nothing but ill-will? For, if Pamphilus could have suddenly drawn his affections away from a woman whom he had loved so many years, I shouldn't count him a man, nor think him staunch and constant enough by half for my daughter.

MYRRHINA. Good husband, no more of the young man, nor of my supposed faults, neither! Go and meet him privately, and ask him whether or no he'll take home his wife. If he says yes, send her away; if not, I think I've taken a wise course with my daughter.

PHIDIPPUS. If he wouldn't take her back, and you knew him to be in fault, wife, I wasn't far off. Pray, why was not I consulted at once? It maddens my heart to find that ye dare do such a thing without leave of me. I charge ye, upon your life, not to let the child stir out of the house. *Aside.*

. . . But what a blockhead am I to think she'll heed what I say! I'll go in myself, and strictly charge my servants to let nobody carry the little creature away.

Exit PHIDIPPUS.

MYRRHINA. Let me die if I don't believe I'm the unhappiest woman in the world. In good truth, I foresee well enough how extremely ill he'd take it if he knew all, since he's so very angry for that little he does know, nor can I conceive how to alter his resolution. . . . And this will be the one evil that could crown all my other disasters: that I should be forced to bring up a child whom we don't know the father of. For when my daughter was raped, 'twas so dark she couldn't discern his face, nor yet win any token from him by which to know him afterwards. Only when the fellow left her, he forced a ring off her finger. Considering the whole matter, I'm strangely afraid Mr Pamphilus when he comes to hear that we are bringing up another man's child instead of his, will no longer conceal what we so desire him to keep private.

Exit MYRRHINA; *and enter* SOSTRATA *and* PAMPHILUS; LACHES *comes to the door and observes them.*

SOSTRATA, *entering.* I know well enough, Pamphilus, you suspect that it was because of my ill humour that your wife left us; deny this as often as you please. But may I never obtain mercy, nor enjoy that comfort which I expect from ye, if ever to my knowledge I did anything to affront her. I always believed you respected me, but now you have given certain proof of it; for your father has been telling me how far you prefer my reputation to your love. And I intend to return you the like compliment, and tell ye how highly I esteem such dutifulness. I believe, my dear son, 'twill be better both for you and for me, if I retire into the country with your father, as I am fully resolved, so my presence will be no affliction to you, nor any excuse for your wife's staying away.

PAMPHILUS. Pray, Madam, what do ye mean by this? Shall her silly freaks drive you into the country? It must not be, nor can I endure that the envious world should say: ''Twas done because of his wilfulness, and not because of his mother's good nature. Besides, I wouldn't for ever so much have ye banished, upon my account, from the company of your friends and relations, and from all the diversions of the town.

SOSTRATA. Truly, Son, I now relish these enjoyments but little. Time was, indeed, when I had my fill of them, but I'm grown at last quite weary of such gambols . . . At present my chief care is to keep my old age from becoming such a burden to others that they may wish for my end. Here I find I'm despised without cause, and 'tis time to retreat. By this means, I fancy, I shall cut off all cause of discontent, clear myself of suspicions, and please them all. Pray, therefore, let me avoid those scandals from which we women generally suffer.

PAMPHILUS, *aside*. How happy I should be—were it not for this cursed rape—to have such a mother, and such a wife!

SOSTRATA. Good, dear boy, as the case stands, try to bear with this inconvenience. If all other things are to your pleasure, and your wife is as good as I take her to be, grant me this one request, my child: bring her home!

PAMPHILUS. Ah! I'm very unhappy.

SOSTRATA. And I too: for I'm as much concerned by this evil affair as you can be, my dear child, for the very soul of ye!

LACHES *appears and goes up to them.*

LACHES. Well, wife, I overheard all your discourse. How prudent to accept the occasion with good grace when you know that force would follow otherwise.

SOSTRATA. May my prudence be blessed then!

LACHES. Come now: we'll march into the country, and there let us both bear with each other's crotchets.

SOSTRATA. I hope we shall.

LACHES. Go in then, and pack up what things you may need. I'm determined upon this.

SOSTRATA. I shall obey your orders.

Exit SOSTRATA.

PAMPHILUS, *concernedly.* But Sir!

LACHES. Well, Pamphilus.

PAMPHILUS. Would ye send my mother into the country? By no means!

LACHES. Why not?

PAMPHILUS. Because, Sir, as yet I'm not resolved what to do with my wife.

LACHES. How! What can ye do but take her home again?

PAMPHILUS, *aside.* That I would do with all my heart, and can hardly persuade myself against it. But I'll not retreat one foot from my intent, but even take the course I think most consonant with my honour.

To LACHES.

I presume, Sir, they'll become better friends if she stays in her father's house?

LACHES. That's more than you can foretell. However, it should not matter a pin to you whether they be friends or foes, when once your mother's out of the way. The truth of it is: we old folks are poor company for you young ones, and therefore we might as well go our ways. In short, Pamphilus, your mother and I are become words of scorn to ye: *The Old Man,* and *The Old Woman.* . . . But yonder comes my brother, in the critical minute. Let's speak with him!

Enter PHIDIPPUS *at the other end of the stage.* LACHES *moves towards him.*

PHIDIPPUS, *to* PHILUMENA, *within.* Truth, Daughter, I'm angry with you, and very much too, for in sober sadness 'twas a very scurvy trick to play. Though ye plead that your mother forced ye, yet I'm sure that her excuse was a bad one.

LACHES. O Brother, you're come at the best time in the world!

PHIDIPPUS. Why so?

PAMPHILUS, *aside.* What answer shall I give them, or how be able to keep this secret?

LACHES. You may tell your daughter that my wife's going into the country; so now she needn't be afraid of coming home to her husband.

PHIDIPPUS. Poh! Your wife's innocent of everything. 'Tis mine that's the prime mover in all this . . .

PAMPHILUS, *aside.* Nay, then the case is altered.

PHIDIPPUS. And has caused all this ado, Mr Laches.

PAMPHILUS, *aside.* Let them cause what ado they please, if only I'm not obliged to take her home again!

PHIDIPPUS. Now, Pamphilus, I wish nothing more, if it can be brought about, than that there may be a lasting alliance between us. If you're of another mind, so be it. Pray, however, take the child.

PAMPHILUS, *aside.* He knows of that too; I'm past all hope.

LACHES, *hastily.* The child! Prithee, what child?

PHIDIPPUS. Why, we have a grandson, Brother; for my daughter, when she left your house, was big-bellied it seems, and I never so much as knew of it until now.

LACHES. In truth, as I'm an honest man, I'm heartily glad 'tis born, and that your daughter's well. . . . But what a strange sort of a woman is your wife, Pam! What odd kind of fancies she has to keep things from us so long! I vow, I can't say how unhandsome it appears.

PHIDIPPUS. Truly, Brother, I'm as little pleased at these proceedings as you.

PAMPHILUS, *aside*. My mind was in suspense before, but now 'tis fixed! Shall she bring a brat with her that's none of mine?

LACHES. Come, come, Pam, is all this discourse nothing to you?

PAMPHILUS, *aside*. I'm ruined!

LACHES. I've often wished for that happy day when you would have a child to call you father. 'Tis come at last, Heaven be praised!

PAMPHILUS, *aside*. Beyond redemption!

LACHES. Take home your wife, without any further grumbling.

PAMPHILUS. Truly, Sir, had she intended to have children by me, or to have continued as my wife, I'm certain she'd never have hidden what I understand she has. But now, since I plainly understand that she has withdrawn her love from me, I can't believe we shall ever hereafter agree well. Why should I take her back again?

LACHES. Pho! The young girl did all by her mother's persuasion. And, is that such a strange thing? Do ye expect to find any woman in the world without her fault? Have not men their failings too?

PHIDIPPUS. Well, look to it yourselves, both of ye, whether ye think to take her or leave her. I can't answer for all that my foolish wife does. For my own part, do what you will, you shan't find me unreasonable in either case. Meanwhile, what shall we do with the child?

LACHES. A wise query, in truth! Whichever way the business may go, send the child hither, since 'tis his, and we shall nurse it as ours.

PAMPHILUS. Shall I bring up a child of which the mother takes no loving care?

LACHES, *angrily*. What's that you say? Not bring it up, Pamphilus? Good-now, shall we make away with it? . . . Why, this is downright madness; upon my life, I can keep my temper no longer! Now you force me to say what I wouldn't have said else before your father-in-law.

PAMPHILUS *weeps.*

. . . Do ye think I don't know what all this snivelling and all this disorder means?

In another tone.

First ye pretend that you can't have her home, because of your mother. Then your mother promises to leave the whole house to yourselves. Since that excuse won't hold good now, forsooth, you say the child's born without your knowledge. You're mightily mistaken if ye think I don't know whom you hanker after. How long did I wink at your keeping a miss, in hopes of bringing ye over to a wife at last? How patiently did I bear your lavish expenses that way? I urged ye, I entreated ye to marry, told ye 'twas high time, and by much persuasion you did. Then you obeyed me, as your duty obliged ye to do; but now you're in with your whore again and will ruin your wife to pleasure her. I plainly see you are relapsing into your old course of debaucheries.

PAMPHILUS. Who, I, Sir?

LACHES. Yes, you; and let me tell ye, 'tis base to invent sham reasons for quarrelling with your wife, so that when once she's out of sight, you may the more easily live with your strumpet. Philumena was well aware of this, I warrant, or what other reason had she to leave the house?

PHIDIPPUS. He has hit upon it! Certainly that's the reason.

PAMPHILUS. If you please, Sir, I'll swear upon my oath, that the matter is not at all as you imagine.

LACHES. For shame! Take home your wife then, or give us a better reason why you won't.

PAMPHILUS. 'Tis not convenient at the present time.

LACHES. Take care of the child then who, I hope, has done no wrong! We'll consider the mother afterwards.

PAMPHILUS, *aside, walking apart.* I'm miserable on every account. My father has so confounded me by argument, that

I know not where to turn. I'll e'en step out of the way.
I do myself but little good by staying where I am. Yet
they'll hardly dare bring up the child without my order,
especially since my mother-in-law will second me in the
design of exposing it.

PAMPHILUS *stands off.*

LACHES. Do ye steal away? What! You give us no direct
answer? Don't ye think he's crack-brained, Brother? . . .
Well, 'tis no matter. Send the child to me, and I'll bring
him up.

PHIDIPPUS. With all my heart. . . . I don't wonder that my
daughter is not pleased with these fine doings! Women
are fretful creatures and can't forgive such affronts. I know
the cause of their quarrel—my wife told me of it herself,
but I wouldn't mention it in his presence, nor would I believe it at first—but now 'tis as clear as the sun. Your
Pamphilus is a downright marriage-hater.

LACHES. What should I do in the case? What would ye
advise?

PHIDIPPUS. What? Why, first I think 'tis best for us to visit
Madam Bacchis, his miss. Let us discourse with her calmly,
then bring the charge home to her. And if that won't do,
let us threaten her that if ever she has anything more to
do with your son . . .

LACHES. I'll follow your advice.

Goes towards his own house.

Soho, you there within!

Enter a BOY.

Step over to my neighbour Madam Bacchis, and tell her
I'd speak with her presently, if it be convenient.

Exit BOY.

And I must ask you, Brother, to stand by me in this
business.

PHIDIPPUS. Ah, Sir, I've often told ye, and am still of the same
mind, that I desire nothing so much as a lasting alliance
between us—if it be possible to bring that about, and I

hope it may . . . But would you have me stay here to meet your son's miss?

LACHES. No; rather go and provide a good nurse for the child.

Exit PHIDIPPUS.

End of the Fourth Act

ACT FIVE

LACHES *remains; enter* BACCHIS *on the other side of the stage, with two* WAITING-MAIDS, *and* LACHES'S BOY

BACCHIS, *entering.* I'll be sworn 'tis no small matter that makes Mr Laches send to speak with me now. Yet, in truth, I'm mightily mistaken if I don't guess what the business is.

LACHES, *to himself.* I must take special care that my passion neither hinders me from bending her to my wishes, nor makes me do in haste what I may repent at leisure. . . . I'll accost her . . . Mrs Bacchis, your servant!

BACCHIS. Yours, good Mr Laches.

Exit BOY.

LACHES. Truth, I don't doubt but that you somewhat wonder why I sent to speak with ye.

BACCHIS. And really when I consider that question myself, I fear lest the scandal of my trade should prejudice you against me. For, as to my honest behaviour in it, I defy the world to accuse . . .

LACHES. If it be so, you've no reason to be afraid of me, young woman; for I'm of an age in which a false step is not so easily pardonable as in the young, and I'm therefore the more cautious to do nothing rash. If you always do what you can justify as honest, 'twould be very unhandsome of me to offer ye any injury—and very unjust, since you don't deserve it.

BACCHIS. Upon my word I'm extremely obliged to ye for that remark; for, after an injury's done, begging a woman's pardon is never sufficient amends. . . . But pray, Sir, what is your pleasure?

LACHES. I hear you entertain my son Pamphilus . . .

BACCHIS, *interrupting*. Sir . . .

LACHES. Hear me out! . . . Before he married, I winked at your amours.

Here BACCHIS *is going to speak.*

. . . Hold, I haven't spoken all my mind yet. . . . Now he's married, you'd do well to find yourself a more constant lover; for Pamphilus will not always have the same inclinations nor, troth, you the same beauty.

BACCHIS. Pray, Sir, who reports this?

LACHES. His mother-in-law.

BACCHIS. That I entertain Mr Pamphilus?

LACHES. Yes, you! For which reason she has taken her daughter home, and would have secretly made away with the child she has by him.

BACCHIS. Sir, if I knew anything more sacred than an oath to convince ye, I'd freely offer it to ye, swearing that I have never had anything to do with your son since he married.

LACHES. Thou art a dainty fine girl! But can ye guess what further favour I'd desire of ye?

BACCHIS. What is it, good Sir?

LACHES. Only step in there . . .

Pointing to PHIDIPPUS's *house.*

. . . and offer to satisfy the women of the house upon oath, and so clear yourself of all scandal.

BACCHIS. I'll obey you, Sir! But in good earnest, there's not another girl in my circumstances would consent to show her face before a young married woman upon such an errand. 'Tis only that I scorn to see your son scandalized upon a false charge, or undeservedly thought inconstant by women who should have a better opinion of him. He has done me many a good turn, and now I'll do him one!

LACHES. Your smooth tongue has made me conceive a more favourable opinion of ye; for I confess it wasn't only their surmises: indeed, I thought as ill of ye myself. . . . Since I've now found ye otherwise than we took ye to be, pray continue so, and you may find a friend of me. But, if ye don't . . . Well, I say no more for fear of vexing ye. . . . This I'll advise ye, that you'd better try what I can do as your friend, than as your enemy.

BACCHIS. I'll do my best, Sir, to satisfy ye.

Enter at a distance PHIDIPPUS *with a* NURSE.

PHIDIPPUS, *to the* NURSE. I won't allow ye to lack for anything—you shall have freely whatever my house will afford. But when you've eaten and drunk sufficiently, pray let the child suck its bellyful!

Exit NURSE.

LACHES. See, there comes our son's father-in-law! He has got him a nurse for the child. . . . Brother! Here's Madam Bacchis swears by all the Gods . . .

PHIDIPPUS. Is that she?

LACHES. Yes.

PHIDIPPUS. Truth these sort of creatures care little for the Gods; and the Gods as little for them.

BACCHIS. Take my servants here, rack the truth out of them if ye please. As the matter now stands, and I'm pledged to reconcile Mr Pamphilus and his Lady; which if I do, I shall get me credit by being the only person of my profession who would have undertaken such a task.

LACHES, *to* PHIDIPPUS, *walking on one side*. I find upon examination that our wives were mightily out in their conjectures. However, let's make use of this woman now, for when your wife once learns her mistake, she'll be soon pacified. And if Pamphilus be angry because his wife was brought to bed privately, that's a mere trifle—he'll be soothed down in a trice. And, edad, I can see nothing in this business that's worth falling out about.

PHIDIPPUS. Troth, would it were as you say!

LACHES. Examine her yourself, since she's here. She'll satisfy ye, I'll engage my oath for it.

PHIDIPPUS. What need for all this? Don't ye know my opinion of this matter already? Let her but satisfy the women, and I'm content.

LACHES, *going to* BACCHIS. Truth, Madam Bacchis, I must desire ye to be as good as your word to me.

BACCHIS. Would ye have me go in, Sir, about this business?

LACHES. Yes; and satisfy them, that they may believe it too.

BACCHIS. I will, Sir; but I'm sure to be no welcome guest there. A young woman, parted from her husband upon this account, will be a mortal enemy to a courtesan.

LACHES. Once they know on what errand you are come, they'll be your friends.

PHIDIPPUS. I'll give my word for that too, when they come to know your business. For you'll clear them of a mistake, and yourself of all suspicion.

BACCHIS. Alack-a-day, I'm so ashamed to look Madam Philumena in the face!

To her MAIDS.

Come, both of ye, after me!

Exeunt PHIDIPPUS, BACCHIS, *with her two* MAIDS.

LACHES, *alone.*

LACHES. What could I have wished for more than what has happened to this woman; that she might procure friends at no cost to herself, and do me a kindness into the bargain? For if in reality she has withdrawn herself from Pamphilus, it will be very much to her interest, reputation, and immortal honour. This one act will make my son for ever grateful, and gain her our friendship too.

Exit LACHES.

Enter PARMENO *at a distance.*

PARMENO. On my conscience, this master of mine counts my labour worth nothing; he wouldn't else have sent me upon a fool's errand as far as the Tower, where I've loitered away a whole day in gaping for Callidemides the Myconian landlord. There I sat all day like a simpleton, asking everybody that came by: 'Pray, Sir, are you a Myconian?' 'No,' says he. 'Is your name Callidemides?' quoth I. 'No,' quoth he. 'Are you acquainted with one Mr Pamphilus?' All answered in the negative. Upon my soul, there's no such man in the world! Faith, at last I was damnably ashamed of myself, and fairly slunk away . . .

Enter BACCHIS *and her* MAIDS.

But what's the meaning of Madam Bacchis's coming out of our father-in-law's? What has she to do there?

BACCHIS. O Parmeno! You couldn't come in a better time! You must run for your master Pamphilus in all haste.

PARMENO. What for?

BACCHIS. Tell him, I'd pray him to step hither a little.

PARMENO. To you, Madam?

BACCHIS. No, to his lady.

PARMENO. What's to do with her?

BACCHIS. Nothing that concerns you; therefore don't be so inquisitive.

PARMENO. Shall I say nothing else?

BACCHIS. Yes; tell him that Madam Myrrhina challenges the ring he once gave me, and says 'twas her daughter's.

PARMENO. I understand ye. Does the business require such haste?

BACCHIS. Yes, indeed! He'll be here in a trice, when you tell him of it. . . . What, are you asleep?

PARMENO. Not in the least; nor I suppose am like to be today; for I have spent hours of it already in running and trapesing all over the town.

Exit PARMENO.

BACCHIS, *to herself*. What great satisfaction has my coming procured Mr Pamphilus today! How many blessings have I brought him! And from how many troubles have I freed him! I have preserved the life of the child which his womenfolk and he himself proposed to make away with; recovered for him the love of his wife, whom he was just about to cast off, and cleared him from the unjust suspicions of both his fathers. . . . This is the ring—

Showing a ring on her hand.

—which has procured him all this good fortune! For I remembered, now, how about nine months ago, he came one evening alone to my house, much out of breath, and drunk as a lord. The sight of him almost put me into a fit. 'Prithee, my dear Pam,' said I, 'for love's sake, why art thou so strangely disordered? Where got ye this ring? Prithee, tell me!' He tried to talk of something else; but I grew more suspicious, and urged him to confess the truth. At last my gentleman tells me that, coming along the street, he met with a young woman he knew not, and raped her then and there, and in struggling took the ring from her finger. Myrrhina espied it just now on mine, and asked me how I came by it? I told her the whole story; upon which out it came: that Philumena was the gentlewoman he had assaulted, and this the child he had engendered. . . . In truth, I'm glad I should be the occasion of so much joy to him, though others of my trade would have been quite the contrary—for it never advances our interests to have our sparks fond of marriage. But upon my honest word, the smell of a little money would never make me do a base thing. Indeed, I enjoyed him as a very free, jolly, pleasant spark, while it was allowable; and I must say that this match caused me much distress and loss. But my comfort is that I did nothing that I know of, to deserve that misfortune. 'Tis only justice that I should be inconvenienced by the filial duties of a man who has been so good a friend to me.

Enter PAMPHILUS *and* PARMENO *at a distance.*

PAMPHILUS, *to* PARMENO. Go, Parmeno, take care you give me clear and evident proof of this business; and that you don't make me believe myself so extremely fortunate for a moment only.

PARMENO. That trouble's over.

PAMPHILUS. For certain!

PARMENO. Yes, for certain.

PAMPHILUS. I'm in Heaven, if it be so!

PARMENO. You'll find it as I say, I'll warrant ye.

PAMPHILUS. Prithee, not so fast! . . . I fear you may tell me one thing and I mistake its meaning.

PARMENO. Well, Sir . . .

PAMPHILUS. Did you not say that my mother-in-law Myrrhina discovered her own ring upon Madam Bacchis's finger . . .

PARMENO. Right.

PAMPHILUS. And it is the very same I formerly presented to her? And it was she who bade ye run and tell me of it? Did she that?

PARMENO. Yes, she did.

PAMPHILUS. Who alive then is a happier and finer fellow than I? What reward shall I bestow on thee for this kind message? What shall I? What? I can't imagine.

PARMENO. But I can, Sir.

PAMPHILUS. Prithee, what?

PARMENO. Just nothing at all! For I can see nothing either in the message or the messenger that will turn to your advantage.

PAMPHILUS. Shall I suffer thee to go unrewarded, thou who hast rescued me from the jaws of death and brought me to life again? Surely thou canst not think me so ungrateful? But hold! There walks Bacchis before their door, waiting for me, I fancy. . . . I'll go to her.

PAMPHILUS *goes up to* BACCHIS, PARMENO *keeps his distance.*

BACCHIS. Mr Pamphilus, your servant!

PAMPHILUS. Bacchis! My sweet Bacchis! Thou hast brought me back to life, my dear!

BACCHIS. There's good news for you, Sir, and I'm heartily glad of it.

PAMPHILUS. Your actions prove it. I see you are still mistress of your old pleasant way, so that your presence, discourse and conversation will always be charming, wherever you go.

BACCHIS. And you, Sir, as I hope for mercy, are still master of your old sweet temper, and pleasant humour. The world can't show a more accomplished gentleman than you, Mr Pamphilus.

PAMPHILUS. Ha . . . ha . . . he . . . This to me, Bacchis?

BACCHIS. You have made an excellent choice of a wife, Mr Pamphilus; I never saw her till now that I know of. I vow, she's a lovely creature.

PAMPHILUS. Are ye in earnest?

BACCHIS. Let me perish, Sir, if I be not.

PAMPHILUS. But, pray, did ye tell my father anything of this business?

BACCHIS. Not a word.

PAMPHILUS. Nor need ye, not so much as a syllable. I don't desire this should prove like a comedy, where the whole plot is unfolded to everybody. Here only those that should be told all shall learn all; but those that should not, must still be in the dark.

BACCHIS. Nay, more, I'll give a further argument to show how easy 'tis to conceal it. For Madam Myrrhina told her husband that she was satisfied with my depositions, and believed you innocent.

PAMPHILUS. Best of all! I hope all things will succeed according to our wishes.

PARMENO *comes up behind and plucks his master.*

PARMENO. Pray, Sir, mayn't I know what good office I've done ye today? And what you two are debating upon?

PAMPHILUS. No, Sirrah!

PARMENO. But I guess though . . .

Aside.

I rescued him from the jaws of death? How did I do that?

PAMPHILUS. Little dost thou think, Parmeno, what a piece of service thou hast done me today; and from what troubles thou hast freed me.

PARMENO, *fawningly.* Your pardon for that, Sir, I know it well enough, and did it on purpose.

PAMPHILUS. So I fancy.

PARMENO. Do ye think poor Parmeno shall let a day go over his head without serving his friends?

PAMPHILUS. Come on then, honest Parmeno!

PARMENO. I'll follow ye, Sir.

Exeunt PAMPHILUS *and* BACCHIS, *with her* MAIDS.

PARMENO *turns to the spectators.*

By my soul, gentlemen, I've done more good today, without knowing it, than ever I did designedly in all my life. I hope we have pleased ye.

Exit PARMENO.

End *of* THE MOTHER-IN-LAW

THE SELF TORMENTOR

A Comedy acted at the Feast of Cybele, when L. Valerius
Flaccus *and* L. Cornelius Lentulus *were Curule Ediles, by
the Company of* Ambivius Turpio.

It was taken from the Greek of Menander.

Flaccus, *a freedman of* Claudius, *composed the music, which
was performed the first time of acting on unequal flutes;
the second time on two right-handed flutes.*

This play was acted a third time under the Consulship of
Tit. Sempronius *and* M. Juventius.

A.U.C.591   Before Christ 163

DRAMATIS PERSONAE

CHREMES, *an old gentleman near Athens, of a nature somewhat strict and severe, very busy, and a great meddler*

MENEDEMUS, *a gentleman, Chremes's neighbour, the Self-Tormentor, of a melancholy, but softer and milder disposition than the former*

CLITIPHO, *Chremes's son, a hot wild spark, a loose liver, and somewhat stubborn to his parents*

CLINIA, *his friend, Menedemus's son; of a civil, courteous, pliant temper, passionately in love with Antiphila*

SYRUS, *servant to Clitipho, and his instructor; a very sly, subtile, active, intriguing fellow; always plotting against Chremes, and tricking him out of money*

DROMO, *servant to Clinia*

SOSTRATA, *Chremes's wife, of a soft, easy and indulgent nature, very submissive to her husband*

ANTIPHILA, *a young gentlewoman, Clinia's mistress, very innocent, modest, loving, and faithful*

BACCHIS, *a noted courtesan, kept by Clitipho, a haughty, proud, impudent, drinking, expensive miss*

PHRYGIA, *her waiting-maid*

NURSE *to Antiphila*

NON-SPEAKING PARTS:

SERVANTS *of Bacchis's*

WAITING-MAIDS

ACT ONE

SCENE: *The country, outside* CHREMES's *door*
TIME: *Late evening*

Enter CHREMES; *and* MENEDEMUS *carrying a rake, etc.,
upon his shoulders, as he returns from the field*

CHREMES. Though our acquaintance be but very short, (for it
began, ye know, upon your buying a farm so close to mine
—that and little else being the occasion of it) yet either
your own worth, or my being your neighbour—for I esteem
neighbourliness as next door to friendship—makes me so
bold as to tell ye that you do not seem to live as becomes
either your age or your station in life. For, in the name of
Heaven and wonder, what do ye do with yourself? What
are ye at? If I may judge by your appearance, you are
threescore years old at least. I know no gentleman who is
seated in a prettier estate, or is better served than you. And
yet you manage all the business yourself, as if you hadn't a
soul in the world to help ye. However early I go out in the
morning, or however late I come home at night, there I
always find you at it, digging, ploughing, or lugging something or other—in a perpetual fury of haste and without any
regard for your quality or person. I'm very certain you
don't do this for your diversion. . . . Perhaps you'll say:
'I hate to see my work go on slowly.' Let me tell ye, neighbour, if you'd bestow but half the pains upon your servants
that you do upon your land, the work would go on ten
times faster.

MENEDEMUS. Chremes, have you so much leisure from your own business that you can meddle with another man's, that doesn't concern ye?

CHREMES. Common humanity, Sir, obliges me to be so concerned. You may take what I say either by way of advice, or by way of enquiry; so that if you do well, then I may follow your example; but if ill, I may divert you from your error.

MENEDEMUS. I have reason for these things; you may do as you please.

CHREMES. Can any man have reason to torment himself?

MENEDEMUS. I have.

CHREMES. Were there any just occasion for this toiling and moiling of yours, I shouldn't be against it. Therefore I would gladly know what it is, and what ye have done to deserve so ill of yourself.

MENEDEMUS. Hey-ho!

Weeps.

CHREMES. Never weep for a matter, but divulge to me whatever it may be. Out with it, fear nothing, but depend upon my good offices. I'll either condole with ye, or advise ye, or assist ye in whatever I can.

MENEDEMUS. Would ye needs know it then?

CHREMES. Yes, for the very reason I have just told ye.

MENEDEMUS. I'll speak out then.

CHREMES. But pray, Sir, set down your tools in the meantime, and don't tire yourself so.

MENEDEMUS. By no means.

CHREMES. Pray, what is your design in this?

MENEDEMUS. Ah! Leave me alone, for I may not indulge myself one minute.

CHREMES. Indeed, Sir, but I won't leave you alone.

He forces the rake, etc., from him.

MENEDEMUS. Ah! That's not fair!

CHREMES. Bless me! What a weight's here!

MENEDEMUS. I deserve it all.

CHREMES. Come, come; out with it now.

MENEDEMUS. I have an only son, a youth. . . . What did I say I have? Ah, Chremes! I had one indeed, but whether or not I have him now I know not.

CHREMES. Why do ye say so?

MENEDEMUS. I'll tell ye, Sir. . . . Hard by dwells a poor old Corinthian woman of whose daughter my son began to be so fond that it had like to have been a match; but all this without my knowledge. When once I found out the intrigue, I began to take him to task; and not with the tenderness due to the weaknesses of youth, but extremely sharp I was. After the common, ranting way of fathers, I was every day taunting him. 'How now,' said I, 'do ye think to live in this vile fashion, and keep a mistress so openly while I am living? No, Clinia, you're mightily mistaken, and don't know me, if you think so. I shall look upon ye as my son, so long as ye do what ye ought; but if otherwise, I know what I ought to do, and you shall find it done. This intrigue is only the effects of too much idleness. When I was at your years, I didn't give my mind to women, but was forced to go as a soldier into Asia, where the war won me both riches and honour too.' At last matters came to such a pass that the poor boy, hearing the same things impressed upon him so often and so gravely, was persuaded; and, Mr Chremes, judging my age and prudence to be better guides than his own, he shipped off for Asia, and there took service under the King of Persia . . .

CHREMES. How's that, Sir?

MENEDEMUS, *weeping*. He stole away without my knowledge, and has been gone a whole quarter of a year.

CHREMES. You're both to blame. Yet what he has done shows both a noble heart and a brave spirit.

MENEDEMUS. When I heard of this from some of his cronies I went home brimful of sorrow, my mind half distracted, not knowing where to turn my head for grief: I sat me down, my servants all attended my beck, some helped to undress me, others ran to lay the cloth and get my supper ready, and all were most diligent to assuage my grief. At sight of which I began to muse: 'Alas!' thought I, 'must so many sweat and toil for me alone? Must so many strive to humour me? Must so many women spend their time in adorning my house and me? Shall all these vast expenses be for me alone—for me whose cruelty has driven hence my son, my only son, who ought to have an equal share with me, or more, since youth can better relish these enjoyments? If I still follow this course of life, no plague too great can light upon my head. While he thus lives in penury abroad, banished from home by my severity, I'll revenge his wrong upon myself: I'll labour, spare, pinch, and scrape up all for him.' With that I put my resolution in practice; for I've rid the house of all its furnishings, leaving neither spare dish nor bed for anybody's use: and of all my maids and men too, except a few to till my land, which were no expense to me. I exposed them all for sale, and put 'House to be Sold' over the door. Thus I raised the sum of two or three thousand pounds, and bought this farm, where I toil and moil every day. I'm fully persuaded, neighbour, that I do less injury to my poor child while I'm in as much misery as he is; nor ought I to take any manner of pleasure till he return safe to share it with me.

CHREMES. I believe you to be an indulgent father, and him a dutiful son if rightly treated. But indeed you didn't understand him, nor he you; and where understanding is lacking, love is lost. You never told him how much you valued him, nor had he that confidence in you which he was entitled to feel. Otherwise, things had never come to this.

MENEDEMUS. Very true, Sir, I confess; but I'm most in fault.

CHREMES. In truth, Sir, I still hope for the best, and do verily believe you'll see him safe at home before long.

MENEDEMUS. Oh! Heavens grant I may!

CHREMES. I'll warrant ye will, Sir. . . . But this is Bacchus's Day; and I should be glad of your company at supper tonight, if you could conveniently come.

MENEDEMUS. I must be excused from that pleasure.

CHREMES. Why so? . . . Pray, Sir, give yourself some little refreshment. I'm sure your absent son would gladly have it so.

MENEDEMUS. I see no reason why I who forced hardship upon him should escape the same myself.

CHREMES. Is that your resolution?

MENEDEMUS. 'Tis so, Sir.

CHREMES. Then good night to ye, Sir.

MENEDEMUS. And to you too.

Exit MENEDEMUS, *with his rake upon his shoulder.*

CHREMES, *alone.* I profess the poor gentleman has forced tears from me, and I can only pity him . . . But the sun sinks, and 'tis time for me to invite my neighbour Phania to supper. I'll call in and see if he's at home . . .

Steps to PHANIA's *door and returns.*

Oh, he needed not to be reminded, for I hear he's at our house already. It seems that I make my guests wait for me now: I'll go to them without delay. . . . But why does the door open again? . . . Who's that comes out of my house? I'll step a little to one side.

He retires.

Enter CLITIPHO.

CLITIPHO, *to* CLINIA *indoors at* CHREMES's *house.* As yet you needn't fear, Clinia. They haven't been long away. I'm confident she'll be here, and the messenger too in a short time. Therefore shake off these baseless fears, that so torment ye.

CHREMES, *aside.* To whom does my son talk?

CLITIPHO. Oh! here's my father, just as I was wishing for him; I'll approach him. . . . Sir, I'm glad I've met with ye.

CHREMES. Why, what's the matter?

CLITIPHO. Sir, d'ye know our neighbour Mr Menedemus?

CHREMES. Yes, very well.

CLITIPHO. And ye know that he has a son too?

CHREMES. Yes, I hear he's in Asia.

CLITIPHO. No longer, Sir! He's now at our house.

CHREMES. Indeed!

CLITIPHO. I happened to meet him as he landed, and brought him hither to supper. He and I have been intimate from our very childhood.

CHREMES. Your news pleases me strangely. . . . What would I not give now that Mr Menedemus had come when I invited him, that I might have been the first to surprise him with these joyful tidings. I believe it isn't too late yet.

CLITIPHO. O Sir, have a care what ye do. It won't be proper.

CHREMES. Why not?

CLITIPHO. Because he's in a great quandary what to do with himself. He's just come ashore, and dismally fears both his father's displeasure and the inconstancy of his mistress whom he loves with all his heart. She was the sole occasion of all this stir and his parting from Mr Menedemus.

CHREMES. I know it.

CLITIPHO. He has just now sent his footboy to fetch her from the city, and I sent our Syrus along with him.

CHREMES. What says the young man to the world?

CLITIPHO. What, Sir? That he's the greatest wretch alive in it.

CHREMES. He the greatest! No man less so. Does he lack for anything that the world calls good? His father's well, his country at peace, he has plentiful store of friends, relations of good quality, and a rich estate. Such things always prove good or bad, according as the man is; being blessings to those who know how to use them, but plagues to them who don't.

CLITIPHO. But, Sir, his father was always a cross old gentleman. I'm afraid of nothing so much as that passion should make him treat his son worse than he deserves.

CHREMES. What, he cross?

Aside.

. . . I'll say no more, though 'tis convenient that the lad should stand in some awe of his father.

CLITIPHO. What's that you say to yourself, Sir?

CHREMES. I say, that however the case stood, he should have stayed at home. If his father seemed a little more harsh than agreed with his debauched inclinations, he should have taken it patiently; for whom should he humour, if not his own father? Which is most proper, think ye, that the father should be ruled by the son, or the son by his father? As for the young man's complaining that he's been ill used, 'tis no such matter. For the severities of parents (I mean such as are not wholly brutal) are very much the same; namely, they won't suffer their sons always to be at the bawdy-house or always at the tavern, or allow them excessive spending money. And yet all this is for their children's good. For when a young man is quite drenched in debauchery, all that he does will stink of it. And son, take this for a rule: never buy commonsense at great expense in town, when it can be given you freely at home.

CLITIPHO. I fancy that is good advice.

CHREMES. I'll see how supper goes forward. You know how late it is; therefore don't be out of earshot.

Exit CHREMES.

CLITIPHO, *alone*. What unconscionable creatures these same fathers are, to expect their children should turn philosophers in the nursery, without so much as tasting the extravagances of youth. They measure us by their own jaded appetites, forgetting how hot they were formerly . . . Well, if ever heaven send me a son of my own, he shall find an extremely loving father in me. He shan't be afraid to make me his confessor, but be sure that I'll give him absolution. I'll not do as my father does, who slily insinuates his moral counsels by a side-wind. It vexes me, for when he begins to tope and be mellow, he'll recount all his old pranks. But now he reads me a lecture about buying commonsense at home! A crafty gentleman i' faith! He little knows that he preaches to the wind. My mistress's words stick twice as long in my stomach than all his preachments. 'Give me this fine thing, and buy me that,' she cries. And i' faith, I can't answer a word; there's none so damnably caught as I . . . Although this Mr Clinia verily has enough trouble upon his hands, yet his mistress is well and modestly brought up, and unacquainted with the tricks of the town; whereas mine's an imperious, craving, stately dame, damnably expensive, and as proud as the Devil. When she asks me for anything, I nod in answer; for to say that I have nothing for her, she accounts a mortal sin:

I did but lately these damned tricks espy,
Yet kept all troubles from my daddy's eye.

Exit CLITIPHO.

End of the First Act

ACT TWO

Enter CLINIA *as from* CHREMES'S *house, with* CLITIPHO *coming behind him at a distance*

CLINIA, *to himself.* Had there been any good news for me about my mistress, I'm sure they'd have been here before now; but I'm horribly afraid somebody has been tampering with her in my absence. There are a thousand circumstances favouring such an evil event that rack my mind: opportunity, place, her tender age, and a wicked mother who would pawn her soul for half-a-piece.

CLITIPHO. Mr Clinia . . .

CLINIA. What a wretch am I!

CLITIPHO. Have a care, Sir, that none of your father's family come out of doors and see you here.

CLINIA. I'll look to that. . . . But I fear there's some mischief in the wind, for my mind misgives me strangely.

CLITIPHO. Do ye usually judge of things before ye know what things they are?

CLINIA. Why, if there hadn't been some unluckiness brewing, we should have seen them before now.

CLITIPHO. They'll be here in a minute, Sir.

CLINIA. But when will that minute come?

CLITIPHO. You don't consider that she lives a great way off;

and when women, ye know, fall once to powdering and combing, they're an age rigging themselves out.

CLINIA. Ah, Clitipho, I'm very uneasy.

CLITIPHO. Bear up, man! Yonder come Dromo and Syrus both together.

Enter SYRUS *and* DROMO *at another part of the stage, talking together.*

SYRUS, *to* DROMO. . . . Say'st thou so my lad? Ha!

DROMO. Just as I tell ye.

SYRUS. But hold . . .

Looking about him.

While we go twattling on, we've lost the women.

CLITIPHO. Do ye hear that, Clinia? Your mistress will be here presently.

CLINIA. Yes, I do hear at last, and am now come to some life and sense again, Clitipho.

DROMO, *to* SYRUS. Faith, I don't wonder they lag behind, having drawn so great a train at their heels.

CLINIA, *overhearing* DROMO. Confusion! How came she by such a train?

CLITIPHO. Do ye ask me, Sir?

SYRUS, *to* DROMO. Truth, we did not do well to leave them so, for they carry things of considerable value about them . . .

CLINIA. All's past recovery.

SYRUS. Such as jewels and fine clothes. . . . Besides, 'tis somewhat duskish, and they know not a step of the way. In sober sadness we've acted like a couple of fools. Prithee, Dromo, do you go back and meet them. Make haste; what do ye stay for?

Exit DROMO.

CLINIA, *aside.* Oh cursed misfortune! How basely have my hopes deceived me!

CLITIPHO. What's the matter? What makes ye so sorrowful now?

CLINIA. 'So sorrowful' say ye? . . . Don't ye hear what a

train of servants, what jewels and fine clothes she brings
with her—when I left her but one girl to wait upon her?
Where should she have got all this, think ye?

CLITIPHO. Pho! Now I know your sickness.

SYRUS, *to himself.* Bless me! what a damnable crew is coming! I'm sure our house will scarce hold them all. What
a plaguey deal will they eat and drink, and to what woeful
expense will they put our old master! . . . But hold, here
are the sparks I wanted!

CLINIA. O Heavens! What's become of true faith? While for
your sake, Antiphila, I fled my native country like a rambling madman, you have feathered your nest finely, and
left me in the midst of all my troubles—you who are the
cause of all my troubles. You, I say, who are the cause of
my foul disgrace, and of my being so heedless of my father's wishes. Now I'm ashamed and troubled to the soul;
for when he read me such good lectures upon the tricks
of those creatures, I neglected his advice, and he could
not make me leave her. But now leave her I must. When
it might have been much to my advantage, then I
wouldn't, so miserable a creature am I.

SYRUS, *aside.* Faith, Mr Clinia has misunderstood every syllable of our talk.

To CLINIA.

Hark ye, Sir; you think worse of your mistress than she
deserves: or, so far as we can gather from circumstances,
she's still the same woman, and her heart as true to you
as ever.

CLINIA. How's that? Prithee, tell me! For I'd desire nothing
in the world sooner than to find my jealousies falsely
grounded.

SYRUS. In the first place (so that you may be sure to know
all) the old Corinthian woman who passed for your mistress's mother was in no degree related to her; and she's
now dead and gone to her long home. This by chance I
heard Antiphila tell the other woman as I was coming
along.

CLITIPHO, *hastily*. Prithee, what other was that?

SYRUS. Good Sir, have patience, and let me first finish my story, and then I'll come to yours.

CLITIPHO. Dispatch it quickly, then.

SYRUS. To begin: when we reached the house, Dromo knocks at the door. Out comes an old woman. As soon as she had opened it, Dromo whips in, and I after him. The old woman bolts the door, and falls hard to work again. And now or never was the time, Sir, to learn how your mistress had spent her time in your absence; for we dropped upon her unawares. It gave an opportunity of making a guess at their common practices, which shed the best light upon character. We found her in mourning—for the old woman who had died, I suppose. She had no rich or gaudy attire on, but went dressed like those homely dames that have no gallants to greet. Nor was she daubed over with nasty paint, but her hair loosely dishevelled, and carelessly thrown about her shoulders.

CLINIA *is going to speak*.

Forbear!

CLINIA. Prithee, honest boy, don't feed me with a fool's hope.

SYRUS. Well, Sir, the old woman she spun; besides her, there was a slut at a loom, wearing patched clothes, and very nasty.

CLITIPHO. If this be true, Mr Clinia, as I fancy it is, thou art the happiest man alive. Didn't you hear how sluttish and nasty he said the maid was? When the confidante goes in rags 'tis a certain sign that the mistress is honest; for the manner of the town is to see the chambermaid first, before paying court to the mistress.

CLINIA. Prithee, dear rogue, on with your story, but have a care not to curry favour by any deceit. What said she, when you first mentioned me?

SYRUS. When I told her you were ashore and desired her company forthwith, she immediately threw aside her work and couldn't speak for crying; which, you may be sure, was all for your sake.

CLINIA. As I hope for mercy, I'm so transported, I scarce know where I am; I was in such a fright but a moment ago.

CLITIPHO. I knew, Sir, that there was nothing amiss . . . Now 'tis my turn, Syrus. Let's know who that other person was.

SYRUS. We have brought Madam Bacchis, your mistress, Sir.

CLITIPHO, *in a passion.* How? . . . Bacchis, do ye say? Why, ye cursed dog, whither do ye take her?

SYRUS. Whither do I take her? Why, to our house, Sir.

CLITIPHO, *hastily.* What, to my father's, Sirrah?

SYRUS. Yes, to your father's.

CLITIPHO. To see the impudence of this rascal!

SYRUS. Hark ye, Sir! Faint heart never won fair lady.

CLITIPHO. Tell me, Sirrah, do you seek to advance your own reputation at my cost? If you step but the least awry, I'm lost to all intents and purposes. . . . And what will ye do, then?

SYRUS. But, Sir . . .

CLITIPHO. But, what?

SYRUS. I'll tell ye, if you'll give me leave.

CLINIA. Prithee, give him leave.

CLITIPHO. Well, then . . .

SYRUS. The case is thus . . . As if . . .

CLITIPHO. Pox, he's going to tell a story nine hours long.

CLINIA. I think so too. . . . Therefore, Syrus, leave fooling, and come to the point.

SYRUS, *to* CLITIPHO. In truth, Sir, I can bear it no longer. You have grown so troublesome that there's no dealing with you . . .

CLINIA, *to* CLITIPHO. Faith, you should give him a hearing, though. Pray be silent a little.

SYRUS. You desire to keep a mistress, Sir—to bed with her, and be able to give her presents; yet you wouldn't run any hazard on her account. Really you're wondrous wise, if it is wisdom to aim at that which can never be. You must either take the hazard with the prize, or lose the prize and run no hazard. Now, Sir, take whichever side seems best to ye. Yet, for all that, I believe the plot I've hatched is both well contrived and safe: by which, first, you'll enjoy your mistress's company under your father's nose, without the least danger; and then by the self-same means I shall trick the old man out of what you promised her—the money for which you've so often dunned me. And what the Deuce would you have more?

CLITIPHO. Nothing: provided it be as you say.

SYRUS. Hang your 'provideds'! Can't you risk the hazard?

CLITIPHO. Well, come on then! Your plot, how is it laid?

SYRUS. Your mistress shall pass as this gentleman's.

CLITIPHO. Very fine! . . . But, prithee, what shall we do with his own? Shall she be fastened upon his back too, as though one wasn't enough to ruin his credit?

SYRUS. We'll send her to your mother's.

CLITIPHO. What to do there?

SYRUS. Faith, Sir, it would take up nine hours to give ye the why's and wherefore's. Let it be enough that I have reason for this.

CLINIA. That's reasonable.

CLITIPHO. Mere stuff! I can see nothing as yet that would remove my suspicions.

SYRUS. Hold, Sir! If you're afraid of this plot, I've another buzzing in my head, too, which I'm sure you'll both own to be safe enough.

CLITIPHO. I beseech you, then, let it out for us!

CLINIA. And in an instant!

SYRUS, *scornfully*. I'll go out to meet the women, and pray them to face about and march home again.

CLITIPHO. Hah! What's that you say?

SYRUS. I'll so rid you of your fears that you may be sure to sleep sound in a whole skin . . .

Is going off in disgust.

CLITIPHO, *to* CLINIA. What had I best do now?

CLINIA. What you, Sir? Why, make good use of . . .

CLITIPHO. Hark ye, Syrus, tell me truly what I should do!

SYRUS. Away from me! You'll wish you had listened to me, when 'tis too late.

CLINIA. Here's a fair opportunity offered. Make good use of it while you may; you aren't sure of having the like again.

CLITIPHO. Why, Syrus, I say!

SYRUS. Bawl till your heart ache, I'm on my way now.

CLITIPHO, *to* CLINIA. In good earnest, you're in the right there.

Aloud.

But hark ye, Syrus, Syrus, I say; soho, Syrus! . . . No, Syrus; I throw myself, my love, my reputation too, into your hands. I'll leave all to your discretion, but pray discharge the matter well.

SYRUS. That's a plea worth laughing at, i' faith! As though my fortune wasn't as much at stake as yours. If an unlucky cast of the dice should spoil all our designs, you'll escape with no worse than a reprimand, but poor Pilgarlick here must be beaten to rags. Wherefore, I must watch my business very closely. But meanwhile you must ask this gentleman to squire your mistress.

CLINIA. He may be sure of my assistance. And as the case stands I am obliged to furnish it.

CLITIPHO. Oh, Sir, my heart goes out to ye!

CLINIA. You must take care that Bacchis plays her part to perfection.

SYRUS. Why, yes. Already she has her lines off by heart, cues and all.

CLITIPHO. For my part, I wonder how you contrived to wheedle her here so soon. Often she scorns the best of us.

SYRUS. I came upon her in a very critical minute, which gave me my advantage. For who should I find in her house, but a sneaking Captain who begged her for one single night of love. She managed this poor devil with such artifice as to enflame his greedy appetite by keeping him at bay, and at the same time to do you a signal piece of service. . . . But hark ye, Sir, beware of making any false step! You know how plaguey sharp-sighted your father is in these intrigues, and I know how hard it is for you to keep yourself under control. You must take mighty care of all double-meaning expressions, of casting amorous looks over your left shoulder; of fighting, spitting, humming and jeering . . .

CLITIPHO. Faith, I'll act the part rarely.

SYRUS. See that you do, then!

CLITIPHO. . . . You yourself shall admire me for it.

SYRUS. But see how quickly the ladies come after us!

CLITIPHO. Where are they?

To SYRUS *holding him.*

Why do ye hold me, boy?

SYRUS. You've nothing to do with her now.

CLITIPHO. Right, not before my father. . . . But until then . . .

SYRUS. No, not until then, neither.

CLITIPHO. Nay, let me go.

SYRUS, *still holding him.* Not a step, I say.

CLITIPHO. Prithee, for one minute!

SYRUS. That I forbid, too.

CLITIPHO. A civil respect, at least.

SYRUS. Get you gone, if you've any wisdom in your noddle.

CLITIPHO. Well, I'm going, but what must Clinia do?

SYRUS. He must stay here.

CLITIPHO. He shall have a fine time of it!

SYRUS. March off, I say!

CLITIPHO *walks on a little on one side.*

Enter at a distance BACCHIS, ANTIPHILA, DROMO, WAITING-MAIDS, *etc.*

BACCHIS. In truth, dear Antiphila, I must commend ye, and think ye very happy, that ye take pains to make your good behaviour so wholly agree with your beauty. As I'm a sinner, I don't wonder that all the sparks of the town should be ready to die for ye, when your discourse reveals the sweetness of your heart. For my part, when I come to consider the life and behaviour of such women as you, who do not bed down with every coxcomb, I don't wonder to find ye so modest and virtuous, and ourselves so very unlike ye. For you virtue is the best rule to follow, but our gallants won't suffer a woman as I am to be thus. Our beauty makes them adore us for awhile, but when that decays they are mad for a new face; so that unless we lay by money while we yet can, we shall find ourselves at the end pining in a desert for the rest of our days. Whereas you, madam, love a man whose age and nature correspond with your own; he wholly keeps himself to you, and by mutual consent the bond is made so firm that nothing can ever separate your hearts.

ANTIPHILA. I'm little acquainted with others; myself I know well enough. I always take care that my dear Clinia's happiness should be the foundation of my own.

CLINIA, *overhearing*. Ah, my dear Antiphila, 'tis for thy sake alone that I'm come home again; for while I was from thee, none of all the hardships I underwent could compare with my being deprived of thy sweet company.

SYRUS, *to* CLITIPHO *peeping from his covert*. I believe him, Sir.

CLITIPHO. I can scarce contain myself, old boy! Is it not a plaguey thing to be debarred from one's own delights, hah?

SYRUS, *to* CLITIPHO. Unless you be speedily gone, I warrant your father will make ye smart for this.

BACCHIS. What young gentleman's that who ogles us so?

ANTIPHILA, *seeing* CLINIA. Oh, lend me your hand, I beseech ye!

BACCHIS. For heaven's sake, what ails ye, my dear?

ANTIPHILA. I'm going . . .

Faints away.

BACCHIS. Help! Alas, poor soul!

ANTIPHILA *recovers a little.*

How came this fit upon ye, my poor child?

ANTIPHILA, *in a soft tone.* Do I see my Clinia, or do I dream?

BACCHIS. Who's that you see?

CLINIA. My life, my soul! Heaven bless thee . . .

Embracing ANTIPHILA.

ANTIPHILA. And thee also, my dear long-wished-for Clinia.

CLINIA. How is it, my dear?

ANTIPHILA. Well, since I have got you again, my darling.

CLINIA, *embracing.* And have I got you again, my duck, within these arms? You, for whom I have so passionately longed.

SYRUS. Come, come, turn in! The old man and his supper await ye.

Exeunt.

End of the Second Act

ACT THREE

CHREMES *alone*

CHREMES. 'Tis just break of day. Why shouldn't I knock at my neighbour's door now, and give him the first news of his son's return, though the young man I fancy will hardly thank me for it? But when I see the poor gentleman take on so extremely about his son's absence, how can I find it in my heart to deny him this unexpected comfort? And his son will be never the worse for it neither: I shall assist the old man to the utmost of my power. And as I perceive that his son and mine help one another all they can, and go hand in glove together, so it is no more than reasonable that we, their fathers, should do each other all the good offices that lie in our power.

Enter MENEDEMUS *on one side of the stage with a rake, etc., upon his shoulder.*

MENEDEMUS, *to himself.* Either I'm born under the curse of an unlucky planet, or else that old saying's worthless which declares that Time cures all things. For this absence of my son afflicts me every day more and more. The longer he's away, the more I desire to see him again, and the more I miss him.

CHREMES, *to himself.* Oh, yonder's the gentleman himself coming from home; I'll go and discourse with him. . . . Good morrow to ye, neighbour, I'm come to ye with such news that I believe you'd be heartily desirous to hear what it is.

MENEDEMUS. Why, Sir, have ye heard anything of my son then?

CHREMES. He's safe and sound, Sir.

MENEDEMUS. Where is he, I beseech ye?

CHREMES. At my house, Sir.

MENEDEMUS. What, my son!

CHREMES. Yes, your son.

MENEDEMUS. Is he come, then?

CHREMES. Yes, indeed.

MENEDEMUS. My boy Clinia come home?

Throws down his rake, etc.

CHREMES. Even so.

MENEDEMUS. Let's be going then. . . . I beseech ye, Sir, bring me to the sight of him.

CHREMES. But he wouldn't for the world have ye know he's come back. He avoids your presence because of what he has done, and now fears you will be more severe upon him than ever.

MENEDEMUS. And didn't you tell him that I was quite another man?

CHREMES. Not I, Sir.

MENEDEMUS. Why didn't ye?

CHREMES. Because if he finds that you give way so easily and softly, it will be the worse for him and you too.

MENEDEMUS. It can't be helped. I've been too severe a father already.

CHREMES. Ah, Sir, you are always upon the extremes: either too generous, or too sparing. You run into the same inconveniences by one as by the other. Formerly you forced your son out of doors rather than suffer him to keep a mistress, though he was then contented with a little, and would gladly have snapped at any kindness. But when she was forced, by his desertion, to become a woman of the

town, and now can't be kept without a mint of money—
now you give him his full liberty. Let me tell you how she
is arrayed for the ruin of mankind: she carries at her heels
no less than ten or a dozen waiting-maids, with a great
luggage of golden trappings. Were a prince her gallant and
desirous to maintain her, he'd be hard put to it. Don't
think that your son Clinia can do the like at your expense!

MENEDEMUS. Is she at your house too?

CHREMES. At my house say ye? . . . Yes, to my cost, I've made
but one banquet for her and her retinue; and i' faith,
if I make another, I shall be forced by poverty to flee
my country. To omit other charges, what a cursed deal
of wine has been wasted only by her tasting and sipping.
She cries: 'Good old Father, this wine is too rough; pray,
let's have some that is smoother.' I pierced every cask and
pipe in my cellar, and my servants were all as busy as so
many bees. This was but one night's work! What will become of you, then, when they descend upon ye every
day? As I'm a living soul, Sir, I heartily pity your condition.

MENEDEMUS. Let him do as he lists. Let him take the money,
spend it, make ducks and drakes of it. I'm resolved to bear
all losses, so be it only that I can have him at home with
me.

CHREMES. Though you seem firmly set upon it, I believe it
will be better to conceal your design, however far you indulge him.

MENEDEMUS. What would ye have me do?

CHREMES. Anything rather than what you intend. Can't you
let him have money at second-hand, by allowing your own
servant to cheat ye of it? And the truth is, I have an inkling that they plan some such thing already, and are contriving how to do it with dispatch. My man Syrus whispers
with yours, and our two sons lay their heads together too.
'Tis better to lose a pound this way than a penny in the
other. It isn't so much the money, neighbour, that is to be
taken thought of, as the manner of giving it him with the
least danger. For if once he finds which way the stream

runs, and learns that you had rather part with your life and money too, than lose him, then fie! what a vast gap do you lay open to his debaucheries? This way your life will become a burden to ye; for too much liberty corrupts an angel. Whatsoever whim comes into his mind, whip! he'll follow it without considering whether his demands be reasonable or not. You'll be mortified to see your estate go to ruin, and your son spoiled into the bargain. If you refuse him a farthing, he'll fall to the same old dog-trick, which he has found works best upon ye, and threaten to be gone, forsooth.

MENEDEMUS. All this seems true and probable enough.

CHREMES. Truth, Sir, I couldn't sleep one wink this night for racking my brains how to restore your son to you.

MENEDEMUS. Your hand, Sir . . . I hope, Sir, you'll continue as you've begun?

CHREMES. I'm ready to serve ye.

MENEDEMUS. Do ye know what I mean, Sir?

CHREMES. Let's hear it.

MENEDEMUS. That you'd encourage them in the design, which you perceive they plan, of getting the money from me. For I long to give my boy what he wants; and even more so to have a sight of him.

CHREMES. I'll do my best, Sir, I must take my Syrus in hand and teach him his lesson. . . . But hold, somebody's coming out of my house! . . . You had best get out of the way, for fear they see we are plotting together. Moreover, a little business calls me hence now; for my neighbours, Simus and Crito, have a dispute about some lands, and I am to be their arbiter; but I'll go tell them they must not expect me today, as I promised them. Tarry, though; I'll be back again in a minute.

MENEDEMUS. Pray, Sir, do.

Exit CHREMES.

MENEDEMUS, *alone*. Bless me! Of what an odd composition men are made! To think that they should see further and judge better of other people's affairs than their own . . .

It may be because in our own concerns we are too much possessed by our passions of joy or grief. This same Chremes now, how much wiser he seems to be on my behalf, than I am myself.

Going off.

Enter CHREMES.

CHREMES, *to* MENEDEMUS, *as he is going off*. I have made my excuses to my neighbours, that I may have more leisure to serve you.

Exit MENEDEMUS *with his rake, etc., upon his shoulder.*
Enter SYRUS *at a distance.*

SYRUS, *to himself*. Well, friend Syrus, whichever way we take, money must be had by hook or by crook; and our old fox must be trapped too.

CHREMES, *aside, partly hearing*. I perceive I wasn't mistaken when I said they were about some such design. Clinia's man is a poor dull tool, but mine is sharp; he must undertake the business.

SYRUS, *aside*. Whose tongue's that? Zookers! All's spoiled! Did he hear me, or no?

CHREMES. Syrus!

SYRUS. Why, is it you, Sir?

CHREMES. What's your business here?

SYRUS. No great matter. . . . You're a brave man, Sir, to be stirring so early, after such a rattle as you had last night.

CHREMES. Why, there was no hard drinking.

SYRUS. No hard drinking, say ye? Marry, you must be heart of oak.

CHREMES. No more of that.

SYRUS. This wench of Clinia's is a good sort of a wench, and pleasant enough.

CHREMES. Ay, so I found.

SYRUS. And, in truth, has a very good face too.

CHREMES. So, so.

SYRUS. Though not comparable to the women in your young

days; but really, as looks go now, she is very fine. I don't wonder Clinia is so desperately smitten. But he has a father, our next neighbour, a covetous, miserable, griping old hunks. Do ye know him, Sir? Being so plaguey afraid he should be starved himself, he has turned his poor son out of the paddock at the roadside. Don't you know what I say to be true?

CHREMES. Ay, why not . . . But there's a rascal I know who deserves the lash.

SYRUS, *fearfully*. What rascal, Sir?

CHREMES. That dull rogue, Clinia's man . . .

SYRUS, *aside*. Faith, Syrus, I was plaguily afraid for thee!

CHREMES.   . . . who allowed all this.

SYRUS. What could he do?

CHREMES. What could he do? Why, he might have found out some device to help the young gentleman get money for his mistress. Thus he would have saved the stingy old fellow from all this vexation, whether he wished it or not.

SYRUS. You're pleased to jest, Sir.

CHREMES. 'Twas no more than his duty, Syrus!

SYRUS. Pray, Sir, do you approve of slaves who trick their own masters?

CHREMES. Yes, if there be just occasion for so doing.

SYRUS, *aside*. Very well, i' faith.

CHREMES. Sometimes a little trickery saves a great deal of trouble. In this case, it would have kept his only son from rambling overseas.

SYRUS, *aside*. Faith, I can't tell whether he's in jest or in earnest . . . However, he encourages me to do what I had already had in mind.

CHREMES. And now, Syrus, why does the fellow idle away his time? Unless he acts soon, his master Mr Clinia will be forced to march off once more, as not being able to defray his mistress's charges? Won't he make one raid upon the old man's pocket?

SYRUS. The fellow's a fool, God bless him!

CHREMES. You should give him one push for the young gentleman's sake.

SYRUS. Sir, I'd do it with all speed, if you'd but give me the word: for I'm a complete master of that art . . .

CHREMES. So much the better.

SYRUS. . . . I don't usually fail, Sir.

CHREMES. Why, then, to work!

SYRUS. But pray, Sir, take care to remember this, what you have said. For you know we are all subject to failings, and if it should chance one day to be your son's case . . .

CHREMES. I hope I shall have no occasion to remember.

SYRUS. Troth, so do I; nor do I mention this, because I suspect any such thing. But I do say it again, that if matters should chance to happen so, you mightn't . . . You see he's young; and edad, if that time once came, I should cheat ye most nobly.

CHREMES. We'll talk of that when the time comes. Keep to your present cue!

Exit CHREMES.

SYRUS, *alone.* Well, I never heard any master talk better than mine did. Nor could I have hoped to find such a broad toleration for roguery. . . . But who comes out of our house there?

Re-enter CHREMES *with* CLITIPHO.

CHREMES, *to* CLITIPHO, *entering.* What impudence is this, I pray? Is this your trade, Clitipho? Do these things become you? Hah!

CLITIPHO. What have I done, Sir?

CHREMES. Didn't I see ye just now with your hand in a courtesan's bosom?

SYRUS, *aside, listening.* All is revealed, and I'm lost!

CLITIPHO. Who, I, Sir?

CHREMES. Those very eyes of yours confess it! Come, don't stand in a lie. You deal basely by Mr Clinia in not keeping your hands from fumbling; for 'tis a great affront to acknowledge a gentleman as a friend, while playing an underhand game with his mistress. And you were strangely uncivil last night at supper too.

SYRUS, *to* CHREMES. You're in the right there, Sir.

CHREMES. And troublesome, too. As I'm a living soul, I was miserably afraid it might cost you a duel. I know these lovers: they take very seriously what to others may be nothing.

CLITIPHO. But, Sir, he has a deep confidence in me, and knows I won't play him an unhandsome trick.

CHREMES. What then? But you might have left them together a little while. Lovers have a thousand things to say and do, which your presence will disturb. I know this of my own experience. For I have never a friend in the world, Clitipho, to whom I should dare trust all my private actions. I'm afraid of my superiors, and ashamed of my equals, lest these should take me for a fool, and those for a debauchee. . . . Suppose he should resemble me in this? For it is our duty to know when and where to please a friend.

SYRUS, *aside to* CLITIPHO. Do ye understand what he says?

CLITIPHO, *aside.* Ay, to my sorrow!

SYRUS, *aside.* Didn't I warn you, Clitipho, to play the part of a very staid and reserved gentleman?

CLITIPHO. Prithee, hold your tongue!

SYRUS. You are in the right, Sir.

CHREMES. I swear, Syrus, I'm ashamed of him.

SYRUS. So I believe, Sir; and with good reason too, for it grieves me also very much.

CLITIPHO, *angrily.* What, will you never have done?

SYRUS. Faith, Sir, I speak as I think.

CLITIPHO, *to* CHREMES. Mustn't I come near them, then?

CHREMES. Yes, in a civil way, but not as you do.

SYRUS, *aside.* Our plot's on the point of sinking. He'll betray all before we get one bag of money.

To CHREMES.

Pray, Sir, will ye be pleased to take a fool's counsel for once?

CHREMES. What's that?

SYRUS. I would have you order your son to withdraw a little.

CLITIPHO, *angrily*. Whither, I pray?

SYRUS. Whither? Why, whither you please, make room for the lovers and take a walk the while.

CLITIPHO. I take a walk! To what place?

SYRUS. Pish! As if ye needed any direction! Take this way, or that way, or which way you please.

CHREMES. He is right, I require you to leave us.

CLITIPHO. Confound ye for a dog! Sending me off to the Devil's arse!

SYRUS, *aside to* CLITIPHO. Keep your hands to yourself another time!

Exit CLITIPHO.

SYRUS. What say ye, Sir? What do ye think will become of this son of yours, if ye don't give him due correction with the utmost authority of a father?

CHREMES. Let me deal with that.

SYRUS. Ay, Sir, and now's the time you must watch him.

CHREMES. I warrant ye I will.

SYRUS. Ay, so you had best; for he heeds me less and less every day.

CHREMES. But hark ye, Syrus! Have ye considered the business of which I told ye? Have ye found any plot yet that pleases your mind?

SYRUS. You mean about the cheating of Menedemus? S't, Sir! I've just now stumbled upon one.

CHREMES. Thou art a brave lad! Prithee, what is it?

SYRUS. I'll tell ye, Sir! But in no order, just as one thing brings out another.

CHREMES. What then, Boy?

SYRUS. This same Bacchis is a plaguey jade.

CHREMES. So I thought.

SYRUS, *aside.* Yes, if you knew all. . . . But observe what a whore's trick she's going to play. Here lived an old Corinthian woman, to whom this Bacchis had lent above thirty pounds . . .

CHREMES. Very well!

SYRUS. This old woman's now dead and gone, leaving Bacchis, her young daughter, in security for the debt.

CHREMES. So then?

SYRUS. Bacchis brought this poor girl along with the rest; and she's now in your lady's apartment.

CHREMES. Well! How then?

SYRUS. She now tempts Clinia to buy the girl for his pleasure; but demands the full sum of thirty pounds . . .

CHREMES. Does she so?

SYRUS. Whoo! Do ye question it?

CHREMES. I did . . . But what do ye mean to do next?

SYRUS. Who, I, Sir? . . . I'll away to Mr Menedemus's, tell him that this girl was spirited away from Caria, that she's one of a rich and noble family, and that he'll get the Lord knows what if he'll put down the money to ransom her.

CHREMES. You've missed the mark.

SYRUS. Why so, Sir?

CHREMES. I'll forecast Menedemus's reply: 'I'll have nothing to do with her.' What do ye do then?

SYRUS. Pray, Sir, take a happier view of the matter.

CHREMES. There's no occasion for that.

SYRUS. No occasion, Sir?

CHREMES. No, marry there isn't.

SYRUS. Why, Sir? I don't take your meaning.

CHREMES. I'll tell you presently. . . . Stay, stay, a little? What's this bustle at the door?

End of the Third Act

ACT FOUR

Enter at a distance SOSTRATA, *with a ring on her hand; and the* NURSE

SOSTRATA, *to the* NURSE *entering.* If I'm not mightily mistaken, this is the very ring my infant daughter had about her when we had her exposed.

CHREMES. What means my woman by this talk, Syrus?

SOSTRATA. How is it, Nurse? Is it not the same, think ye?

NURSE. Truly, Madam, I said 'twas the very same, as soon as ever I clapped eyes upon it.

SOSTRATA. But did you view it well?

NURSE. Oh, very carefully, Madam.

SOSTRATA. You go in, Nurse, and bring me word whether she has finished bathing herself; in the meantime I'll wait here for my husband.

Exit NURSE.

SYRUS, *to* CHREMES. She wants you, Sir! You had best step in and see what she needs. I can't guess why she's so in the dumps. 'Tisn't for nothing, I'm sure; I fear the worst.

CHREMES. Pshaw! What should it be? Is she big with child again? Nay, she's only big with fool, and wants to be delivered.

SOSTRATA. Hah, my good old man!

CHREMES. And my good old woman too!

SOSTRATA. I was looking for thee, my bird.

CHREMES. Well now, tell me your pleasure.

SOSTRATA. First I beg ye to believe that I wouldn't ever disobey your commands.

CHREMES. That's hard to believe, but if you'd have me believe it, for once I will.

SYRUS, *aside.* This excusing herself beforehand bodes some plaguey mischief.

SOSTRATA. Don't you remember, when I was once brought to bed, you strictly charged me not to bring the child up, if it proved to be a girl . . .

CHREMES. I smell out the business! You have saved and reared the child—isn't that so?

SYRUS, *aside.* If that be true, 'twill make a damned hole in my master's pocket.

SOSTRATA. No such matter! I gave our child to an old Corinthian woman, a good honest neighbour of ours, to expose it.

CHREMES. Bless us! Was there ever such a silly soul?

SOSTRATA. Ah me! What hurt have I done you?

CHREMES. 'What hurt?' she asks.

SOSTRATA. Indeed, dear husband, if I have offended, 'twas done in ignorance.

CHREMES, *angrily.* Yes, indeed! I know this well enough, without your owning to it, that everything you do is done ignorantly and foolishly. How many blunders have you committed in this one matter! First, had you obeyed my authority, the girl should have been at once made away with, and you wouldn't have come to me with an idle report of her death, when you did all ye could to save her. But let that pass, 'twas a mother's tender pity; I bear with it. But how rarely you've considered the consequences! Pray study the case. 'Tis most manifest that you've handed your child over to this old woman, either to become a common prostitute, or to be advertised for public sale. I fancy you thought anything would serve the case, if only her life were saved! But why should a man trouble his head with fools like you, who are lost to any sense of justice, honesty or reason. Be it better or worse, for them or against them, they see nothing but what they wish to see.

SOSTRATA. My dear Chremes! I was much to blame, I confess. But now let me beg of ye, as nature has made you the wiser of us two, to be also the more generous, and let your goodness protect my folly.

CHREMES. Well, I'll forgive you this fault! But in sober sadness, wife, my good nature will ruin ye. Now let's hear the whole story, whatever it be.

SOSTRATA. We women are always foolish and superstitious; so when I gave the child to be exposed, I took a ring off my finger and sent it with her; that, though she died, she might at least carry away some token of our kindness.

CHREMES. That's well! So you saved the child's life, and your own conscience too!

SOSTRATA, *showing a ring*. Look ye, this is the very ring!

CHREMES. How came ye by it?

SOSTRATA. The young gentlewoman that Bacchis brought with her . . .

SYRUS, *aside*. How!

CHREMES. What says she of it?

SOSTRATA. . . . She gave it me to hold, while she went to the bath. At first I took no notice of the ring; but when I eyed it more narrowly, I knew it again, and came running in all haste to acquaint you.

CHREMES. And what have ye gathered from this gentlewoman about the matter?

SOSTRATA. I am quite in the dark, unless you'll examine her herself, inquiring where she got it, and what she can inform you about it.

SYRUS, *aside*. My plot's countermined. I find there's more in the wind than I could wish for. If this be true, she's certainly my master's daughter.

CHREMES. Is the old Corinthian alive—the woman to whom ye delivered the child?

SOSTRATA. I don't know.

CHREMES. How did she say she had disposed of it?

SOSTRATA. She said she had done exactly as I ordered her.

CHREMES. What's her name, that we may hunt her up?

SOSTRATA. Philtere.

SYRUS, *aside.* The very same: she's found, as surely as I'm lost.

CHREMES. Come, wife, let's retire.

SOSTRATA. How things happen beyond my expectation! I was extremely afraid you'd prove as severe now, as long ago when you gave me your orders.

CHREMES. If a man's estate won't afford it he can't always do as he would. Now my circumstances are such, that I should be glad of a daughter: formerly 'twas otherwise. *Exeunt all but* SYRUS.

SYRUS. If I am not very much mistaken, I'm in a fair way to be utterly routed; all my forces are so miserably reduced that I shall never come off safe, unless I can keep old Mr Menedemus from perceiving this young woman to be his son's mistress. For 'tis idle to hope for a bag of money, or to think of winning anything from the old fellow. I shall come off well enough if I can creep away with a whole hide. It pierces my very heart to see such a delicate morsel suddenly snatched out of my very mouth. . . . Where shall I go? . . . Or what shall I invent? . . . I must find some new platform! . . . Hang it, diligence outdoes the Devil. . . . Suppose I try this way? . . . Pox, it won't do! . . . Suppose that way? . . . 'Twill be the same. . . . Nay, but I believe this other will serve. . . . No! . . . Yes, best of all! I have it: I believe I shall once more lay my hands upon that damned runagate money. *Enter* CLINIA, *at a distance.*

CLINIA, *to himself.* From this time forward nothing can happen to disquiet me; such is the happiness I'm surprised into! I'll so wholly yield to my father's pleasure now that I'll be far better than he himself could wish.

SYRUS, *aside*. I wasn't beside the mark, I see. From what this spark says, the gentlewoman is really proved to be Mr Chremes's daughter . . .

To CLINIA.

I'm heartily glad, Sir, that things have fallen out so favourably to your desires.

CLINIA. Prithee, honest boy, did you hear of it too?

SYRUS. Yes, I was present at the discovery.

CLINIA. Did ye ever know anyone so fortunate as I?

SYRUS. No, Sir.

CLINIA. Let me die if I'm half so glad for my own sake as for hers, who deserves every blessing however great!

SYRUS. I believe she does, too. Now, Clinia, your turn comes to do us a small kindness, pray remember your friend, Mr Clitipho, and take care that his mistress be still concealed from our old gentleman.

CLINIA, *not minding him*. Gods!

SYRUS. Forbear these raptures.

CLINIA. . . . Shall my dear Antiphila be mine then?

SYRUS. Won't ye let me speak, Sir?

CLINIA. What would ye have me do, old soul? I'm so transported—prithee, bear with me!

SYRUS. Faith, so I will; but sore against my will.

CLINIA, *still not minding him*. We shall live as happy as the Gods . . .

SYRUS. My labour's lost, I see.

CLINIA. Now speak, I'm listening to ye.

SYRUS. But by and by you won't.

CLINIA. Yes, but I will.

SYRUS. I tell ye, Sir, some care must be taken to secure your friend's interests. Now, if you go away and leave Bacchis at our house, my old master will immediately discover her to be Mr Clitipho's mistress; but if ye take her along with ye, he will be as much in the dark as ever he was.

CLINIA. Ah, but Syrus, nothing could work more against my wedding than this! For with Bacchis at my side, how can I speak to my father of Antiphila? Do you heed what I say?

SYRUS. Yes.

CLINIA. What shall I say to him? What excuse can I offer?

SYRUS. Nay, Sir, I wouldn't have you say one word of untruth; but plainly tell him the whole business.

CLINIA. How!

SYRUS. I'd have you acquaint him of your passion for Antiphila, and beg leave to marry her; confessing that this Bacchis is Clitipho's mistress.

CLINIA. You demand of me nothing but what is just, reasonable and easy. I suppose you'd have me beg my father to conceal all from your old Mr Chremes?

SYRUS. You mistake me; I'd have your father truthfully tell my master the whole story, from top to bottom.

CLINIA. How! Are you mad or drunk? In truth, you'll plainly ruin Clitipho. Prithee, tell me how he can have his interests secured, as ye say?

SYRUS. Oh, I reckon this a masterpiece of my cunning. Here I triumph in having such a mighty knack and faculty at juggling that I can cheat both of them by telling the truth. For when your old gentleman informs my old gentleman about his son's mistress, he shall be laughed at as a simpleton.

CLINIA. Nay, once more you destroy all my hopes of matrimony. For so long as Mr Chremes believes Bacchis to be my mistress, he'll never venture to bestow his daughter upon me. Perhaps you don't care whether I sink or swim, if only you can serve Clitipho's turn?

SYRUS. What a pox! Do ye think I'd have ye act this part forever? A single day, that's all, will serve my purpose and let me finger the money. I desire not an hour longer.

CLINIA. Will a single day suffice? But what if his father should find out all in the meantime?

SYRUS. Right! And what if the sky should fall?

CLINIA. I dread what will come of this.

SYRUS. Dread! Fiddle-sticks! As if you weren't able to slip your neck out of the collar whenever you pleased. You may clear yourself by making a full confession.

CLINIA. Well, come on then, let Bacchis be brought over.

SYRUS. That's a true friend. . . . Here she comes.

Enter BACCHIS *and* PHRYGIA.

BACCHIS, *to* PHRYGIA, *entering*. I' faith, this rogue's impudent devices have brought me hither to a good purpose. It was thirty guineas he promised me. And if he fools me now, let him fawn and cringe until his heart aches for me to come again, but I'll not do it. Or else I'll make an assignation, and appoint a time (of which he'll be sure to tell his master) and when Clitipho's mind is big with hopes, I'll baffle them by not coming at all; and then Syrus's back shall be soundly lashed for my fault.

CLINIA, *overhearing*. She promises very fairly, Syrus.

SYRUS. Do ye think she jests, Sir? She'll perform what she says, if I don't oblige her.

BACCHIS, *to* PHRYGIA. They're in a dead sleep, sure; but I'll rouse them with a vengeance. . . . Hark ye, Phrygia, did you take notice of Charinus's house, which the man showed us just now?

PHRYGIA. I did, Madam.

BACCHIS. 'Tis the very next house on the right-hand.

PHRYGIA. I remember it.

BACCHIS. Run thither at full speed. For the Captain celebrates Bacchus's feast there in Charinus's company.

SYRUS, *aside*. What the Devil shall we do now?

BACCHIS. Tell him I'm here sore against my will, being restrained by force. But I'll soon get rid of my oppressors and straightway come to him.

PHRYGIA, *going off*.

SYRUS. 'Sdeath! I'm at my last prayers.

Aside.

Stay, Madam, stay, where are you sending her, I beseech ye? Call her back!

BACCHIS, *to* PHRYGIA. Get you gone, I say!

SYRUS. The guineas are waiting for you, Madam.

BACCHIS. Then I'll stay.

PHRYGIA *returns.*

SYRUS. You shall receive them in a minute.

BACCHIS. As you please. Do ye find me in such haste for them?

SYRUS. Pray, Madam, do you know what you must do?

BACCHIS. What?

SYRUS. You must just step over to Mr Menedemus's house and take all your train with you.

BACCHIS, *angrily.* Ye impudent dog, what do ye mean? Why?

SYRUS. To coin money for your ladyship's use.

BACCHIS. Do ye think me a fit person to hoodwink?

SYRUS. No, I'm in earnest, Madam.

BACCHIS. Have I any business there with you?

SYRUS. No, Madam, but there I'll pay you the money.

BACCHIS. Let's be going then!

SYRUS. Come this way, Madam.

Exit BACCHIS, *let out by* CLINIA *and* PHRYGIA, *who follow.*

SYRUS. Soho, Dromo!

Enter DROMO.

DROMO. Who calls?

SYRUS. 'Tis I.

DROMO. What's the matter?

SYRUS. Bring over all Bacchis's servants to your house quickly.

DROMO. Why so?

SYRUS. Don't wait to ask questions, let them carry all their baggage with them too. The old gentleman will think his expenses are lessened as soon as he finds his house clear of the lumber. Faith, he little thinks he shall pay for it in the long run. As for you, Dromo, if you have any wit, take not the least notice of what you see or hear.

DROMO. You'll find me a perfect deaf mute.

Exit DROMO, *and presently re-enters with* BACCHIS'S SERVANTS, *and their luggage, crossing the stage. After them enter* CHREMES.

CHREMES, *to himself.* As I'm a sinner, I can't help pitying my unfortunate neighbour Menedemus, to see him forced to maintain this creature with all her train. I'm satisfied he won't resent it at first, because of his longing for his son's company. But when he once finds such vast expenses continuing daily, and sees no end to them, he'll wish his boy in the farthest Indies. . . . Oh, here comes Syrus very seasonably, too!

SYRUS, *aside.* Why don't I take my cutlass and board him? Ha, Sir!

CHREMES. What makes you so merry?

SYRUS. I've wished for your appearance this half hour.

CHREMES. I fancy you've been tampering with the old gentleman?

SYRUS. You mean in the manner we discussed a short while ago? Ay, Sir, no sooner said than done.

CHREMES. In good earnest!

SYRUS. Yes, Sir, in good earnest.

CHREMES. Faith, I can't forbear caressing thee. Come hither, ye little rogue, I'll remember thee for this. Edad, I will!

SYRUS. Ah, Sir, if you knew how prettily the notion jumped into my noddle.

CHREMES. Pho! Do ye pride yourself because of your good luck?

SYRUS. Troth, not I. I only speak the truth.

CHREMES. Let's hear it then.

SYRUS. Clinia has told his father that Bacchis is your son's mistress; and that he brought her hither only to cast a mist before your eyes.

CHREMES. Very well!

SYRUS. Pray tell me what ye think of it.

CHREMES. 'Twas admirably done, I swear.

SYRUS, *aside*. Ay, if you knew all.

Aloud.

. . . But mark what plot's behind! . . . Then Clinia tells him that he has seen your daughter, is much taken with her, and has a mind to marry her.

CHREMES. What, she whom we've just found to be ours?

SYRUS. Yes, Sir! . . . And he'll desire his father to win your consent.

CHREMES. Why so, Syrus? I don't understand any reason for it.

SYRUS. Pshaw! You're so dull of apprehension.

CHREMES. Likely enough.

SYRUS. His father is to give him money for the wedding, to . . . you take me, Sir?

CHREMES. To buy him a wedding shirt, I warrant.

SYRUS. Right, right.

CHREMES. But I neither give him my daughter, nor my promise.

SYRUS. No, Sir? Why not?

CHREMES. Why not, say ye? Do ye think I'll marry her to a rascal, who . . .

SYRUS. Please yourself about that! I didn't say you should let him have her for good and all; only that you should pretend it.

CHREMES. I hate such pretences. . . . Plot as you please, so as you don't include me in the plot. Shall I promise to give my daughter, when I don't intend to do any such thing?

SYRUS. I was in hopes you might.

CHREMES. Not a bit of it.

SYRUS. In truth, it might have been done cleverly. I should never have undertaken this plot, but that you urged me.

CHREMES. I grant that.

SYRUS. Nevertheless, Sir, my intentions were good.

CHREMES. I'd have ye do your best to cheat Menedemus, by all means; but then I'd have ye go another way to work.

SYRUS. So I will, Sir, we'll find out one. . . . As for the money that I told ye your daughter owes to Bacchis, that must be paid down upon the nail. Neither will you (I presume) shrug the debt off by saying: 'What is it to me? Did Bacchis lend me the money? Was it done by my orders? Why should the Old Corinthian put my daughter in pawn without my consent?' As for that, the old saying's true: 'You may have much law on your side, but little equity.'

CHREMES. I'll have none of these deceptions.

SYRUS. Though others may dishonour their obligations, it won't look well in you, for the whole town counts you a rich man, whose word is his bond.

CHREMES. Well, then, I'll pay the money myself.

SYRUS. You'd better order your son to do that.

CHREMES. Why so?

SYRUS. Because he now passes as Madam Bacchis's gallant.

CHREMES. What of that?

SYRUS. Why, if he pay the money himself, there will seem to be some truth in it; and I shall be able the more dexterously to bring about my own design. . . . Oh, yonder's your son! You'd best step in and fetch the money.

CHREMES. So I will!

Exit CHREMES.

Enter CLITIPHO *at another part of the stage.*

CLITIPHO, *to himself.* There's nothing so easy but it becomes hard to an unwilling mind. Though this walk I have taken be but a little one, yet how faint it has made me! And now I dread nothing so much as to be sent on another fool's errand, and not allowed to come near my dear Bacchis . . .

Angrily, to SYRUS.

Now all the gods confound thee for a rogue, with all thy fine tricks and inventions! Thou art always framing some damned villainy with which to plague me!

SYRUS, *huffingly.* Keep your curses to yourself! Your foolish and greedy ill-nature has nearly brought my neck to a halter.

CLITIPHO. Upon my soul, I wish it had! I'm sure 'twas no more than you deserved.

SYRUS. Than I deserved! How so, pray? I'm glad I know so much of your mind before giving ye the money I have just got ready for ye.

CLITIPHO. What could I have said less? You brought my mistress hither, and then would not suffer me to come near her.

SYRUS. Well, I have done. I'm in good temper again. . . . But can you guess where your mistress is?

CLITIPHO. Why, at our house?

SYRUS. No, but she isn't.

CLITIPHO. Where then, pray?

SYRUS. At Mr Clinia's.

CLITIPHO. All's lost!

SYRUS. Courage, Sir; you yourself shall take in the money promised her.

CLITIPHO. Thou pratest like a fool; where should I have such a sum?

SYRUS. From your own daddy.

CLITIPHO, *smilingly.* You banter me.

SYRUS. You'll soon see whether I banter or no.

CLITIPHO. Nay, then I'm made forever, Syrus? . . . Dear rogue, let me buss thee!

SYRUS. 'S't! There comes your father. . . . Have a care you don't play the fool, and show surprise at the matter; observe the course I set you; do as you're bid, and ask no questions.

Enter CHREMES, *with a bag of money.*

CHREMES. Where's this Clitipho now?

SYRUS, *aside to* CLITIPHO. Stay here, Sir!

CLITIPHO. Here he is, Sir.

CHREMES, *to* SYRUS. Have you told him his business?

SYRUS. Most of it, Sir.

CHREMES, *to* CLITIPHO. Here, take this money and carry it to her.

SYRUS, *aside to* CLITIPHO. Zookers: Why do ye stand like a post? Why don't ye take it?

CLITIPHO. Give it me, if you please, Sir!

CHREMES gives him the money.

SYRUS, *to* CLITIPHO. Follow me as fast as you can . . .

To CHREMES.

But you, Sir, be pleased to stay here a minute until we come back, for we've no occasion to tarry long there.

Exeunt CLITIPHO *and* SYRUS.

CHREMES alone.

CHREMES. So my daughter has got thirty good pounds out of me already, to be written off against her account for board and keep. I suppose another thirty must follow to buy her fine clothes. After this comes a rounder sum for a marriage portion. Well! This same custom is the Devil. Now must I leave all my other business to find some honest fellow who will be my son-in-law and ease me out of that money I've been so long scraping together.

To him enter MENEDEMUS.

MENEDEMUS, *to* CLINIA, *within.* Dear child, I now think myself the happiest father in the world, since I find you so well reformed.

CHREMES, *overhearing, aside.* How sweetly he's mistaken!

MENEDEMUS. Chremes! 'Twas you I wanted. . . . Now, Sir, you may be the making of my son, and myself, and my family; and I beg you'll do as I ask.

CHREMES. Good Sir, what would you have me do?

MENEDEMUS. It seems you have found yourself a daughter today. . . . My son Clinia desires your consent to marry her.

CHREMES. Bless me! What sort of a strange man are you?

MENEDEMUS. What do ye mean?

CHREMES. Have ye so soon forgotten the trick we talked of just now, which was to cheat you of your money?

MENEDEMUS. I remember it.

CHREMES. Why 'tis that they're now at work upon . . .

MENEDEMUS. What say you, Chremes?

CHREMES. . . . I'll warrant ye, this Bacchis at your house is my son's mistress too; is she not?

MENEDEMUS. They say so.

CHREMES. And you believe it?

MENEDEMUS. Yes, that I do.

CHREMES. Then they pretend that your son desires to be married. So that when I've promised him my daughter, you may allow him money to buy wedding-clothes, and the like.

MENEDEMUS. So that's the business then! He wants it for his mistress.

CHREMES. No doubt of it.

MENEDEMUS. Alas, unhappy man! My joys are nipped in the bud. And yet I'd rather endure anything than part with him again. . . . What answer, Sir, shall I carry from ye, that he may not perceive I've found it out, or lay it to heart?

CHREMES. To heart, say ye? Pshaw! Menedemus, you cocker him too much by half!

MENEDEMUS. Let it be so; I'm gone too far to draw back. Sir, I only beg the continuance of your favours.

CHREMES. You may tell him we met and discoursed of the match.

MENEDEMUS. Well, and what more?

CHREMES. . . . That I'm ready to do anything. That I like him for a son-in-law; and lastly, if you please, you may tell him that I've given my consent.

MENEDEMUS. Ah, that's what I'd have.

CHREMES. That he may ask ye for the money so soon as he pleases, and that you will part with it eagerly, according to your wish.

MENEDEMUS. That's what I shall do, indeed.

CHREMES. In truth, so far as I can see, you'll quickly tire of gratifying this greedy son of yours; so, if you have your wits about ye, pray give it him cautiously, and little by little.

MENEDEMUS. So I will.

CHREMES. You had best go in and see how much he asks. I shall be at home, if you want me.

MENEDEMUS. That would be to my pleasure; for whatever I do I shall make you acquainted with it.

End of the Fourth Act

ACT FIVE

MENEDEMUS. For my part, I must own myself to be somewhat simple-minded, and slow-witted. But my neighbour
Chremes here, this same assistant, counsellor, and sage dir-
ector of mine, outdoes me by a bar and a half. The hon-
ourable titles of Fool, Blockhead, Clodpate, Ass, and Dolt,
may well enough be applied to me, but they won't fit
him, for *his* folly is beyond expression.

Enter CHREMES *at another part of the stage.*

CHREMES, *to* SOSTRATA, *within.* Prithee, wife, don't tire out
the Gods with being so unmannerly overthankful for having found you your daughter—unless you measure them by
yourself, and fancy they can't understand a thing without
hearing it a hundred times over!

To himself.

. . . But in the meantime, what the deuce makes Clitipho
and Syrus tarry so long at Menedemus's?

MENEDEMUS. Who do ye say tarry so long, Chremes?

CHREMES. Hah, Mr Menedemus! Are you come hither again?
. . . Well, Sir, did ye tell your son what I said?

MENEDEMUS. Every syllable, Sir.

CHREMES. And what answer made he?

MENEDEMUS. He seemed transported with joy, just as if he had a mind to be married.

CHREMES. Ha, ha, ha!

MENEDEMUS. What do ye laugh at?

CHREMES. My man Syrus's trick has just come into my mind.

MENEDEMUS. Indeed!

CHREMES. This cunning rogue has a knack of fixing other people's faces as well as his own.

MENEDEMUS. You mean that my son only counterfeits his joy?

CHREMES. Yes, Sir.

MENEDEMUS. This same suspicion came in my head too.

CHREMES *laughs*. Ha, he's a well-pickled rogue!

MENEDEMUS, *jeeringly*. You'd say so too if you knew all.

CHREMES. Say ye so?

MENEDEMUS. Pray, Sir, give me a hearing.

CHREMES. But hold; first I desire to know how much you've thrown away upon them. For I warrant ye that as soon as you told your son I had promised him my daughter, Dromo will have clapped in a word, saying that the bride wanted wedding-clothes, jewels, attendance, and the like, so that you might pay out money for them.
Laughs again.

MENEDEMUS. Not a word.

CHREMES, *in amaze*. How! Not a word!

MENEDEMUS. No, indeed!

CHREMES. Nor your son, neither?

MENEDEMUS. Not a tittle, Sir, but was only most urgent to have the match struck up today.

CHREMES. You amaze me! . . . But what of my man Syrus? Did he say nothing either?

MENEDEMUS. Nothing at all.

CHREMES. How so, I beseech ye?

MENEDEMUS. Nay, I can't tell. . . . But I wonder that you should see other things so clearly, and not this.
Jeeringly.

Pshaw! Syrus has fixed your son's face too, and so admirably well that no man could suspect this Bacchis to be my boy's mistress.

CHREMES. How's that!

MENEDEMUS. I'll not say a word of their kissing and embracing; for that, I reckon, is nothing.

CHREMES. What more could they do to counterfeit their affection?

MENEDEMUS. Pish!

CHREMES. What is it, I beseech ye?

MENEDEMUS. Well, listen then! . . . I've a little withdrawing room at the back part of my house, where a bed had been brought in and made up.

CHREMES. What followed?

MENEDEMUS. What? . . . Why, thither went Clitipho.

CHREMES. All alone?

MENEDEMUS. Yes, alone.

CHREMES, *aside*. My mind misgives me strangely.

MENEDEMUS. Immediately after him went Bacchis.

CHREMES. All alone too!

MENEDEMUS. Ay, all alone too.

CHREMES. I'm ruined.

MENEDEMUS. As soon as they were within, they made fast the door.

CHREMES. How . . . Was your son an observer all the while?

MENEDEMUS. Why not? He and I watched the play together.

CHREMES. Ah, Menedemus, then she's certainly become my son's whore, and I am absolutely undone.

MENEDEMUS. How so?

CHREMES. I'll have scarce sufficient money left to keep house for ten days.

MENEDEMUS. What? Are ye concerned that your son should help his friend a little?

CHREMES. No, but I fear he may take over your son's she-friend.

MENEDEMUS. Yes, he may do that, indeed.

CHREMES. Do ye question your son's honour? . . . Do ye know anyone of such a base and poor spirit as to allow his own mistress to be led off before his eyes, and to be . . .

MENEDEMUS. Ha, ha, he! Why not?

Jeeringly.

That I might be the more easily imposed upon?

CHREMES. Do ye jeer me, Sir? . . . Now have I right good reason to curse my own stupidity? How many signs have they not given me to discover the imposture? What things have I been an eye-witness to? Fool that I am!

In a passion.

. . . But as I'm a living soul, they shan't go off scot-free! For immediately I'll . . .

MENEDEMUS, *interrupting.* Have ye no control of your passions? Have ye no regard for yourself? I had thought that my example might be of use to ye.

CHREMES. I am quite distracted by my anger, Menedemus.

MENEDEMUS. That you should say so now! Isn't it your greatest failing to advise others, and be so wise in their concerns, and yet can't help yourself at home?

CHREMES. What course shall I take?

MENEDEMUS. Use the qualities that you said I was so defective in . . . Make your son understand that you are his father, and that he may safely trust all his secrets, wants, and desires to you alone, lest he seek consolation elsewhere, crying: 'Goodbye, Father!'

CHREMES. Ay, let him go jogging to Jericho for all I care, rather than indulge his debaucheries here and bring me down to my last crust. I' faith, Menedemus, if I continue thus to supply all his extravagancies, I shall quickly come to hedging and ditching like yourself.

MENEDEMUS. What a great many troubles will ye pull down upon your head, if you don't look about ye! Would you show yourself a rigid father, and drive him to an extremity —but pardon him at last, when he won't give ye one good word of thanks for your pains?

CHREMES. Ah, Sir! You can't conceive how much this counsel sinks into my heart!

MENEDEMUS. Do as you please with it. . . . But what say ye to my proposal? Will you marry your daughter to my son? Or have ye another in mind, whom you like better?

CHREMES. No, I favour him for a son-in-law, and I favour the alliance too.

MENEDEMUS. What portion shall I tell him you'll give with her? . . . What? No answer?

CHREMES, *pausing.* Money, say ye?
Shakes his head.

MENEDEMUS. Yes, Sir.

CHREMES, *sighing.* Ah, Sir!

MENEDEMUS. Come, Chremes, don't trouble yourself, though it be but a trifle. You and I will not quarrel about the size of the portion.

CHREMES. I proposed, indeed, to give her no more than three hundred pounds, which was all that my estate would bear. But if you have my welfare at heart, and that of my estate, and that of my son, you may tell him I've promised to give him my entire substance for a portion.

MENEDEMUS, *surprised.* What project have ye in mind now?

CHREMES. Prithee, pretend to wonder at my decision, and ask my son too why I take it.

MENEDEMUS. I do so wonder in all good conscience. Why take you it?

CHREMES. Why, to curb his appetites, now solely bent upon luxury and debauchery, and bring him to such a pass that he shan't know where to turn.

MENEDEMUS. What do ye mean?

CHREMES. Pray, Sir, let me have my whim in this matter!

MENEDEMUS. Well! . . . But would you truly have me tell him so?

CHREMES. Yes.

MENEDEMUS. Then I will, Sir.

CHREMES. Now, Sir, let your son get ready, and send for his

bride. As for mine, I'll upbraid him to some tune, as fathers should do to their children. And as for that dog Syrus . . .

While CHREMES *speaks the next lines, exit* MENEDEMUS.

CHREMES *walks about in a huff.* As I'm a living man, I'll so lace his jacket and curry his hide for him, that he shall remember it as long as he has an hour to breathe. . . . Damned rogue, to think to make a butt and laughing-stock of me! I'll be hanged if the rascal would have dared serve a poor friendless widow as ill as he has served me.

Re-enters MENEDEMUS, *with* CLITIPHO *and* SYRUS *following after.*

CLITIPHO, *to* MENEDEMUS. I beseech ye, Mr Menedemus, has it come to this then, that my father so suddenly casts off all natural affection? For what offence? What grievous crime have I, miserable fellow, committed? I do no more than all young persons commonly do.

MENEDEMUS, *to* CLITIPHO. I'm aware that this seems most hard and severe for those that bear the burden; and I myself feel as you do, though I know not why, and can give no reason for it, apart from my particular liking for ye.

CLITIPHO. Didn't ye say my father was nigh?

MENEDEMUS. Yes, there he walks.

Exit MENEDEMUS.

CHREMES. What do ye blame me for, Clitipho? What I have done was to cure thy sluggish nature, and curb thy rashness. When I found you to be set upon present enjoyment, without considering the future, I took means to secure you from want, and my estate from ruin. And seeing that I could not make ye my heir (as nature prompted me) I had recourse to your nearest relations, making over and trusting all my substance to their hands. At their house you'll always find sanctuary from your misadventures, and be supplied with diet, clothes, and a room to hide your head in.

CLITIPHO. Woe's me!

CHREMES. This is better, than to appoint you my heir and so to let Bacchis run away with everything.

SYRUS, *aside.* I'm undone! What a storm have my rogueries raised before I was aware!

CLITIPHO. Would to God I were dead.

CHREMES. Pray learn first what it is to live; when you've tried that, and don't like it, then die if it pleases you.

SYRUS. Good Sir, will you listen to one word from me?

CHREMES. Speak then!

SYRUS. But may I speak freely, Sir?

CHREMES. Speak, I say!

SYRUS. What injustice and madness is this, that Mr Clitipho should be punished for my offence?

CHREMES. 'Tis done; don't you meddle in this matter! Nobody impeaches you, Syrus; therefore you needn't seek out a sanctuary, or a friend to plead for ye.

SYRUS. Pray, Sir, what's your design?

CHREMES. I'm now neither angry with you nor with him. Nor ought you to be with me, for what I have done.

Exit CHREMES *hastily.*

SYRUS. He's flung himself off! Pox! Would that I had asked him . . .

CLITIPHO. What, Syrus?

SYRUS. . . . Where I should find fodder for my belly, since he has turned us out of doors? You, it seems, may take refuge at your sister's.

CLITIPHO. Am I reduced to this then, that I must starve for lack of bread?

SYRUS. However, while there's life there's hope . . .

CLITIPHO. Of what?

SYRUS. . . . Of a full stomach to come.

CLITIPHO. Are you so cheerful and pert in time of adversity, and not give me one push up this steep hill?

SYRUS. Yes, Sir, I'm ready to help thee, and my mind hammered at the matter all the time your father was reading you his lecture. . . . And, as far as I can perceive . . .

CLITIPHO. Prithee, what?

SYRUS, *pausing*. You shall have it presently.

CLITIPHO. Pray what is it?

SYRUS. The case is thus! For my part, I don't believe that you are any son of theirs.

CLITIPHO, *hastily*. How's that, Syrus? Art thou mad?

SYRUS. I'll tell ye the reasons for my belief. Judge of them as you please. . . . While they had no child but you, and you alone were all their joy, they then cockered you up and gave ye anything. But now they have found a daughter, they take the occasion to send you packing.

CLITIPHO. That seems very probable.

SYRUS. Do ye think that otherwise he'd have been so damned mad about a peccadillo?

CLITIPHO. Nay, I can't think so.

SYRUS. There's another business to be well considered. All mothers, you know, are pleaders for their sons' faults, and constantly take their parts against the fathers. But here we see no such matter.

CLITIPHO. Very true, faith! Therefore, good boy, tell me what to do.

SYRUS. Put it to them that they should resolve this doubt for ye, and don't mince matters. If the belief be false, you'll work upon their affections; if true, you'll know whose son you are.

CLITIPHO. Your counsel's good, I'll follow it.

Exit CLITIPHO.

SYRUS, *alone*. Egad this was a lucky hit; for the less hope the spark has, the sooner he'll make his peace with his father, and surrender at discretion. . . . Perhaps the fancy may take him to tie himself in marriage; but no thanks to poor Turlygood here!

Strikes himself on the head.

What noise is that? . . . Oh, 'tis the old man coming back. . . . I must scamper for it. . . . Considering what has been done, I wonder he didn't order me to be trussed up for a flogging before now. . . . I'll betake me to Mr

Menedemus's and persuade him to beg me off. I'll never trust this old fellow my master.

Exit SYRUS.

Enter CHREMES *and* SOSTRATA.

SOSTRATA. In truth, my dear husband, if you be not very cautious, you'll cause the boy to do himself some mischief. And I can only wonder how such a whim came into your head.

CHREMES. Must you be a woman still? Can't I do anything but you try to thwart me, Mrs Impertinence? Were I to ask ye what's amiss in my project, or upon what account I undertook it, you could not answer me a word. Why therefore do ye so confidently oppose me, ye old fool?

SOSTRATA. Can't I answer ye?

CHREMES. Yes, yes, you can! I'd rather grant that than tell the story a hundred times over.

SOSTRATA. What an unreasonable thing it is that I should stand mute at such a time as this? Why do ye make me?

CHREMES. I don't make ye; say whatever you please! I'll do as I wish for all that.

SOSTRATA. Will ye so?

CHREMES. Yes, by Cock, so will I.

SOSTRATA. You don't consider the ill consequence that must follow. He'll think himself a foundling.

CHREMES. A foundling, say ye?

SOSTRATA. Indeed, dear husband, he will.

CHREMES. And you may say so, too.

SOSTRATA. Oh, I beseech ye, let them that hate us most say such cruel things! How can I deny that he's my son, when he is my son?

CHREMES. What, are ye afraid you can't prove him to be your son whenever you please?

SOSTRATA. What, because he's so like my new-found daughter?

CHREMES. No; but because he's so like you in character, which is a more convincing argument by half. That way you'll soon prove him your own: for he resembles ye extremely. There's not one ill quality in him, but you have it too: indeed, there's not another woman upon God's earth who could have born such a son. . . . But here he comes. . . . How grave he looks! When you view him thoroughly, you'll know what to think of him.

Enter CLITIPHO.

CLITIPHO, *to* SOSTRATA. If there was ever a time, Mother, when you took delight and pleasure in calling me son, I'd entreat you to bring it to remembrance, and take pity upon a wretch who craves to know who are his parents.

SOSTRATA. For heaven's sake, dear child, never so much as imagine you had your being from any but us too!

CLITIPHO. I can't help it.

Sighing.

SOSTRATA, *weeping.* Ah me! How could ye find in your heart to ask me such a question? As I hope for your prosperity when we are dead and gone, you are mine and his; and take good heed (if you've any love for your mother) that I never hear such a word from you again!

CHREMES. And, jackanapes, if you have any reverence for your father, let me see no more of these tricks, or you had better go eat your nails.

CLITIPHO. What tricks, Sir?

CHREMES. If you must needs know, I'll tell ye. The tricks of an impertinent, idle, cheating, drinking, whoring, consuming, debauchee! . . . Believe what I say, and don't doubt that I am your father!

SOSTRATA. Do these harsh words come from a father's mouth?

CHREMES. No! Though you had been born from a fertile brain as Pallas Athene, they say, sprang from mighty Jove's, I'd not endure to be disgraced by your lewd tricks.

SOSTRATA. Gods forbid that!

CHREMES. I know not what the Gods will do, but I'll endeavour to prevent the worst.

To CLITIPHO.

You look about for parents, whom you didn't lack; but not at all for what you lack extremely, which is how to obey your parents, and to preserve by soberness what they have won by industry. How could ye have the impudence to cheat your father, and bring before his very face your . . . I am ashamed to name the filthy word before your mother, though you were not ashamed to be filthy with her in Mr Menedemus's house.

CLITIPHO, *aside*. Alas! How mad am I with myself! How ashamed of myself! I can't so much as begin to see which way to pacify him.

Enter MENEDEMUS.

MENEDEMUS, *to himself, entering*. In truth, Chremes handles the poor young gentleman too severely, and too roughly. Therefore I'm come to repair the breach. . . . Oh, best of all, there they are!

CHREMES. Oh, Mr Menedemus, why haven't ye sent for my daughter? And what of the contract we agreed to draw about the portion?

SOSTRATA. For God's sake, husband, never do that!

CLITIPHO, *kneeling*. Dear Father! I beseech ye to pardon me.

MENEDEMUS. Pray do, Mr Chremes; let his repentance persuade ye so far at last.

CHREMES. Shall I in my right senses make over my whole estate to that baggage Bacchis? I'll be damned first!

MENEDEMUS. We'll take care to prevent any such thing.

CLITIPHO, *still kneeling*. Sir, if you value my life, forgive me!

SOSTRATA. Come, come sweet husband, do!

MENEDEMUS. Prithee, Mr Chremes, don't be so obstinate!

CHREMES. What means all this? . . . Well, I perceive I cannot do what I designed.

MENEDEMUS. Now you speak like a worthy gentleman.

CHREMES. But upon this one condition: that my son shall do as I think most proper for him.

CLITIPHO. I'll do anything, Sir! Pray command me!

CHREMES. I'd have ye marry.

CLITIPHO. I'll offer no excuses.

MENEDEMUS. I'll engage my own word that he shall do so.

CHREMES. But he himself does not undertake it.

CLITIPHO, *aside*. My case is desperate!

SOSTRATA. What do ye boggle at, Clitipho?

CHREMES. Nay, let him take his own way.

MENEDEMUS. He shall do as you desire him.

SOSTRATA. Fools find marriage a bugbear; but they who have tried it find a blessing there.

CLITIPHO, *to* CHREMES. Well, I'll obey your pleasure, Sir.

SOSTRATA, *to* CLITIPHO. In good faith, my boy, I've a fine girl in my eye for thee, with whom you can't fail to be pleased. 'Tis our neighbour Phanacrates's daughter.

CLITIPHO. Pho! That carrot-pated, wall-eyed, pimple-faced hook-nosed creature? It goes against the grain, Sir.

CHREMES. Look ye now, how choice his tastes are grown! You would think that he had taken deep thought on the matter already.

SOSTRATA, *to* CLITIPHO. I'll tell ye of another, then.

CLITIPHO. No need of that, Sir! Since I must marry, I have a girl in my eye, who pleases me very well.

SOSTRATA. That's my good boy!

CLITIPHO. Aribonides's daughter.

SOSTRATA. That's as well as I could wish.

CLITIPHO, *to* CHREMES. Now, Sir, I've one favour to beg.

CHREMES. What's that?

CLITIPHO. To pardon Syrus for all that he has done on my account.

CHREMES. Well, I will.

Turns to the spectators.

Gentlemen, fare ye well, and give us your approbation!
Exeunt all.

End of THE SELF TORMENTOR

THE EUNUCH

A Comedy acted at the Feast of Cybele, when L. Posthumius Albinus *and* L. Cornelius Merula *were Curule Ediles, by the Company of* L. Ambivius Turpio *and* L. Attilius Prenestae.

Flaccus, *a freedman of* Claudius, *composed the music, which was performed upon two right-handed flutes.*

It was taken from the Greek of Menander.

Acted twice, under the Consulship of M. Valerius *and* C. Fannius.

A.U.C.593   Before Christ 161

DRAMATIS PERSONAE

LACHES, *father to Phaedria and Chaerea*

PHAEDRIA, *his eldest son, a gentleman of a soft and easy temper, fondly in love with Thais*

CHAEREA, *his younger brother, a hot, wild, amorous youth, wantonly in love with Pamphila*

ANTIPHO, *a young gentleman, Chaerea's confidant*

CHREMES, *a young country squire; somewhat blunt in speech and behaviour, and unacquainted with the tricks of the town*

THRASO, *a proud, self-conceited, pedantic, bragging, hectoring, clownish officer, one that believes himself a great wit, and a man of courage, when at the same time he's both coward and coxcomb*

GNATHO, *the parasite, a hanger-on of the Captain's, a crafty, sly, insinuating, wheedling, buffooning fellow, always extolling the Captain's wit and valour, and by an ingenious equivocating sort of flattery, abusing the Captain to his very face*

PARMENO, *servant to Phaedria, and his counsellor, a bold, cunning, intriguing fellow, and a downright woman-hater*

DORUS, *the Eunuch*

SANGA, *servant to Thraso*

THAIS, *a noble courtesan, kept by Phaedria, a good-natured creature, of a flattering, insinuating, winning disposition*

PYTHIA, *her maid, very busy and faithful, a mortal enemy to Parmeno*

DORIA, *another servant to Thais*

SOPHRONA, *a nurse*

NON-SPEAKING PARTS:

PAMPHILA

SIMALIO
DORAX } *servants to the Captain*
SYRISCUS

A NEGRESS

WAITING-MAID *to Pamphila*

ACT ONE

SCENE: *The street before* SIMO'S *door*

Enter PHAEDRIA *attended by* PARMENO

PHAEDRIA, *entering.* What's to be done now? Shan't I go to Thais? . . . Why not, when she now sends for me so kindly? . . . Or shall I resolve never to put up with the affronts of a jilting mistress? . . . First she shuts me out, now she invites me in . . . Go? No, that I won't, pox on it, though she'd beg it on her knees.

Angrily.

PARMENO. Truth, Sir, if you could hold out in this matter, 'twould be the best and bravest thing you ever did; but if you begin with indignation against her, and your heart will not serve ye to go through with it; if you faint in the enterprise, and go in before you're sent for, or before you're so much as reconciled, and sneakingly tell her: 'I'm so entirely devoted to you, that I cannot live an hour without you,' why then your goose is cooked! She'll ride you to death when she has you at her mercy; wherefore I'd have you think twice, and once again before it be too late. For alas! Sir, what use is there for reason or moderation in a case that will allow of neither? For love, you know, is strangely whimsical; containing affronts, jealousies, jars, parleys, wars, then peace again. Now, for you to ask advice on the rules of love, is no better than to ask advice on the rules of madness . . . As for your present resolutions while your blood is up and you cry: 'What! go to her when she prefers a rival to me, and even refuses me entrance to her house? Never persuade me to it. I'll die first: I'll make her know I'm no lapdog of hers.' . . . Why, in good faith, Sir, one pitiful hypocritical drop of a tear, which this creature can with difficulty squeeze out of her eyes, hard though she rub them, will confound all this bluster, bring you to your whining *Peccavi* and make you submit to her mercy.

PHAEDRIA. Oh, horrid shame! . . . Now I see that she's a cursèd jilt, and I a miserable fool! I'm sick of it; yet I die with love. I perish with my knowledge and senses about me, aware of every circumstance, yet utterly at a loss what to do.

PARMENO. What should you do, Sir, but free yourself from her as cheaply as you can? If you can't draw all the good cards, make the best of a bad game, and don't vex yourself about lost stakes.

PHAEDRIA. D'ye think that's the best way?

PARMENO. Ay, Sir, if you'd only recognize it . . . Add no more troubles to those that love has already brought on ye; and bear what's befallen ye like a man . . .

Enter THAIS *at some distance.*

Aside.

Ah, yonder comes the caterpillar that eats all our harvest, and leaves us to starve.

THAIS, *to herself.* Unhappy woman! I am very much afraid that Phaedria should take it otherwise than I intended, that I did not admit him yesterday.

PHAEDRIA. Ah, Parmeno! I'm come over in a cold sweat at the very sight of her.

PARMENO. Brisk up, Sir, and go nearer. She carries fire enough to warm ye with a vengeance.

THAIS, *overhearing.* How now, Phaedria! What, are you here? And waiting at the door, too? Why didn't you come in without any more ado?

PARMENO, *aside*. The Devil a word she speaks of her shutting the door upon me.

THAIS. What, speechless, my dear?

PHAEDRIA, *scornfully*. Well asked, madam! For these doors always stood wide open for me, and I ranked the highest in your ladyship's favours.

THAIS, *clapping him on the cheek with her fan*. Let these things pass from your mind, my dear.

PHAEDRIA, *angrily*. 'Pass!' you say. . . .

More mildly.

Ah, Thais, Thais, would that you and I did but love equally, and went at an even pace; so that either what you've done might trouble you as much as it has troubled me, or that I might concern myself as little as you do.

THAIS, *interrupting*. Prithee don't fret thyself, my pretty Phaedria, for I swear by this light it wasn't because I loved or cared for anybody more than thy dear self. But as the circumstances stood, 'twas a thing I could not avoid.

PARMENO, *jeeringly*. Likely enough . . . She, poor soul, shut me out of doors, out of stark love and kindness!

THAIS, *to* PARMENO. Say ye so, Parmeno? . . . Well, go on; . . .

To PHAEDRIA.

. . . but prithee, my dear, do but hear why I sent for ye.

PHAEDRIA. I'll hear ye, for once.

THAIS. First, let me know whether this man here is discreet.

PARMENO. Meaning me, Madam? . . . The rarest fellow in the world for discretion. But we must enter into articles about keeping your secrets. If your story be true, I am as mute as a fish; but if it be a lie, a foppery, or a sham, 'twill out in an instant, for I'm as full of holes, as a sieve. Therefore, pray Madam, not a word of falsehood, as you hope for secrecy.

THAIS. My mother was born on Samos, but lived at Rhodes.

PARMENO, *aside*. Mum, mum, for that.

THAIS. There it was that a certain merchant presented her with a fine young girl, kidnapped from Attica.

PHAEDRIA. Was she a gentlewoman?

THAIS. I suppose so. We couldn't tell for certain. She told us her parents' names. As for her place of birth, and other proofs of identity, she forgot them, nor because of her age could it be otherwise expected. The merchant added, that he understood from the pirates (of whom he bought her) that she was stolen from Sunio, hard by Athens . . . My mother took charge of her, gave her the best education she could, and bred her up like her own child; so that this girl and I were generally taken for sisters. I came hither in company with that merchant (the only man with whom I was then concerned), who died and left me all that I now possess.

PARMENO, *interrupting*. If any of this be untrue, out it will gush.

THAIS. Why should you suspect me of lying?

PARMENO. Because, forsooth, you are not the woman to eat from one dish only, and nor was he your sole gallant. For this gentleman's pocket has supplied you with money for many an amour.

THAIS. But can't you let me go on with my story?

To PHAEDRIA.

While things stood thus, Captain Thraso, who began to take some liking to me, marched into Caria; meantime, I had got acquainted with thee, my dear rogue. And thou knowest how dearly I have loved thee ever since, even to trusting thee with my greatest secrets . . .

PHAEDRIA. Parmeno will let that tale gush out with the rest.

PARMENO. You may swear to that, Sir.

THAIS. For love's sake, dear hearts, hear me out! Not long afterwards my mother died at Rhodes. Now my uncle, you must know, was a worldly man, and perceiving the slave girl was well-shaped, and had a good hand at the lute, hoped to make money by her, and forthwith exposed her to sale. As good luck would have it, my friend, Captain

Thraso, being there, buys her as a gift for me, being perfectly ignorant of the whole affair. He's just come to town, and perceiving what's between you and me, he invents many excuses to delay his parting from her as long as he can. But he says, that if only he could persuade himself I loved him better than you, and if he were not miserably afraid that when I once got the girl, I should send him off, he'd part with her at once. This he's still afraid of, but so far as I can see he hankers after her himself.

PHAEDRIA. And has it got no further than hankering?

THAIS. No, for I've made strict enquiry. . . . Now, my dear Phaedria, I've a thousand reasons for wishing to wheedle her from him. First, because she passes as my sister; and second because I'm a lonesome woman, with neither friend nor kin, and I hope by this business to provide myself with friends at least. Therefore if you love me, help me out in the management of it! Let this swaggering Captain be Lord of Misrule for two or three days.

Fawningly.

. . . What, no answer?

PHAEDRIA. Thou basest and most ungrateful of thy sex. . . . What shall I answer thee?

Walks about in a passion.

PARMENO, *aside.* O rare master of mine! Thanks be to God, say I! He's himself again! Edad, thou art a man every inch of thee.

PHAEDRIA. As if I didn't understand your designs!

In another tone, mocking her.

'A young girl was kidnapped hence . . . my mother bred her up like her own child . . . she passed for my sister . . . I'd fain wheedle her out of him, . . . and thus provide myself with friends . . .' All this stuff is to shift me from your chamber, and take in your Captain, forsooth. But why, I pray?

Scornfully.

Only because he's more in your ladyship's favour than I

am; and you're plaguily afraid this girl will put your nose out of joint, and steal your lusty stallion from you.

THAIS. Who, I afraid of that?

PHAEDRIA. Ay, you! Why else should you be so concerned? Is he the only person who has made you presents? Did ye ever find me close-fisted? The other day you asked for a negro maid—didn't I go post haste and buy you one? And then you'd have your eunuch, forsooth, purely because ladies of quality have them. This I got too. Yesterday I paid down on the nail no less than fifty guineas for the two of them. Though I'm slighted by ye, yet you see I didn't forget ye; and my good nature's finely rewarded.

THAIS, *fawningly*. How's this, my Phaedria! No, though I should be glad indeed to have this sister of mine—and I believe I might easily get her this way—yet rather than vex thee, I'll forgo my desires and do what thou wouldst have me do.

PHAEDRIA. O that these words came from your heart! 'Rather than vex thee.' Could I but believe them sincerely, I could then bear anything.

PARMENO, *aside*. He staggers! One damned wheedling has undone him in a trice.

THAIS. Ah dear! Don't I then speak from my heart? When did I ever deny you a request, though it were made but jestingly.

Weeping.

And yet I can't for my soul win the favour of your absence for two short days.

PHAEDRIA. Ay, if it were but two short days . . . But what if that two should be enlarged to twenty?

THAIS. Indeed, Sir, it shall be no more than two or . . .

PHAEDRIA, *interrupting*. Or what? No more of that!

THAIS. It shall be no longer by a minute. Let me persuade thee for once.

PHAEDRIA, *coldly*. Well, then, for once I shall be persuaded.

THAIS. Now I love thee most wonderfully, thou hast so obliged me.

PHAEDRIA. Well, I'll away into the country, and there kill these two days by process of pining. . . . That's my resolution, since my cruel dear must have her way . . . And, Parmeno, take care to deliver the eunuch and the negress in my absence.

PARMENO. I will, Sir.

PHAEDRIA. Goodbye my dearest Thais, for two long days.

THAIS. Goodbye to thee, my sweet creature. Have you any other commands?

PHAEDRIA. What can I desire further than that though the Captain have your company, yet your heart may be at another place. Let me both night and day be the entertainment of your love, your wishes, your dreams, your expectations, your thoughts, your hopes, your pleasure, your all! In fine: let your heart be as much mine, as mine is yours.

Exeunt PHAEDRIA *and* PARMENO.

THAIS, *alone.* Dear heart! I'm afraid Phaedria believes not one word of what I have said, but takes me for one of your jilting creatures of the town. But I, who know my own heart best, am sure that I am devising no cheats; nor is there any soul I love so fondly and tenderly as this gentleman. Whatsoever I have done in the case was purely for the sake of the poor girl, whose brother, a person of some repute, I hope that I have at last found out. He appointed today to give me a visit. I'll step in and await his coming.

Exit THAIS.

End of the First Act

ACT TWO

Enter PHAEDRIA, *attended by* PARMENO

PHAEDRIA. Do as I ordered ye! Let the slaves be carried to my mistress.

PARMENO. So they shall, Sir.

PHAEDRIA. But with care, then!

PARMENO. It shall be done.

PHAEDRIA. But with speed too!

PARMENO. With speed also.

PHAEDRIA. Have I made my orders clear enough?

PARMENO. Ah! that's a question indeed!

Angrily.

As though 'twas so hard a piece of business. . . . For my part, Sir, I wish with all my soul that you were as sure of winning a thousand pounds, as ye are of losing these gifts.

PHAEDRIA. Prithee, don't trouble your head about those things; for if I lose them, I lose myself too, which is by far the greater loss.

PARMENO. It shan't trouble me, but I'll do your business effectually. . . . Have ye any further commands?

PHAEDRIA. Be sure you set off the presents with all the compliments you can muster; and give my rival all the inconvenience imaginable.

PARMENO. Pshaw, I'd have done that without your bidding.

PHAEDRIA. Well, I'll into the country.

Offers to go.

PARMENO, *jeeringly.* I fancy you will.

PHAEDRIA, *returning.* But, hark ye, Parmeno!

PARMENO. What's your pleasure, Sir?

PHAEDRIA. Dost really think I can have so much power over myself as to hold out for so long a time?

PARMENO. Who, you, Sir? No, i' faith! For either you'll change your mind within the hour, or else your lack of sleep will send ye back hither at midnight with a 'why not?'

PHAEDRIA. I'll tire myself as much as I can, that I may sleep whether I desire it or no.

PARMENO. It won't do, Sir. Tire yourself as much as ye please, but you'll be none the nearer to sleep.

PHAEDRIA. All this signifies nothing, Parmeno. . . . I must break the neck of this unmanly weakness. I indulge myself too much. In short, do ye think I can't live without her three whole days, if occasion serve?

PARMENO, *jeeringly.* How, Sir! For three live-long days? For shame, Sir!

PHAEDRIA. Nay, I'm fully resolved upon it, however.

Exit PHAEDRIA.

PARMENO, *alone.* Heavens! what a plaguey thing is this! Can love alter men so strangely, that you can't know them for the same? Never a gentleman in town had a better head-piece, a graver carriage, and was less given to the flesh than this master of mine . . .

Enter GNATHO *leading* PAMPHILA, *attended by her* WAITING-MAID; *at a distance from* PARMENO.

. . . But who comes yonder in the name of goodness? Ha, ha, 'tis that wheedling rascal Gnatho, a hanger-on of the Captain's. He has taken the young gentlewoman by the wrist, as a present to his lady. . . . Bless me! what a smug-faced little rogue she is. No wonder if I cut but a poor

figure today when I present my rotten old eunuch. . . .
Why, this creature cuts out Thais herself!

Walks up and down before the door.

GNATHO, *to himself.* Bless me! to see the difference between
one man and another, betwixt a fool and a philosopher!
And why I say it is this. As I was coming along today,
I stumbled upon a man of my own rank and quality, an
honest fellow too, I warrant, who had made shift to
squander an estate, as I had done before him. Seeing such
a rough, nasty, meagre fellow, tricked out with rags and
rheumatism, I asked him: 'What's the meaning of this fine
dress?' 'Alas,' said he, 'I had an estate once, but played
the fool and couldn't keep it, and here you see to what I
am sunk. All my friends and acquaintances avoid me as
they would the plague.' Here I began to eye him with
scorn. 'Why you whoreson blockhead,' said I, 'is it to come
to that then, that you have stripped yourself of all pride?
Say: have ye diced away your brains and your money together? Why, do but look on me, who was once in the
same case as you! How neat and genteel my clothes, how
strong and lusty my person! I have all the Indies at my
command, though estates I possess none; I can scarce call
a groat my own, yet I lack for nothing.'

In another tone.

'But,' says he, 'I'm of such an unlucky character, that neither playing the buffoon nor allowing myself to be kicked
about agrees with me.' 'How's that,' said I, 'do ye think
that's the way? No, you're plaguily wide of the mark. In
the old days this might have done well enough, but we
now have another fashion, and perhaps I was its inventor.
There's a sort of people in town who pretend to be first
rate wits, and yet have no more brains than a maggot.
Now these are the men I seek out; but I am not their
Merry-Andrew to make them sport, instead I merrily make
sport of them, though at the same time I praise them to
the skies. If they say anything, I applaud. If they unsay it,
I commend them for their sagacity. What they deny, I
deny; what they affirm, I affirm. In fine, I've brought my-

self to agree with them in everything; by which means I
get many a sweet morsel, and earn many a bright penny.'

PARMENO, *aside.* A very pretty fellow, upon my word! Give
him a fool, and he'll make a madman of him.

GNATHO. While this chat lasted we came to the market-place,
where I was joyfully hailed by a troop of Confectioners,
Fishmongers, Butchers, Cooks, Pastrymen, Fishermen,
Poulterers—all of my old cronies to whom I had been a
good customer before I spent my estate, and who still honour me. They complimented me with hat in hand, invited
me to supper, and said they were very glad to see my
worship. When my poor hunger-starved comrade saw how
high I stood in their books, and how easily I lived, he
begged me for heaven's sake to teach him a little of my
art. 'Follow me,' quoth I, 'and be my pupil! And, as all
the sects of philosophers borrow their names from their
masters, be called a Gnathonic, and study at my knees the
Arts of Wheedling.'

PARMENO, *aside.* What it is to live at ease, and be fed at
another man's table!

GNATHO. But hold, I'm plaguey backward in taking this gift
to Madam Thais, and inviting her to dine . . .

Advances towards the door, and sees PARMENO.

Yonder's Parmeno, our rival's servant, all in the dumps too!
Our business goes swimmingly; these fellows will be left
out in the cold. . . . I'm resolved to have some sport with
this poor rogue.

PARMENO, *aside.* I warrant they think this gift will make the
lady theirs for ever.

GNATHO, *jeeringly.* My own dear friend! Gnatho's thy very
humble servant. Well, what are you upon now?

PARMENO, *surlily.* Upon my legs.

GNATHO. I see that . . . But don't you see something here
that offends your eyesight?

Pointing to PAMPHILA.

PARMENO, *surlily.* Yes, yourself.

GNATHO. That I believe. . . . But is there nothing else?

PARMENO. Why, what should there be?

GNATHO. Because, my friend, you seem to be a trifle out of humour.

PARMENO. Not in the least.

GNATHO. Nay, I wouldn't have ye be so. . . . But what think ye of this gift? Hah!

PARMENO. Why, she's tolerable.

GNATHO, *softly*. I've galled him, I see.

PARMENO, *aside, overhearing*. How plaguily he's mistaken!

GNATHO. Won't Madam Thais be mightily taken with this gift, think ye?

PARMENO. As much as to say you have put our nose out of joint. But hark ye, friend, every dog has his day; and there is a time for all things.

GNATHO. Now, Parmeno, I am prepared to give thee a six months holiday that will save thee the trouble of trotting up and down, and sitting up till four or five in the morning. Is that not a prodigious service?

PARMENO. To me it seems a damnable one.

GNATHO. It is thus that I always oblige friends.

PARMENO. You do well.

GNATHO. But perhaps I detain ye, Sir; your business possibly calls ye elsewhere?

PARMENO. No, I'm at my journey's end.

GNATHO. Then, Sir, pray do me the favour of introducing me to the lady.

PARMENO. Very good: this gift will be your passport.

GNATHO. Do ye wish to have any one sent out to ye?

Exit GNATHO, PAMPHILA *and the* WAITING-MAID.

PARMENO, *alone*. Once these two days are over, I'll take care that you may knock for admittance until your heart aches. Though now you find the doors fly open at a touch of your little finger.

Re-enter GNATHO.

GNATHO. What, here still, my own friend? Do ye keep guard

here, that no message by a civil messenger can pass privately between the Captain and the lady?

Exit GNATHO.

PARMENO, *alone*. Very wittily spoken! These wonderful fine things must please the Captain.

Seeing CHAEREA.

But behold, I see my master's younger son making this way. . . . I wonder what brings him from his post at Piraeus, when he's on duty there . . . There's something more than ordinary in the wind. . . . And he's in great haste too . . . I can't guess what makes him cast his eyes about so wildly.

Enter CHAEREA *at a distance from* PARMENO, *out of breath, and looking about him.*

CHAEREA, *to himself.* I'm undone! The pretty creature's lost! . . . And so am I . . . who have unluckily missed her. Where shall I look? How shall I trace her? Of whom shall I inquire? In what blind alley shall I range? . . . I'm in a strange quandary. . . . I've this comfort left, that she can't remain long *incognito* wherever she may be . . . The most charming beauty! From this moment I've done with all everyday lasses and faces: they will never please me again.

PARMENO, *aside*. Heyday! Here's another man whining and languishing for love, or I'm much mistook. . . . The Old Gentleman, their father, is finely blest in his boys! If this spark once takes up the sport of love, he'll be so maddened by it that Mr Phaedria will seem a simple child by comparison.

CHAEREA. The Devil damn that old curmudgeon for interrupting my journey; and damn me too for listening to him, when I should have taken no notice. . . . Ho! here's Parmeno! Well met, old friend!

PARMENO. Why so concerned, and yet so gay? And whither bound?

CHAEREA. Who, I? Truth, I can't tell whence I come, nor where I'm going. I've lost my senses.

PARMENO. How so, I beseech ye?

CHAEREA. I'm in love, man.

PARMENO. Heyday!

CHAEREA. Nay, old boy, show what a man you are! Thou knowest how often thou once promised me: 'Master Chaerea, do but find out a wench you have a mind to, and I'll show what a talent I have at intriguing.' You remember it was when I used to steal you tasty morsels from my father's pantry, and nobody ever the wiser, ye rogue!

PARMENO. Pshaw, no more of that!

CHAEREA. Why, i' faith, 'twas even so. Therefore, prithee, now be as good as thy word, at least if you think it worth the expense of your brains. . . . This pretty creature isn't at all like our town ladies, whose mothers saddle their backs and lace in their waists, to make them better shaped. And if any of them chance to grow somewhat plumper than the rest, the mothers presently cry: 'She looks like a prize-fighter!' and then her diet must be shortened; and though she be naturally fat and lusty, yet they'll make her as slender as a broom-stick. By this means one woodcock or another is caught in their snare.

PARMENO. And what shape has yours, I beseech ye?

CHAEREA. Such beauty the world never saw!

PARMENO. Heyday!

CHAEREA. Her complexion true and natural. Her body sound, strong, and plump as a partridge.

PARMENO. How old, think ye?

CHAEREA. About sixteen.

PARMENO. In the very prime, i' faith.

CHAEREA. Now, help me to this sweet creature, either by force, fraud, or wheedle; I don't care which way, so long as I may enjoy her.

PARMENO. But who is this sweet creature?

CHAEREA. Faith, I know not.

PARMENO. Whence came she?

CHAEREA. I can't tell.

PARMENO. Where does she live?

CHAEREA. I can't tell you that, neither.

PARMENO. Where did you see her?

CHAEREA. In the street here.

PARMENO. How came you to lose her?

CHAEREA. That's what I was cursing at when I met you. I cannot believe that the man lives whose good fortune has ever left him so miserably in the lurch. What a disaster was here! . . . I'm in utter wretchedness.

PARMENO. How came you to miss her, Sir?

CHAEREA. Why, don't ye know old Archimedes, my father's kinsman and companion?

PARMENO. Yes, very well.

CHAEREA. I ran full tilt into this fellow, as I was hot upon the scent of my pretty creature.

PARMENO. Faith, 'twas a little unseasonable.

CHAEREA. Nay, but devilish unfortunate; lighter matters than this may pass for unseasonable. For I can safely swear that I hadn't seen him these six months, and now I must be detained by him when I never desired his company less. Wasn't this a damned accident? Hah! What say you?

PARMENO. As you say, Sir, 'twas a damned accident.

CHAEREA. I ran on, but he comes hobbling after me, with his chin and his knees close together, his joints shaking in his hide, hanging his jaw like an old horse, and groaning like a rotten sheep. He bawls out: 'Soho, Chaerea, Soho? 'tis you I would speak with.' . . . With that I made a halt. 'D'ye know,' says he, 'what's my business with ye?' 'No, pray tell me, Sir.' 'Oh,' said he, 'my lawsuit is heard tomorrow.' 'And what then?' said I. 'Why, be sure,' quoth he, 'to tell your father that he must be in court without fail.' I think he was a whole hour by the clock in telling this. I asked him whether he had any further business. He said: 'None at all!' Away marched I. And looking for this young creature, I found she had vanished down this street.

PARMENO, *aside*. My life on it! That must have been the same girl who was presented to Thais.

CHAEREA. I ran to the end of the street, but she was nowhere to be seen.

PARMENO. Had she any attendance with her?

CHAEREA. Yes, a man and a waiting-maid.

PARMENO, *aside*. The very same, i' faith . . .

Aloud.

Set your heart at rest, Sir, your business is in good hands.

CHAEREA. Surely thy wits are wool-gathering?

PARMENO. No, I know what I say.

CHAEREA. Why, canst thou tell me who she is? . . . Did ye see her?

PARMENO. I did see her, I know her too. More than that, I can tell where she's gone.

CHAEREA. Ah, dear rogue! Thou truly knowest her?

PARMENO. Yes, Sir.

CHAEREA. And canst tell where she's gone, too?

PARMENO. She was brought hither as a gift to Madam Thais.

CHAEREA. Is any man living able to afford so rich a gift?

PARMENO. Yes: Captain Thraso, your brother's rival.

CHAEREA. For ought I see, my brother will find it hard to trump that and take the trick.

PARMENO. Ay, i' faith! So you'd swear indeed, if you knew what a pitiful card he intends to play.

CHAEREA. What card's that, prithee?

PARMENO. A eunuch.

CHAEREA. What? That ugly-looking creature he bought yesterday? The haggish fellow?

PARMENO. That's he, Sir.

CHAEREA. Certainly my brother and his gift will be kicked to the Devil. . . . But I never knew before that Madam Thais was our neighbour.

PARMENO. Why, she's lately removed thither.

CHAEREA. Unlucky whelp that I am! That I should never see Thais! But prithee, tell me, is she such a beauty as they report?

PARMENO. Every jot.

CHAEREA. But falls far short of the girl who is now given her —I wager my life.

PARMENO. Ay, she's another thing altogether.

CHAEREA. Prithee, honest boy, do what ye can to bring us together.

PARMENO. I shall do my best to help ye. What would ye have me do more?

Going off.

CHAEREA. Whither away now?

PARMENO. Why, home, to fetch the eunuch, and a negress besides: according to your brother's orders I am to present them to Madam Thais.

CHAEREA. Oh, the luck of this same miserable eunuch, to enter her house where the other beauty is!

PARMENO. How so, Sir?

CHAEREA. Do ye ask that? Why, he'll always be blest with the sight of his companion. They'll talk together, live together, and now and then perhaps bed together.

PARMENO. What would you say now, if you were to be that same blessed creature?

CHAEREA, *hastily*. What, I? I do not understand you. Speak, dear rogue!

PARMENO. Suppose you take the eunuch's clothes . . .

CHAEREA. His clothes! And how then?

PARMENO. And be conveyed thither in his stead . . .

CHAEREA. On, on boy!

PARMENO. And give out that you are he.

CHAEREA. I smell your design.

PARMENO. Thus you may enjoy all those rare blessings that you fancy just now would befall another. You may eat and drink with her, sit by her, toy with her, and . . . bed with her. For not a creature in that house can know what you are, or whence you came. And besides, your youth and your smooth cheeks will let you pass for a complete eunuch.

CHAEREA. Spoken like an angel, and advised like an oracle! *Hugs* PARMENO, *and is carrying him off.*

Come away, boy, let's be about it immediately, equip me to rights now, and bring me to her as fast as if your life hung upon it.

PARMENO, *struggling.* Hold Sir! . . . What d'ye mean? I did but jest.

CHAEREA. Pshaw! That's nonsense.

PARMENO. I'm ruined! How like a fool have I spoken! Where d'ye thrust me, Sir? . . . Faith, you had almost pushed me on my nose . . . 'Tis you I address, Sir. Pray, tarry!

CHAEREA. Nay, I say: let's go.

PARMENO. Are ye resolved upon it then?

CHAEREA. Absolutely!

PARMENO. Have a care you don't make more haste than good speed.

CHAEREA. No, no, trust me for that.

PARMENO. Ah, but my bones will smart for this! Oh! 'tis a horrible villainy!

CHAEREA. Villainy d'ye call it, for a man to visit a bawdy-house and pay a company of jilts in their own coin? Why, if it be their trade to abuse, torment and trepan innocent young men, should not we with justice and equity plague them in return? Shan't I rather play tricks upon them, than upon my father? This I should be blamed for; as for t'other, it will be said: 'He paid them in their own coin.'

PARMENO. How's this? Well, if ye be fully bent upon it, why, then take your own course; but don't lay the blame at my door afterwards.

CHAEREA. That I won't do.

PARMENO. And is it your will to play the game thus?

CHAEREA. It is my will to have it so, and it must be so, and it shall be so; and what I have said, I shall stand by.

PARMENO. Well, then follow me.

CHAEREA. Venus and Cupid favour the design!
Exeunt both.

End of the Second Act

ACT THREE

Enter THRASO *and* GNATHO

THRASO. Well, and was she so very thankful then?

GNATHO. O yes, Sir, most hugely.

THRASO. And glad at heart, say ye?

GNATHO. O yes, but not so much for the gift as for the giver; and of him, let me tell ye, she's plaguily proud.

Enter PARMENO *at a distance.*

PARMENO, *to himself.* I'm watching for a fair opportunity to bring my gifts in too. . . . But hold! Here's Captain Bell-swagger Thraso.

Retires to one side.

THRASO. Really I am a lucky man! Everything that I do comes off most wonderfully well.

GNATHO. I have observed as much.

THRASO. The King of Persia, whenever I did him a kindness, never failed to show me gratitude and love. Nor does he unbend so to everyone.

GNATHO. A tongue as smart as yours brings its possessor all the glory for which others toil in vain.

THRASO. Right, boy.

GNATHO. The King has you in his confidence, then?

THRASO. Right again.

GNATHO. And loves to have you at Court.

THRASO. No doubt of it. . . . Nay more, he has trusted his whole army to my generalship, and follows my advice in everything.

GNATHO. Prodigious!

THRASO. Then if he chanced to be weary of company or business, and had a mind to take a little ease . . . as though . . . you know what I mean.

GNATHO. Yes, Sir. As though when he had a mind to rid his stomach, if a body may so say, of all weighty concerns . . .

THRASO. Right, then would he dine in private with me.

GNATHO. Ay, marry, Sir! That is a King indeed.

THRASO. Ay, he's a man in a thousand . . .

GNATHO. Or in a million . . .

Aside.

. . . if he chooses you for his favourite.

THRASO. All the officers of Persia grumbled at me behind my back. I cared not a straw, though they envied me damnably. But above all, one who had the charge of the Indian Elephants. This fellow being more troublesome than the rest: 'Prithee, Strato,' said I, 'why account yourself so plaguey big? Is it because you are lord over a pack of beasts?'

GNATHO. Neatly said, i' faith, and shrewdly . . . Bless me, there you overthrew man and beast. . . . What said he, Sir?

THRASO. Not a word.

GNATHO. Nay, I don't know how he could have found a choking retort to that.

PARMENO, *aside*. Bless me! This Captain's the blindest coxcomb I ever saw, and t'other the vilest rascal.

THRASO. What think ye, Gnatho? Did I ever tell ye how I took down the young Rhodian spark at a feast?

GNATHO. Never, Sir, let's hear it, I pray!

Aside.

He has told it a thousand times.

THRASO. This Rhodian stripling was with me at the said feast, where by chance I had taken a small girl. He began to be sweet upon her, and jeered upon me too. 'How now, you impudent sauce-box,' said I, 'you're a hare yourself, and are you hunting game?'

GNATHO. Ha, ha, he!

THRASO. What's the matter? Hah?

GNATHO. Very fine, sharp, and delicate; that couldn't have been bettered. . . . But, pray Sir, was this jest all your own? I took it for an old one.

THRASO. Why, did you ever hear of it before?

GNATHO. Yes, Sir, very often: it has gone the rounds like wildfire.

THRASO. I'll assure you, 'twas all my own.

GNATHO. Yet I'm sorry you were so sharp upon the foolish young gentleman.

PARMENO, *aside.* Ah, the Devil take thee for a rascal.

GNATHO. Pray, Sir, what did he say then?

THRASO. He was quite dashed out of countenance; and the whole company almost died with laughing. After that, everybody was plaguey careful not to meddle with me.

GNATHO. And well they might be.

THRASO. . . . But hark ye, Gnatho, had I best rid Thais of the jealousy she feels for my being in love with Pamphila?

GNATHO. Let that be the least of your thoughts; rather give her more cause to be jealous!

THRASO. Why so?

GNATHO. Don't ye understand me, Sir? Should she but speak a word about Phaedria, or commend his virtues on purpose to plague you . . .

THRASO. I have it.

GNATHO. Your only way to prevent that, is: whenever she names Phaedria, be sure you cast Pamphila in her teeth. If she cries: 'Let's have Phaedria to be merry with us,' do you answer: 'And Pamphila to give us a song.' If she praise his person, extol her beauty. And be sure give her a tit for every tat; that will vex her to the heart . . .

THRASO. Ay, if she loved me, this might do well, Gnatho.

GNATHO. As long as she desires and loves your gifts, you may wager your life she loves you, and still you may venture to tease her. She'll always be afraid lest any harsh word should turn the stream of your bounty another way.

To them enter THAIS, *attended by* PYTHIA.

THAIS. I fancied I heard the Captain's tongue just now. . . . Oh, here he is . . . My dear hero, welcome!

Hugs him.

THRASO. Oh, my sweet Thais, my dear honey, how is it? . . . Don't ye love me now for giving you this pretty wench?

PARMENO, *aside.* Admirable, i' faith! How nobly he opens the campaign.

THAIS. Oh, Sir, I'm eternally obliged to you for the gift.

GNATHO. Let's go in to supper, I say! Why this dallying?

PARMENO, *aside.* Here's another hero, too! Faith, one would swear he was the Captain's bastard, they're so like one another.

THRASO, *to* GNATHO. As soon as you will, for I am ready.

PARMENO, *advancing nearer.* I'll speak to her, and make as though I had just come from home . . .

Aside to THAIS.

Are you going abroad, Madam?

THAIS, *to him.* Oh, Parmeno! Truth, you are come at a very lucky time: I was just going out.

PARMENO. Whither, Madam?

THAIS, *aside to him.* Why, don't ye see this gentleman here?

PARMENO, *softly.* I do see him, to my sorrow . . .

Aloud.

When you please, Madam, my master's gifts are at your service.

THRASO. What? Do we tarry? Why don't we jog on?

PARMENO, *to* THRASO. May it please your honour, by your

leave: first let me make my presents as I was ordered, and have a little harmless chat with my lady.

THRASO, *jeeringly.* Very special presents! I'll warrant ye they are not to be named in the same breath with mine.

PARMENO. Trial will show . . .

Goes towards LACHES's *house.*

Soho! within there! Send out the persons I ordered.

Enter the NEGRESS.

Come, lass, advance a step! . . . She comes from as far as Prester John's country.

THRASO. I can sell you as good for seven or eight guineas.

GNATHO. Ay, and better too.

PARMENO, *to them within.* You sir, Dorus, where are ye? Stand forth, boy. . . . Here's your eunuch for ye then . . . see what a pretty look he has got, and in the flower of his youth, too.

Enter CHAEREA, *dressed up like the eunuch.*

THRASO. As I hope to be saved, a very likely fellow!

PARMENO. What say ye now, Mr Gnatho? Do ye espy any faults here? . . . And you, noble Captain? . . . What, never a word? . . . That's commendation enough of all conscience. Try him in the schools, in the field, in music, or where you will, you'll find he has the education of a gentleman.

THRASO, *aside to* GNATHO. That eunuch would serve a man's needs well enough, even were he sober.

PARMENO. And yet, Madam, the gentleman who made these presents doesn't desire to be your only favourite, nor that all others should be thrust out of doors for his sake. He doesn't tell you romantic stories of his fights and duels, nor yet boast of his wounds and scars; neither does he stand in your light, as does a certain person who shall be nameless. But when it shall be no trouble to you, Madam, whenever you please, and whenever your ladyship is at leisure, he will esteem it a favour to be admitted.

THRASO. 'Tis evident this fellow has gone to some poor Grub-street hack for rhetoric to plead his master's case.

GNATHO. Faith, likely enough! For he wouldn't have kept this fellow so long, had he a shilling in his pocket to hire him a better.

PARMENO. Peace, dog! . . . Thou art not worthy to be kicked! . . . If you can stoop to flatter him . . .

Pointing to THRASO.

. . . thus, you'd be content to do the most sordid thing in the world for a livelihood.

THRASO, *angrily*. Shall we stay to hear this fellow chatter?

THAIS. I'll just step in with these, and give my maids their orders, and be back again in an instant.

Exeunt THAIS, CHAEREA, *the* NEGRESS, *and* PYTHIA.

THRASO, *to* GNATHO. I'll go ahead . . . But do you stay and wait for Madam Thais.

PARMENO. Fie! Is it beneath a general's dignity to escort his own mistress?

THRASO, *to* PARMENO. Why should I spend my breath upon thee? . . . Like master like man.

Exit PARMENO.

GNATHO. Ha, ha, he! . . .

THRASO, *somewhat surlily*. What do ye laugh at?

GNATHO. Why, at your witty rejoinder! Besides, you put me in mind of the Rhodian stripling, and I couldn't forbear. . . . But here's Madam Thais again.

Re-enter THAIS, PYTHIA, *and* ATTENDANTS.

THRASO. Run home, and see that all the rooms be got ready.

GNATHO. I go, Sir.

Exit GNATHO.

THAIS, *to* PYTHIA. Be sure, Pythia, take care to do what I bid ye . . . If Mr Chremes should chance to come today, desire him to stay a little; if he can't oblige me, then ask him to come another time. And if he can't do that, send him over to the Captain's to me.

PYTHIA. I will, Madam.

THAIS. Hold . . . I had something else to say . . . let me see . . . O, I remember it . . . Be sure you make much of the young gentlewoman, and remain within doors.

Exit PYTHIA.

THRASO. Now let's march.

THAIS, *to the* ATTENDANTS. Do you follow me!

As they go off one way, enter CHREMES *alone another way.*

CHREMES. In truth, the more I think and chew upon this business, the more I fear that this Thais should play me some dog's trick or other; I find myself damnably wheedled by her. When she first sent for me, any man might have wondered what business I had there; faith, I couldn't tell myself. But when I came, she immediately cast about for excuses to make me tarry. 'I have,' says she, 'just now been at my devotions; and am therefore more fit for discourse on grave and serious matters.' At that my heart misgave me plaguily. She drew up a chair and sat by me, and fawningly tried to make me talk. When discourse presently flagged, she asked me how long had my father and mother been dead. I told her: 'A pretty long while ago.' Then she asked whether I had not a seat at Sunio, and how far from the sea it stood. Pox! I believe she likes the place herself, and has a mind to gull me out of it. And lastly, whether I hadn't lost a young sister thence? And who was in her company at the time? And how she was clothed, and whether I would know her again, and suchlike stuff. I can't imagine why the Devil she asked all these questions, unless she designs to impose herself on me as this lost sister, as an impudent jade of her sort might well do. However, if the child is alive, she will be just sixteen and no more; whereas Thais is somewhat older than myself, so that won't do. Now she sends again, begging me very earnestly to come. Let her either tell me her business plainly or trouble me no more. I'll be hanged if she catches me here a third time. Soho, within there! Soho!

Knocks at the door.

PYTHIA, *within.* Who's there?

CHREMES. 'Tis I, my name's Chremes.

Enter PYTHIA.

PYTHIA. My pretty little squire, is it you?

CHREMES, *aside.* So . . . I said as much! Such wheedling bodes no good.

PYTHIA. My lady humbly desires you to come again to-morrow.

CHREMES. I'm going into the country this afternoon.

PYTHIA. For love's sake, Sir, do as my lady asks.

CHREMES. I tell you plainly: I can't.

PYTHIA. Why then, Sir, stay but a little until my lady returns.

CHREMES. Faith, I don't intend it.

PYTHIA, *fawningly.* Why not, dear Mr Chremes?

CHREMES. Pox take ye for a dissembling baggage!

PYTHIA. Well, if you be firm in your resolve, Sir, I beseech ye to give yourself the trouble of stepping over to where she is.

CHREMES. I don't care if I do that.

PYTHIA, *to them within.* Doria!

Enter DORIA.

Go quickly and show this gentleman over to the Captain's.

Exeunt severally.

Enter ANTIPHO *alone.*

ANTIPHO. Yesterday a knot of good fellows got together with me at Piero, where we agreed to have a club feast today, and chose Chaerea for our steward. The stakes were all laid down, the hour and place resolved upon. But the hour has passed, and at the place they know nothing of any such feast. Our gentleman-steward has given us the slip, and 'faith I can't tell what to say or think of the business. . . . The rest of the company have employed me to hunt about for Chaerea; I think I'd better call in at his father's . . .

Discovering CHAEREA.

But who is that coming out of Thais's house? Is it he, or is it not he? . . . As I live 'tis he! Hey-day! What a toy of a man have we got here? What means his disguise? . . . What unaccountable freak is this? I can't for my life imagine what's the matter. But I am determined to know. *Retires a little on one side.*

Enter CHAEREA *looking cautiously about.*

CHAEREA, *to himself softly.* But is no one here now? Not a mortal! . . . Does nobody dog me? . . . Not so much as my shadow! . . . Shall I now exult in my swelling joys? . . . O Heavens! what would I not give for some kind friend to cut my throat immediately, that in the height of this joy I might end my life without the least dash of misfortune. . . . Thank Heaven that no curious, inquisitive fellow comes up by my side, to deafen and murder me with question upon question at every turn. As: 'Why these transports of joy? Why so wonderful merry? Whither away so fast? Whence come ye? Where got ye this garb? What frolic is this? Are you in your wits, or are ye stark mad?'

ANTIPHO, *aside, advancing nearer.* Faith, I'll even slide up to him, and do him that favour myself.
Aloud.

. . . Chaerea, at what do you chuckle so? What means this fool's coat? Why so merry a smile? Hey, brave lad! What do ye mean? Do ye claim to be in your wits? Why do ye stare at me so?

Here they stare upon each other.

What, never a word?

CHAEREA. Huzza! This is a day of jubilee! Well met, old soul! God take me, there's not a man alive I'd have sooner seen than thy dear self.

ANTIPHO. Prithee, tell me this mighty business.

CHAEREA. And prithee, dear rogue, prepare thyself to receive it with gladness. . . . I suppose you know my brother's mistress?

ANTIPHO. You mean Thais, I suppose?

CHAEREA. The very same.

ANTIPHO. I thought I knew her.

CHAEREA. This day a pretty young girl was presented to her. But why should I stand prating and commending her beauty to thee, my friend, when thou knowest well how severe a critic I am . . . In short, she fired my blood.

ANTIPHO. Say you so?

CHAEREA. Ay, boy, had you but seen her, I'm sure you would explain that she was the mirror of her sex. But, to let irrelevancies be, I was presently in up to the ears; and as good luck would have it, we had a eunuch at home, whom my brother bought for his mistress, but who wasn't yet delivered to her. Our man Parmeno gave me a hint of a design, which I immediately put into execution.

ANTIPHO. And what was that?

CHAEREA. Be patient and you'll hear it sooner. It was to change clothes with the eunuch, and for me to be presented instead of him!

ANTIPHO. What, for the eunuch!

CHAEREA. Even so, old boy.

ANTIPHO. Prithee, what advantage could you gain thereby?

CHAEREA. That's a question worth the asking. Why, to see her, discourse with her, and be alone with the pretty creature I loved, ye rogue! And d'ye make nothing of this now? . . . In short, I was presented to Thais who, as soon as she received me, very joyfully brought me home, and committed the beautiful creature to my charge.

ANTIPHO. To whose charge? To thine?

CHAEREA. Yes, to mine!

ANTIPHO. Marry, she was in safe hands!

CHAEREA. Thais ordered that not a man should come near her save myself, and charged me not to stir a step from her; but she and I should be alone together in the parlour. I looked as if butter wouldn't melt in my mouth, and cried: 'Yes, Madam!'

ANTIPHO. The Lord help thee!

CHAEREA. She told me she was going out to supper; and drew all her train after her, except a few raw new-comers to attend the fair stranger. Those prepared a bath for my angel. I urged them to hasten as much as they could. While they were about it, this sweet creature sat in a withdrawing room, with her eyes cast upon a fair picture of Jupiter, who (as the story goes) came down into Danaë's lap in a shower of gold. I made bold to dart a look that way too, and finding how like his intrigue was to mine, I was ten times the more tickled. To think that a very God should transform himself into a mortal, and privately steal through the tiles of another man's house, and so drop like a shower into his mistress's arms. And what God, thought I, was this? Why, no less a God than the Thunderer himself, who shakes the battlements of Heaven. And should flesh and blood refuse to follow his example? I'll do it, and with all my soul too. While these thoughts were working in my head, they called her away to the bath. She goes, she washes, she comes back, and then they put her to bed. I stood waiting for the word of command. At last comes one to me: 'Prithee, do you, Dorus, take this fan, and cool the young gentlewoman thus, while we are bathing. When we have done, you may bathe too, if you've a mind to it.'

ANTIPHO. I'd have given the whole world almost to have seen thy impudent face at that moment! How you carried yourself, and how like a great booby you managed the fan.

CHAEREA. The words were scarce out of her mouth, but they all rushed out of the room to the bath, and set up a gaggle, as servants do when their master's back is turned. Meanwhile, my dear lady falls into a sweet sleep; with that I cunningly cast a sheep's eye through the fan.

Showing him how he looked.

And took a sidelong glance round the room, to see that the coast was clear . . . Finding all was well, I made fast the door.

ANTIPHO. What then, brave boy?

CHAEREA. How? What then, simpleton?

ANTIPHO. Ay, simpleton indeed!

CHAEREA. Had I neglected such a short, wished-for and unexpected opportunity, when it dropped into my very
mouth, I must then have been a very eunuch indeed!

ANTIPHO. Faith boy, thou art in the right. . . . But in the
meantime, what's become of our club-feast?

CHAEREA. 'Tis just ready.

ANTIPHO. Truth, thou art a brave fellow. But where is it? At
your house?

CHAEREA. No; at old Harry Platters.

ANTIPHO. That's a plaguey way off!

CHAEREA. We must go the faster then, that's all.

ANTIPHO. But won't you change your clothes?

CHAEREA. How can I? Pox on't! I'm banished from home, lest
my brother should see me in this rig and, what's worse,
lest my old Father should return from the country.

ANTIPHO. Why, then let's go to our house, that's the nearest
place I can think of where you may change back into your
proper apparel.

CHAEREA. That's right; let's away then, and lay our heads together, how my dear one may be for ever mine.

ANTIPHO. A match, then!

Exeunt both.

End of the Third Act

ACT FOUR

Enter DORIA *alone, with a casket under her arm*

DORIA. As I'm a living soul, so far as I can gather from this
Captain's mood, I fear he will make some disturbance today, and turn upon my lady. For as soon as Chremes, the
young gentlewoman's brother arrived, my lady asked the
Captain's leave to have him admitted. He began to huff
and grow angry, but yet durst not deny her. Besides, my
lady urged him to make the gentleman welcome at the
table, wishing to detain him until the proper time should
come to tell him about his sister. At last, with a sullen
look, the Captain coldly bids him welcome. The gentleman
stayed, and my lady began to discourse. Then Captain
Huff-cap, imagining that Mr Chremes was a rival brought
there to affront him, thought he would plague her in revenge. 'Hark ye,' says he, 'send for Pamphila to give us a
song.' 'By no means in the world,' cries my lady. 'What
should such a wench do at a feast?' The Captain having
set his mind upon this point, fell to wrangling. Meantime
my cunning lady whips her gold and jewels into this casket, which she slipped into my hand to carry home—a certain sign that she would come away herself so soon as her
business allowed.

Enter PHAEDRIA *at a distance.*

PHAEDRIA. As I was walking along the road to our country

house, a thousand thoughts came running into my head one after another, which I took all in the worst sense (as 'tis usual with people when they are uneasy). To be short, while I was musing on these things, I passed by my house unawares, and had gone half a mile beyond before I perceived it. Upon that I turned back with a heart as heavy as lead. . . . When I came close to the gates again, I stood still, and began to reason thus with myself: 'What! must I be forced to stay here eight-and-forty long hours without her? . . . What of all that? . . . A mere trifle . . . How a trifle? . . . Well, if I can't kiss her hand, 'tis very hard that I can't steal one look at her. If I can't have the one thing, sure I may have the other. 'Tis better to be almost out-distanced than to be quite thrown out of the race.' With that, I went past the gate on purpose. But hold, what makes Pythia run out of doors in such a fright?

Enter PYTHIA *looking about.*

PYTHIA, *to herself.* Where's this cursed, wicked creature? . . . Wretch that I am! Where shall I find him? Or where shall I look for him? . . . That ever any man should have the impudence to practise such a villainy!

PHAEDRIA, *aside.* Alas! my heart misgives me, strangely.

PYTHIA, *to herself.* Nay, more than that, after having abused the girl, he tears her clothes, and drags her up and down by the hair of the head.

PHAEDRIA, *aside.* How's this?

PYTHIA, *to herself.* O that I had but the rogue in my clutches now! . . . How I would claw at the eyes of that whore's-bird!

PHAEDRIA, *aside.* I can't imagine what great disorder has happened here in my absence. . . . I'll e'en step up to her.

To PYTHIA.

What's the matter? Whither in such haste? Whom do ye look for, Pythia?

PYTHIA. Hah, Mr Phaedria! Whom look for, say ye? A curse upon you and your precious presents both together!

PHAEDRIA. Prithee, tell me what's the matter?

PYTHIA. The matter, quoth he? . . . Your eunuch whom you gave us, what wicked work has he made here? He has gone and ravished the young gentlewoman whom the Captain gave my lady.

PHAEDRIA, *in amaze.* What sayest thou?

PYTHIA. I'm quite undone.

PHAEDRIA. Ay, and drunk too, I think.

PYTHIA. Would that the worst of mine enemies were as drunk as I am!

DORIA. O law, Pythia, wasn't it a very prodigious thing, ha?

PHAEDRIA. Thou art certainly mad. . . . How is it possible for a eunuch to do this?

PYTHIA. I can't tell what he was; but 'tis plain what he has done. The poor creature is all in tears, neither can ye get one word from her. This precious rogue is in hiding now. I'm woefully afraid too, that he has stolen something out of the house, when he ran away.

PHAEDRIA. 'Tis a wonder to me such a decrepit beast should get out of sight so soon, unless he has gone to earth at my Father's house.

PYTHIA. Dear Sir, step in and see.

PHAEDRIA. I'll let you know soon enough, if I find him.

Exit PHAEDRIA.

DORIA. O Gemini! Prithee, my dear, did you ever hear of such a horrid prank before? I never did.

PYTHIA. Truly I have heard say that eunuchs are great admirers of fine women, but can do nothing but slobber over them. Yet, like the silly jade I was, I never thought of this: else I should have locked up my gentleman and kept the girl far enough from his reach.

Re-enter PHAEDRIA, *dragging in* DORUS *by the ears.*

PHAEDRIA. Come out, you infamous dog! . . . What, d'ye hang back, runagate scoundrel? . . . Thou damnable bargain, come out of thy kennel!

DORUS. Good Sir!

PHAEDRIA. Do but see what a damned Friday-face the gaol-bird makes? How came you hither again? . . . And why this change of dress, I pray? . . . What answer, dog? If I had waited but a minute longer, Pythia, I should have missed the rogue—you see he's just equipped for the march.

PYTHIA. O dear, Sir, have ye found the rascal?

PHAEDRIA. Found him! Ay.

PYTHIA. That's good luck indeed.

DORIA. Ay, special good luck, upon my word!

PYTHIA. What have ye done with him?

PHAEDRIA. Done with him! Can't ye see what is before your eyes?

PYTHIA. Whom should I see?

PHAEDRIA. This fellow here.

Pointing to DORUS.

PYTHIA. And what of him?

PHAEDRIA. He's the same was sent to your house today.

PYTHIA. I dare swear, Sir, none of our house ever set eye upon the fellow.

PHAEDRIA. Sure they were blind then!

PYTHIA. Pray, Sir, do ye believe this to be the man who was brought to our house?

PHAEDRIA. Believe it? The Devil a one else had I to send!

PYTHIA. Fie! . . . there's no comparison to be made between this and that. The other had a fine air, and looked like a gentleman.

PHAEDRIA. Ay, so you thought, because he had got his gay clothes on; now he has altered his dress, you take him for an ugly creature.

PYTHIA. Pray, Sir, don't persuade me to doubt my senses, as though there were no more difference than that between them. Why, he that we had today was such a fine young fellow, 'twould have done your heart good to see him. This is a dry, decrepit drowsy-headed fumbler, and looks like a weasel.

PHAEDRIA. 'Sdeath! What stuff's this? You've brought me to such a pass, that I know not what I've done myself.

To DORUS.

. . . Come hither, Sirrah! Didn't I buy ye and pay for ye?

DORUS. Yes, if it please your worship.

PYTHIA. Now, pray, Sir, let me have my say with him.

PHAEDRIA. Do so.

PYTHIA. Were you at our house today?

He shakes his head.

Look ye, he denies it . . . He whom Parmeno brought was no more than sixteen years of age.

PHAEDRIA. Well, I'll try again myself. First, Sirrah, tell me how you came by these clothes. What, have you lost your tongue? . . . Ye ugly dog, why don't ye answer me?

DORUS. One Mr Chaerea came . . .

PHAEDRIA. Not my brother, I hope?

DORUS. Yes, Sir.

PHAEDRIA. When?

DORUS. Today.

PHAEDRIA. How long ago?

DORUS. But a little while.

PHAEDRIA. With whom did he come?

DORUS. With Parmeno, if it please your worship.

PHAEDRIA. Did you know him before?

DORUS. No, Sir, nor ever heard his name.

PHAEDRIA. How came ye then to know it was my brother?

DORUS. Parmeno told me so. . . . And 'twas Chaerea gave me these clothes . . .

PHAEDRIA. Confusion!

DORUS. . . . and put on mine, and away they went together.

PYTHIA, *to* PHAEDRIA. So, Sir, who's drunk now? 'Twas I filled your head with stories, wasn't it? Now 'tis as clear as the sun that the poor gentlewoman's ravished.

Weeps.

PHAEDRIA. Away, ye beast. . . . D'ye believe one word this fellow prates?

PYTHIA. A fig for believing! The thing's plain enough itself.

PHAEDRIA, *softly to* DORUS. Come a little this way. D'ye hear me, Sirrah? . . . Nearer yet. . . . That's well. . . . Let me hear this business once again. Did Chaerea take your clothes from ye?

DORUS. He did, Sir.

PHAEDRIA. And put them on himself?

DORUS. Yes, Sir.

PHAEDRIA. And was sent hither in your stead?

DORUS. Yes, that he was.

PHAEDRIA, *aloud in a passion.* Oh heavens! This is the most wicked impudent dog alive.

PYTHIA. Alas, Sir! Are ye not convinced that we have been most basely abused?

PHAEDRIA, *angrily to Pythia.* 'Tis no wonder if a cracked chamber-maid believes this scoundrel.

Softly.

. . . But the truth of it is, I'm somewhat gravelled myself.

Aside to DORUS.

. . . Hark ye, Sirrah, deny all, or I'll cut your throat!

Aloud to DORUS.

. . . Can't I rack the truth out of ye today? Did ye see my brother Chaerea?

DORUS, *fearfully.* No, indeed, Sir.

PHAEDRIA. I see there's nothing to be done without blows. . . . This way, ye dog. . . . First he says one thing, then he denies it.

Aside, to DORUS.

. . . Down on your knees, and ask my pardon.

DORUS, *kneeling.* Good Sir, I beseech ye, forgive me.

PHAEDRIA. Into your kennel then.

Beats him.

DORUS. O! O!

Runs out howling.

PHAEDRIA, *aside*. Faith, I couldn't think how to pass the matter off without this stratagem. . . . But if 'twas my brother Chaerea, the case is past cure.

Aloud to DORUS.

. . . D'ye think, ye rascal, to make a fool of me?

Exit after him.

PYTHIA. I'll wager my life that this damned plot is of Parmeno's contriving.

DORIA. You may swear it.

PYTHIA. I' faith, I'll pay him in his own coin before I sleep. . . . But prithee, Doria, what wouldst thou advise me?

DORIA. You mean, in the case of the young gentlewoman?

PYTHIA. Yes, whether we had best keep the matter to ourselves, or report it.

DORIA. In truth, were I you, I should pay no heed to the eunuch, or to the girl, neither. By that means you'll keep out of harm's way, and oblige our lady besides. You need only say that the eunuch has given us the slip.

PYTHIA. I'll follow your counsel.

DORIA. But yonder comes Mr Chremes . . . My lady isn't far behind them.

PYTHIA. What makes ye think so?

DORIA. Because the Captain and she were almost at daggers drawn when I left them.

PYTHIA. Then away with the casket, quick. . . . I'll learn what has passed from this gentleman.

Enter CHREMES, *half drunk.*

CHREMES, *to himself.* Hey-dazy! . . . I have been finely taken in. . . . This wine has been too much for me. . . . The time I was toping . . . I thought myself as sober as a judge . . . but when I came to try my legs . . . 'Sblud, neither my feet nor my head knew which should go uppermost.

PYTHIA. Oh, Mr Chremes!

CHREMES. Who's that? . . . Oh, the pretty, pretty Pythia!
Why, thou art worth forty of the Pythias I saw last.

PYTHIA. And upon my word, you're forty times more pleasant
than you were before.

CHREMES. The old saying's very true. If it wasn't for meat
and good drink, women might gnaw the sheets. . . . But
your mistress has been home a long time, I suppose?

PYTHIA. Why, has she gone from the Captain's, then?

CHREMES. Oh, a damnable while. . . . They were quarrelling
like dog and cat.

PYTHIA. Didn't she desire ye to follow her?

CHREMES. No, she only tipped me a wink as she went away.

PYTHIA. And wasn't that enough?

CHREMES. No, i' faith; I couldn't tell what her winking and
twinkling meant, until the Captain very civilly gave me
my explanation by thrusting me head and shoulders after
her. . . . But see, here she comes already. . . . I wonder
what Devil brought me hither before her.
    Enter THAIS.

THAIS, *to herself.* I believe this hectoring bully will be back
soon enough, to take away the girl by force.
    Angrily.
Ay, let him come; if he tries to touch her but with one
finger, I'll pluck his eyes out . . . I can abide with his
extravagancies and big words, as long as they are but
words, but i' faith, should he come to action, I'll make him
smart for it.

CHREMES. Ah, Madam, I've been here a long while.

THAIS. My dear Chremes, 'twas you I wanted; aren't you
aware that this quarrel was upon your account—that the
whole business is a concern of yours?

CHREMES. Of mine! Pray how so? As if I had been . . .

THAIS. While I'm taking pains to restore your sister to ye, I'm
forced to bear with these and a thousand such affronts.

CHREMES. Pray, Madam, where is she now?

THAIS. At home, in my house.

CHREMES, *concernedly*. Hah!

THAIS. What's the matter? You needn't fear, for her education hasn't been beneath her station.

CHREMES. What's that you say?

THAIS. Nothing but the truth. I freely give her to ye, and shan't expect a farthing for my pains.

CHREMES. I thank ye, Madam, and I shall endeavour to make ye amends when the time serves.

THAIS. But have a care, Sir, that you don't lose her before you have her, for 'tis she whom the Captain is coming to plunder us of by force of arms. . . . Do ye hear, Pythia, run in quick, and fetch the casket and the tokens!

CHREMES, *discovering* THRASO *and his party.* Do ye see them, Madam?

PYTHIA. Where is the casket laid, Madam?

THAIS. In the chest of drawers. . . . Can ye move no faster, ye baggage?

Exit PYTHIA.

CHREMES. What an army has this fellow mustered up against ye! . . . Lamentable!

THAIS. What, my dear, art thou chicken-hearted?

CHREMES *struts*. Pshaw, I chicken-hearted! I'm as bold as a lion.

THAIS. Ay, and so you need be.

CHREMES. Ah, Madam, I doubt ye take me for a monstrous brave fellow.

THAIS. However, hear this for your comfort, that the fellow you're to deal with is a stranger at Athens, has less interest, less acquaintance, and fewer friends to back him than you.

CHREMES. That I know too: but no wise man stands behind an ass when he kicks. I'd rather prevent a quarrel beforehand, than revenge it afterward. . . . Do you go in and barricade the door, while I run to the Piazza and fetch the constable to keep the peace.

Going off.

THAIS, *catching him by the cloak.* Hold, Sir!

CHREMES. I had better go.

THAIS, *still holding him.* Stand your ground, pray.

CHREMES. Pray let me go, I'll be back again in an instant!

THAIS. Sir, you need call no help . . . Do but tell him she is your sister, and that you lost her when she was young, and have now come to claim her: then show him the tokens.

Re-enter PYTHIA, *with the casket.*

PYTHIA. Here they are, Madam.

THAIS. Do you take 'em, Sir.

CHREMES *takes the casket.*

If he offers the least violence, you may haul him before the magistrate. . . . You understand me?

CHREMES. Yes, very well.

THAIS. Be sure you tell him so with a good courage.

CHREMES. Edad, and so I will!

Struts, and puts his arms akimbo.

THAIS. Up with your cloak, man . . .

Aside.

Dear heart! I've called in a champion who needs a champion himself.

Exeunt on one side. Enter on the other side THRASO, GNATHO, SANGA, SERVANTS *with linkboys, fireforks, shovels, dishclouts, etc.*

THRASO. Prithee, Gnatho, how can a man of honour swallow such a notorious affront as this? I'll rather die upon the spot! Come, Simalio, Dorax, Syriscus, follow your leader! . . . First I'll storm their castle.

GNATHO. Very well said!

THRASO. Then I'll carry off the damsel in triumph.

GNATHO. Better and better.

THRASO. And lastly, I'll put the jilt to severe punishment.

GNATHO. Best of all.

THRASO. Advance, Dorax, with your truncheon, and command the main body. Simalio, command the left wing; and you, Syriscus, the right. . . . Where are the rest? Where's Captain Sanga with his ragged regiment?

SANGA. Here, Sir.

THRASO. Ye lazy son of a whore! Do ye think to engage the enemy with a dishclout? What did ye bring that for?

SANGA. Who, I, Sir? Why, I knew the prowess of my general, and the courage of his soldiers so well, that they could never part without bloody wounds; so I brought this clout to staunch the flow.

THRASO. Where's all the rest of them?

SANGA. The rest, you ask? There's only Sannio left to keep the house from running away.

THRASO. Gnatho, do you marshal them all in rank and file! . . . I'll bring up the rear, and there give the signal for the onset.

GNATHO, *aside*. This shows a prudent general: when he has drawn up his men in battle array, he makes sure of his own retreat.

THRASO. This was the Persian King's way.

CHREMES *and* THAIS *appear above.*

CHREMES. Do ye observe, Madam, what this cut-throat's about? I see my counsel wasn't amiss, when I advised ye to barricade the door.

THAIS. Pshaw! This fellow, whom you take for a hero, is as faint-hearted as a town bully. . . . Bear up, man!

THRASO, *to* GNATHO. What had we best do?

GNATHO. Had we but a mortar now to train upon them, one bomb would make them scamper.

THRASO, *discovering* THAIS. But hold, yonder's the enemy!

GNATHO. Shall we make the assault, noble general?

THRASO. Hold, I say. . . . Wise commanders usually send a summons before they storm; perhaps he'll first surrender upon discretion.

GNATHO. Oh wonderful! What plaguey things these politics are! I am never in your company, but I go away the wiser for it.

THRASO, *to* THAIS. Thais, answer me the first article: when I gave ye Pamphila, didn't ye promise me so many days to myself?

THAIS. What of all that?

THRASO. A pretty question! . . . Didn't ye smuggle in one of your gallants under my very nose? What business had ye together? Why did you slink away with him from my house?

THAIS. Because it was my pleasure.

THRASO. Why, then deliver up Pamphila, unless you'd have her carried off by force.

CHREMES, *angrily*. Deliver her to thee! Touch her if you dare, thou worst of . . . .

GNATHO, *to* CHREMES. Hah, Sir! Have a care! Not a word more!

CHREMES. Dare you prate to me, buffoon?

THRASO. Shan't I touch what's my own?

CHREMES. Thine, villain?

GNATHO, *to* CHREMES. I say once again, have a care, friend! I see you don't know whom you address thus.

CHREMES, *to* GNATHO. Won't you be gone, ye rascal?

To THRASO.

And you, Captain Swashbuckle, don't ye know what is good for ye? If ye give us the least disturbance here, I'll make you remember the place, the day, and the person you have affronted, as long as you breathe.

GNATHO, *to* CHREMES. Poor wretch! I pity ye, that ye should provoke so great a man to be your enemy.

CHREMES. I'll crack your fool's pate for ye, if ye be not gone presently.

GNATHO. Say ye so, Mr Snarl? Are your hands so heavy?

THRASO, *to* CHREMES. Pray, Sir, who are you? What would you have? And what have you to do with the girl?

CHREMES. That ye shall know presently. First, I say she's free-born.

THRASO. So!

CHREMES. And a citizen of Athens.

THRASO. How?

CHREMES. And my sister, too.

THRASO. Oh, impudence!

CHREMES, *jeeringly*. Therefore, Captain, I tell ye, once and for all: lay hands on her if you dare.

To THAIS.

Now, Madam, I'll fetch Sophrona, the nurse, and show her the tokens.

THRASO. Why, Sir! Will you hinder me from enjoying what's my own?

CHREMES. Yes, that I will.

CHREMES *withdraws*.

GNATHO, *to* THRASO. Bear witness, this Chremes owns himself a thief. He lays himself open to the Law's vengeance.

THRASO, *to* THAIS. Do you say the same, too?

THAIS. Fish and find out!

THAIS *withdraws*.

Here THRASO *and* GNATHO *stare at one another*.

THRASO. What shall we do next?

GNATHO. Let us march home again. . . . By and by she'll come fawning like a spaniel to beg your pardon.

THRASO. Think ye so?

GNATHO. Nothing more certain: I know these women well enough. When you will, they won't and when you won't, they will.

THRASO. Thou hast hit it.

GNATHO. Shall I dismiss the army?

THRASO. When you please.

GNATHO, *to* SANGA. Well, Captain, you and your troops are discharged. Now, like a noble general, lead them into winter quarters: for refreshment in the kitchen.

SANGA. Truth, my belly chimed the dinner hour more than forty minutes ago.

GNATHO. Well said, Tom! We need food!

THRASO. Follow your leader.

Exeunt shouting.

End of the Fourth Act

ACT FIVE

THAIS *and* PYTHIA

THAIS, *entering.* Do ye speak in riddles still, ye dirty slut?
In another tone, mocking her.

'I do know, I don't know, he's fled, I heard of it, but was
not there.' Hussy, can't ye tell me the story in plain terms?
The poor girl's gown is rent, she's all in tears, and won't
speak. The eunuch's fled, too? But why? What's been done?
Come! No answer?

PYTHIA. Alas, Madam, what would ye have me say, when
they all affirm that it wasn't a eunuch who was here?

THAIS. Who was it then?

PYTHIA. One Mr Chaerea.

THAIS. What Mr Chaerea?

PYTHIA. The young gentleman, Phaedria's brother.

THAIS. What's that ye say, ye witch?

PYTHIA. Nothing but what is certainly true.

THAIS. Pray, what should he do here? Upon what account
came he hither, pray?

PYTHIA. I can't guess, unless he was in love with Pamphila.

THAIS. 'Sdeath, I'm undone then! All my measures are broken
if this be true. Is it for this that the poor creature so be-
moans herself?

PYTHIA. So, I believe, Madam.

THAIS. How's this, ye baggage? Didn't I give you a particular charge, when I left her with you?

PYTHIA. What could I do in the case? You ordered that she should be wholly committed to his care!

THAIS. Oh, you jade, you set the wolf to keep the sheep! I'm ashamed to the soul to be so cursedly fooled . . .

Seeing CHAEREA *afar off.*

But what fellow's that?

Enter CHAEREA *at a distance, still in the eunuch's dress.*

PYTHIA. 'S't! Madam! Patience, I beseech ye! All's well, we have got our spark within reach of the net!

THAIS. Where is he?

PYTHIA. 'S't! on the left-hand! Don't you see him? Look there, then!

THAIS. I see him.

PYTHIA. Seize him immediately!

THAIS. What can we do to him, fool!

PYTHIA. Do to him, say ye? . . . See, I beseech you what a cursèd impudent look he wears.

THAIS. I see no such thing.

PYTHIA. And with what confidence he comes to us!

CHAEREA, *to himself.* Antipho's father and mother were both at home, as if they'd stayed there on purpose; so that I couldn't possibly get in without being discovered. The time I was in the porch, an acquaintance of mine passed that way. Upon this I took to my heels as fast as I could, ran into a blind alley, then into another, and so to a third. Thus did I dance up and down in a peck of troubles, to prevent my discovery. . . . But hold, is that Thais? The very same! . . . I'm at a plaguey loss what to do. . . . Pshaw, what care I? She can neither hang, draw, nor quarter!

THAIS. Let's up to him. . . . O good Sir Dorus, you're welcome home. Pray tell me, did you run away from us?

CHAEREA. True, as you say, Madam.

Looks simply.

THAIS. And are extremely pleased with this vagary I warrant?

CHAEREA. Not so extremely neither, Madam.

THAIS. D'ye think you shall be pardoned?

CHAEREA. Well, Madam, 'twas but one fault. If you catch me in another, string me up!

THAIS. Why did you run? Were you afraid that I should prove a hard mistress?

CHAEREA. No, indeed, Madam.

THAIS. What then did you fear?

CHAEREA. Why, only that this woman should have told tales of me.
   Pointing to PYTHIA.

THAIS. Why, what have ye done, then?

CHAEREA. A small matter.

PYTHIA, *in a passion.* Impudence! A small matter, d'ye call it? Is ravishing a virgin and citizen so small a matter in your eyes?

CHAEREA. I took her for one of my fellow-servants.

PYTHIA, *in a great fury.* Thy fellow-servants? I can scarce keep my nails out of his eyes . . . Thou devil incarnate! Art thou come to laugh at us too?

THAIS, *to* PYTHIA. Keep off, you madwoman!

PYTHIA. Why, Madam? Why should I not freely tear his hairs out by the root, since he owns himself your servant?

THAIS, *trifling, aside.* Indeed, Mr Chaerea, you've done a very unworthy thing, and which did not become ye! For though I might have richly deserved this affront, yet 'twas dishonourable for you to serve me so. As I live, I know not what course to take about the poor girl; you've so broken all my measures, that I can't possibly return her to her friends, either as I ought to have done, or as I intended. For I wished to win their gratitude and favour by thus obliging them.

CHAEREA. Now, Madam, I hope to see a lasting kindness betwixt us both. For from such bad beginnings as this, the greatest friendships often arise; and who knows but some lucky star has ordered this?

THAIS. Why, truly, I interpret it thus myself, and wish it with all my soul.

CHAEREA. And I beg it may be so. Only believe me: I did not do this thing to affront you, but for pure love.

THAIS. I do believe it, and can therefore pardon it. For I'm not of so hard-hearted a nature, Mr Chaerea, nor yet so inexperienced as not to know something of the power of love.

CHAEREA. As I hope for happiness, Madam, I'm extremely taken with you.

PYTHIA. Faith, Madam, look to yourself then!

CHAEREA. I wouldn't hurt her even if I might.

PYTHIA. I'll trust ye no farther than I can see ye.

THAIS. Cease your prating, fool!

CHAEREA. Now, Madam, I must crave your assistance in this great design. I trust and commit myself wholly to your disposal and beg your protection; let me die, if I don't marry her!

THAIS. But what if your father . . .

CHAEREA. What, he? I'm sure of his consent, once she is proved to be a gentlewoman.

THAIS. If you please to wait a little, her brother will be back; he's but gone to fetch Sophrona, the nurse who brought her up; and so, Sir, you may be present at the disclosure.

CHAEREA. Then I'll stay.

THAIS. Meanwhile, I think we had better go in, than stay here at the door.

CHAEREA. With all my heart.

PYTHIA. D'ye know, Madam, what you're going to do?

THAIS. Why that question?

PYTHIA. Why? Sure you don't intend to take this blade into your house again?

THAIS. Why not?

PYTHIA. Trust me for once, Madam! He'll make some new disturbance.

THAIS. Prithee, no more of your tattling.

PYTHIA. It seems you haven't yet made sufficient trial of him?

CHAEREA. I'll do no harm, good Mistress Pythia.

PYTHIA. I'll not trust ye an inch, good Mr Chaerea . . . unless your head were off.

CHAEREA. But Mistress Pythia, thou shalt be my keeper.

PYTHIA. No, faith! Who will trust themselves with you, either to keep or to be kept? Away with ye!

Enter at a distance CHREMES *and* SOPHRONA.

THAIS. What luck's here! Here comes the brother.

CHAEREA. Alas-a-day! I beseech ye, Madam, let us go in; I wouldn't for the world be seen in the street thus dressed.

THAIS. Why so? Because you're ashamed of it?

CHAEREA. Yes, indeed, I am.

PYTHIA. 'Yes, indeed, I am,' say ye? You blush like a virgin, Mr Chaerea!

Clapping her hands at him.

THAIS. Do you go in, Sir, I'll follow ye.

Exit CHAEREA.

But do you stay here, Pythia, to bring in Mr Chremes.

Exit THAIS.

PYTHIA, *to herself.* What trick now, what mischief can I think of? . . . How shall I contrive to make this rogue Parmeno pay for the damnable fashion in which he cheated us?

CHREMES. Come, bestir yourself, Nurse, a little faster!

SOPHRONA. So I do, you see!

CHREMES. Ay, but you don't advance.

PYTHIA, *to* CHREMES. Have you shown the nurse those tokens?

CHREMES. Yes, all of them.

PYTHIA. Pray, Sir, what says she? Does she know them again?

CHREMES. Ay, and remembers them very well.

PYTHIA. That's good news, in truth, I wish the poor gentlewoman well with all my heart . . . Be pleased to walk
in, my lady has been expecting ye this long time . . .

Exeunt CHREMES *and* SOPHRONA.

Enter PARMENO *at a distance.*

Yonder comes that precious rogue Parmeno! In the name
of Heaven, how unconcernedly the fellow strolls along!
But I believe I know a way to revenge myself on him as
I would wish. First I'll go in and see the truth of this disclosure, then I'll come again and fright the rascal out of
his wits.

Exit PYTHIA.

PARMENO, *alone.* I'm come to see how Chaerea carries on his
intrigue, which, if it be managed cunningly, then what
monuments of praise will be due to me! For, to say nothing of procuring him the person he loves without trouble,
fees, or charges, when the amour might have proved very
difficult and costly to settle with a covetous bawd-mistress,
I've done something for which, I think, I deserve a statue:
I have shown this spark a way to see through all the tricks
and deceptions of these common jilts, that by timely knowledge he may abhor them for ever after. When they're
abroad, forsooth, none are so cleanly, so modish, so genteel, so delicately neat as they. When they feast with their
gallants, how prettily they wipe their mouths; but to ob-
scure the insatiable gluttony, the vile nastiness, the griping
penury of these same jades at home—how greedy of a stale
crust, how eagerly they slobber and swill at a bowl of
stinking pottage—to know all this beforehand may be the
young man's salvation.

PYTHIA, *at the door, overhearing him.* Faith, I'll be even with
you for your rogueries; you shall have small joy, Sirrah,
in making sport with us.

Enter PYTHIA *taking no notice of* PARMENO.

PYTHIA, *entering.* Bless me! What a base unworthy action is
this! Alas for the unfortunate young gentleman betrayed
hither by that wretch Parmeno!

PARMENO, *aside*. What's in the wind now?

PYTHIA, *to herself*. It grieves me to the soul, dear heart. I left the house in haste, to escape the sight of blood. . . . What a dreadful example they say that they'll make of him!

PARMENO, *aside*. Heavens! What new mischief's this! Has my plot miscarried then? . . . I'll even speak to her. . . . What's the matter, Mistress Pythia? What's that you talked of? Who's to be made an example of?

PYTHIA. Do ye ask that, ye desperate fool? Why, you've quite ruined the young gentleman you had brought instead of the eunuch, thinking, I warrant, that you had well tricked us.

PARMENO. How so . . . . what has happened . . . . prithee, tell me!

PYTHIA. I will so. . . . You don't know then, that the girl who was presented to my lady today, is a gentlewoman of this town, and her brother a person of quality?

PARMENO. I know nothing of it.

PYTHIA. But so it proved. . . . And 'twas she whom your poor master ravished. When her brother knew of it, a most bloody-minded fellow . . .

PARMENO, *fearfully*. What did he do?

PYTHIA. . . . First bound him hand and foot, 'twould grieve your heart to see it.

PARMENO. Bound him! Damnation!

PYTHIA. . . . Though my lady begged pardon for him on her knees.

PARMENO, *hastily*. What say ye?

PYTHIA. Now he threatens to take a knife to him and . . . ah! . . . and do a thing I never saw, nor wouldn't for the world.

PARMENO. How can he dare so great a villainy?

PYTHIA. Why so great, I beseech ye?

PARMENO. Why isn't it the greatest of all villainies? . . . Pray who ever heard of one being so served in a common bawdy-house?

PYTHIA. I can't tell that.

PARMENO. That you mayn't say you don't know of it, let me now declare, and forewarn you, that 'tis no less than Mr Phaedria's brother . . .

PYTHIA. How! Prithee, 'tisn't he, is it?

PARMENO. . . . Therefore your lady had best beware lest he come to harm. . . . But why don't I break into the house myself?

Prepares to enter.

PYTHIA. Have a care what you do, Parmeno! You'll do him no good, and ruin yourself into the bargain, for everybody believes that this plot was all your contrivance.

PARMENO, *coming back.* Alas, what shall I do?

Seeing LACHES *at a distance.*

Oh, yonder comes my old master from his country house. . . . Shall I tell him of it, or no?

Ponders.

. . . In truth I will, though certainly I know I shall provide a rod for my own breeches. Necessity knows no law; Mr Laches must rescue his poor son.

PYTHIA. You do well . . . I'll go in. Be sure you tell him the whole tale from beginning to end.

Enter LACHES.

LACHES, *to himself.* I always find the nearness of my country-house to carry this advantage: that I'm never much tired either with the town or country. When I begin to be sick of the one, I shift lodgings to the other. . . . But isn't that our man Parmeno? 'Tis he, as I hope to live. Parmeno! For whom do you wait at this house?

PARMENO, *turning short.* Who's that there? . . . Ah, Sir, you're welcome back to town.

LACHES. For whom d'ye wait, ha?

PARMENO, *aside.* I'm thunderstruck, I can't wag my tongue for fear.

LACHES. Ha! What's the matter? Why do ye shake so? Is all well at home? Prithee, tell me!

PARMENO. First I'd have you be fully satisfied of this one thing, Sir, that whatever has happened, I'm as innocent as a new-born babe.

LACHES. Why, what's the matter?

PARMENO. That's well asked, for I should have told you before . . . Mr Phaedria bought a eunuch, whom he presented to this woman . . .

LACHES. To what woman?

PARMENO. Thais.

LACHES. He buy eunuchs! . . . 'Sblud, I'm undone then! What did he cost?

PARMENO. Fifty pounds.

LACHES. A fearful sum!

PARMENO. Then his brother Chaerea fell in love with a music-wench.

LACHES, *angrily to* PARMENO. How! What! Is he in love too? Does he practice that sport already? And has he left his post at Piraeus to visit the city? . . . One plague upon another!

PARMENO. Pray, Sir, don't you lecture me. I wasn't his counsellor.

LACHES. One more word about yourself, you hangman, and as I live . . . But tell me the whole business quickly!

PARMENO. Mr Chaerea was sent there instead of the eunuch, Sir.

LACHES. Instead of the eunuch!

PARMENO. Very true, Sir, and now they have apprehended him for rape, and bound him hand and foot, and propose . . .

LACHES. Hell and furies!

PARMENO. But mark the impudence of these jades!

LACHES. Why don't I break in upon them?

Exit LACHES.

PARMENO, *alone*. I don't question but I've brought a whole
house upon my head by this day's work; and yet I couldn't
possibly have avoided it. . . . However, I'm pleased that
these strumpets shall be made to smart because of me.
The old gentleman has sought an occasion this half-year
past to make notorious examples of some of them; and
now, I think, he has found one.

Enter PYTHIA.

PYTHIA, *to herself*. I' faith, this was the pleasantest scene I
ever saw in my life: to see the old gentleman come blunder-
ing upon us in such an error! I had all the sport to myself,
because I alone knew his ailment.

PARMENO, *overhearing, aside*. What a plague's here?

PYTHIA, *to herself*. I'm now come to seek out the fool Parmeno . . . But where, in the name of goodness, shall I
find him?

PARMENO, *aside*. Upon my soul, she looks for me.

PYTHIA, *to herself*. O! I see him, I'll be with him in a trice.

PARMENO. What's the matter, Mistress Impertinence? What
tickles you so? Will you never cease your laughter?

PYTHIA. Oh, my sides! . . . I've almost burst my sides with
laughing at thee.

PARMENO. Your reason, pray?

PYTHIA. A pretty question! . . . Faith, thou art the arrantest
ass I ever set my eyes on, or ever shall. 'Tis utterly past
my skill to tell thee what excellent sport thou hast made
within doors. . . . I took thee for a cunning, ingenious
fellow.

PARMENO. How's this?

PYTHIA. Had ye no more wit than to believe what I said?
Were you not enough ashamed of the villainy into which
you enticed the poor gentleman, but that you must carry
tales about him to his father? How foolish did he look,
think ye, when his father surprised him in that disguise?
What, don't you see to what a fine pass you have brought
yourself?

PARMENO. Ha! How's this, you filthy carrion? Did ye tell

me a lie, and then laugh at the humour of it? Do ye think it such fine sport to abuse us, ye jade?

PYTHIA. Oh, the finest sport in the world.

PARMENO. Do ye think you shan't pay dearly for this?

PYTHIA. Perhaps so.

PARMENO. Ay, faith ye shall.

PYTHIA. I fancy as much. . . . These threats may come to-morrow, but you'll be strung up today for turning a young gentleman into a debauchee, and then disclosing the crime. Both father and son will make an excellent example of you for this day's work.

PARMENO. I'm a reprobate.

PYTHIA. And for this you shall be richly rewarded. Now good-bye to ye!

Exit PYTHIA.

PARMENO, *alone.* Like a senseless fool, I've betrayed myself, as rats do with their own squeaking.

Enter THRASO *and* GNATHO, *at another part of the stage.*

GNATHO, *to* THRASO. What's in hand now, Sir? Upon what design are we come hither? What enterprise is next, Sir?

THRASO. I'll even surrender myself to her upon discretion, and do as she bids.

GNATHO. How, Sir?

THRASO. Why should I be less submissive to this lady than Hercules was to Omphale, to whom he was bound as a slave and learned from her to twirl the distaff?

GNATHO. A pat example.

Aside.

. . . Would I could see the slipper flung at your soft head too. But what makes her door open?

Discovering Chaerea.

What mischief's on foot now? . . . I think not I know that face. . . . What makes him cut such capers?

Enter CHAEREA.

CHAEREA, *to himself.* Come, my dear countrymen, was ever

man born under a happier planet than myself? Not one, upon my word! For 'tis plain that the powers above have singled me out to shower down so many blessings upon my head all at once, that the world may know how great their sovereignty is.

PARMENO. Why is he so merry, though?

CHAEREA. My dear Parmeno! 'Tis to thee I'm indebted for the rise, the advancement, and the perfection of my joys. . . . Dost know that my dear sweet creature's been proved a gentlewoman?

PARMENO. I heard it rumoured, Sir.

CHAEREA. . . . And that she's to be my bride?

PARMENO. As I hope to be knighted, that's admirable!

GNATHO, *aside to* THRASO. Do ye hear, Sir, what he says?

CHAEREA. I am heartily glad too that my brother's amours are in such a happy condition. The families are both united now. Thais has put herself under my father's care and protection, and is wholly ours.

PARMENO. Then Mr Phaedria is like to have her for good and all?

CHAEREA. Yes, indeed.

PARMENO. And the mighty Captain's routed—this too is worth laughing at.

CHAEREA. See that my brother knows of all this, as soon as you can, wheresoever he may be.

PARMENO. I'll look for him at home.

Exit PARMENO.

THRASO. Ah, Gnatho, dost thou not think I'm ruined to all intents and purposes?

GNATHO. There's no thinking otherwise.

CHAEREA, *to himself*. Where shall I begin first? Or whom shall I commend most? Him that advised me to do it, or myself who had the heart to venture upon it, or the God of Luck who directed us both, and brought so many fortunate circumstances into the compass of a single day? Or shall I praise the indulgence of my father?

> Great Jove! that dost poor mortals' fate secure,
> Grant that our joy may with our lives endure!

Enter PHAEDRIA.

PHAEDRIA, *to himself.* Bless me! Parmeno tells me wonders. But where's my brother?

CHAEREA. Here, at your service.

PHAEDRIA. I'm extremely glad to hear of your good fortune, brother.

CHAEREA. That I well believe! And truly, brother, there's never a mistress more worthy to be beloved than yours. She has vastly benefited our family.

PHAEDRIA. Hey-day! What is this? You commend her to me?

THRASO, *to* GNATHO. I'm quite undone! The less I hope, the more I love. Good Gnatho, I rely wholly upon thee.

GNATHO. What would you have me do, Sir?

THRASO. Bring it about, either for love or money, that I may continue a little while in Madam Thais's favour.

GNATHO. That will be hard.

THRASO. You can do it, I know, if you lend your mind to the business. If ye perform it, command whatever gift or reward you please—'tis your own.

GNATHO. Shall it be so, Sir?

THRASO. It shall indeed.

GNATHO. Why then, Sir, I shall need free egress and regress into your house, whether you be at home or abroad; and a place at your table, whether invited or not.

THRASO. It shall be so, upon my honour.

GNATHO. Well, I'll make an effort.

PHAEDRIA. Whose tongue's that? . . . O, Captain, is it you?

THRASO. Gentlemen, I'm your humble servant.

PHAEDRIA. Perhaps you know not what has happened at this house.

THRASO. Yes, Sir, I do.

PHAEDRIA. Why come ye scouting in these quarters then?

THRASO. Under your protection, gentlemen.

PHAEDRIA. Do ye know the protection you're to expect? Take this from me, noble Captain: if I find you sauntering here again in the street, you mustn't think to put me off with 'I was looking for a friend, and my business lay this way.' For you can hope for no quarter from me.

GNATHO. Soft, Sir! That's not spoken like a gentleman.

PHAEDRIA. I'll prove no worse than my word.

GNATHO. Indeed, Sir, I didn't think you were so huffy.

PHAEDRIA. You'll find that I am.

GNATHO. Pray be pleased, gentlemen, to permit your servant Gnatho a word or two, and then do what you please in this affair.

PHAEDRIA. Let's hear you, then.

GNATHO. Do you, Captain, move a little on one side.

THRASO *stands off, out of hearing.*

In the first place let me beseech ye both to be persuaded, that whatever I do in the case is purely for my own sake; but if your interest should jibe with mine, then you'll be unwise not to follow my counsel.

PHAEDRIA. Out with it, then.

GNATHO, *fawningly.* What if you took the Captain in amongst ye too?

PHAEDRIA. How amongst us?

GNATHO. Consider a little better, Sir! . . . Why, faith, you and your mistress live very high, for you're used to an easy, splendid life; you've but a small allowance yourself, and Madam Thais will be requiring more. Now, that you may support her, and save your own pocket, there's not a fitter or more convenient utensil than this blunderbuss in the whole world. For first, he has money enough at command, and there's none more prodigal of it than he. Then he's a soft-headed fool, and a half-witted coxcomb, and a fumbling fellow, who snores night and day. You needn't fear that the gentlewoman will fall in love with him; and you may kick him out of doors when you please.

PHAEDRIA, *to* CHAEREA. What had we best do?

GNATHO. Then, Sir, what's best of all, there's no man in the world more obliging and complaisant.

PHAEDRIA. Ten to one, but we may have occasion for this fool some time or other.

CHAEREA. I'm of that mind too.

GNATHO. Gentlemen, I'm obliged to you. . . . One favour more let me beg of you: to admit me also into your retinue. I've been chopping on that block long enough already.

PHAEDRIA. We grant it.

CHAEREA. And with all our hearts.

GNATHO. Then in gratitude, Gentlemen, I will assist you to fleece and jeer the cully to death. Let us drink to it!

CHAEREA. That's well said.

PHAEDRIA. He deserves it.

GNATHO, *to* THRASO. Now, Noble Captain, you may join our company!

THRASO. Prithee, and how do matters stand?

GNATHO, *aside to him.* How? The gentlemen didn't know your worth. When I had informed them of your good qualities, and given you a character such as your noble actions and virtues deserve, your suit was granted.

THRASO, *to* GNATHO. Well hast thou done!

To PHAEDRIA *and* CHAEREA.

Gentlemen, great thanks do I return ye. I never was anywhere but that all kinds of people loved me most dearly.

GNATHO. Didn't I tell ye how choice he was in his expressions? Polite, upon my word!

PHAEDRIA. Now that there's nothing more to be done, you may retire.

Turns to the spectators.

Gentlemen, adieu, one kind applause!

End of THE EUNUCH

THE TRICKS OF PHORMIO

A *Comedy acted at the Roman Sports, when* L. Posthumius Albinus *and* L. Cornelius Merula *were Curule Ediles, by the Company of* L. Ambivius Turpio *and* L. Attilius Prenestae.

Flaccus, *a freedman of* Claudius, *composed the music, which was performed on unequal flutes.*

It was taken from the Greek of Apollodorus, *called* Epidiacazomenos, *and acted four times, under the Consulship of* C. Fannius *and* M. Valerius.

A.U.C.592   Before Christ 161

DRAMATIS PERSONAE

DEMIPHO, *a rich old citizen of Athens, covetous, mistrustful, and petulant*

CHREMES, *Demipho's brother, another citizen of Athens, an old, uxorious, hen-pecked gentleman, who in his youth loved a girl in a corner*

ANTIPHO, *Demipho's son, a good-natured, modest, well-bred young gentleman, very fond of his wife Phanie*

PHAEDRIA, *Chremes's son, an amorous genteel spark of the town, passionately in love with Pamphila, a music-girl*

PHORMIO, *the parasite, a bold, cheating, intriguing, subtle fellow, and one of singular impudence*

GETA, *servant to Antipho, an ingenious, designing, plotting fellow, true to the interest of Antipho and his cousin, Phaedria*

DAVUS, *a servant, an intimate of Geta's*

DORIO, *a covetous, ill-natured, peevish bawd-master, owner of Phaedria's music-girl*

HEGIO
CRATINUS } *three foolish advocates, friends to Demipho*
CRITO

NAUSISTRATA, *Chremes's wife, a haughty imperious woman, who keeps Chremes in awe of her*

SOPHRONA, *nurse to Phanie, a harmless old woman*

NON-SPEAKING PARTS:

DORCIO, *a servant of Demipho's*

PHANIE, *married secretly to Antipho*

SERVANTS

ATTENDANTS

ACT ONE

SCENE: *The street before* DEMIPHO'S *door*
TIME: *Morning*

DAVUS *alone, with a bag of money in his hand*

DAVUS. My very good friend and compatriot Geta came to me
yesterday, asking about a small sum of money he had left
in my hands formerly; he begged me to get it together, so
I have, and am just carrying it to him. His young master,
I hear, has now picked up a wife; and this looks as if
'twere a present for Mrs Bride. What a confounded custom 'tis for those who have but very little, to be always
pampering such as have abundance! All that this poor fellow now has, with much ado, scraped together bit by bit
out of his pitiful allowance must go at one swoop, nobody
ever considering how he has starved himself for it. And
soon poor Geta must be squeezed once again, to give her
ladyship joy of her first-born; and after that again upon
the brat's anniversary day, when 'tis initiated forsooth. The
child is the pretended recipient of all these gifts, but 'tis
the mother runs away with 'em. But isn't that Geta, there?
Enter GETA.

GETA, *to them within.* If a red-haired fellow should enquire
for me. . . .

DAVUS. He's here, spare your breath.

GETA, *turning about.* Ho, Davus! I was just coming to meet
ye.

DAVUS. Here, hold out your hand.

Gives him the bag.

'Tis all good coin, and just what I owed ye.

GETA. Thou art an honest fellow, and 'twas kindly done not to forget me.

DAVUS. Kind indeed, as the world goes now, I'll assure ye; for 'tis come to such a pass, that a man must first pray, and then be thankful, to get again what is his own. But why so concerned?

GETA. You may well ask that! If you did but know the dread and danger I'm in.

DAVUS. And how, pray?

GETA. You shall know, upon promise of secrecy.

DAVUS. Away, simpleton! What! trust me with thy money, and afraid to trust me with a secret! I shouldn't win a pin for my sleeve by dealing falsely with thee now.

GETA. Prithee, hear me then.

DAVUS. Yes, with both ears.

GETA. You know Mr Chremes, our old master's elder brother, don't ye?

DAVUS. Very well.

GETA. And his son Phaedria too?

DAVUS. As well as I know thee.

GETA. It so fell out that the two reverend gentlemen took a journey together, Chremes to Lemnos, and our master to Cilicia—for an old crony of his had wheedled him over there: had sent him letter upon letter, promising him whole mountains of gold, with the Devil and all.

DAVUS. What, to him that already had enough and to spare?

GETA. Never wonder at him, man, 'tis his nature to exceed his wants.

DAVUS. Pox of ill luck! What a pity it is I wasn't born King!

GETA. When the two old gentlemen set out they made me tutor to their sons.

DAVUS. Ah, Geta, that was a hard task for thee.

GETA. Troth, so I found it by woeful experience. My unlucky genius used me very ill that day. At first I tried to be strict with them. But why waste words? My faithfulness to my old masters cost me many a sore drubbing.

DAVUS. As the proverb has it: 'tis hard to kick against the goad!

GETA. Upon that I dropped the reins, and gave the mettlesome pair their heads.

DAVUS. You understood the rules of the market.

GETA. As for our youngster, he was very regular for awhile. But Mr Phaedria immediately picked up his music-girl, and fell head over ears in love. She was kept it seems by a damnable, griping bawd-master. The old gentleman had taken care to keep the young men's pockets empty: so that our amorous spark could do nothing but look fawningly into his mistress's eyes, follow her around town, and perhaps lead her to the Music School and back again. I and my young master, having little else to do, must needs bear him company. Right before the school was a barber's shop, where we commonly awaited her coming out. One day, while we were thus dancing attendance on the girl, in comes a young fellow blubbering so loud that it made us all wonder. We asked what ailed him? 'Why,' said he, 'never till now did I know poverty to be such a sad intolerable burden! Hard by I've just seen a poor girl, crying and taking on most grievously for the death of her mother, by whose dead body she was sitting. She had neither friends, acquaintances, nor relations, to stand by her, or look after the funeral, except for one poor old woman. It grieved me to the very soul, for she was of marvellous beauty.' In short, we were all agog at the story. Mr Antipho presently cried: 'Shall we go and see her?' 'Ay, ay,' says another, 'let's go! Prithee, honest man, bring us to the place!' Away we go, come to her, see her. A pretty rogue i' faith, she was; and what's more, she had nothing of ornament to set off her beauty. Her hair hung about her ears, all out of order, her feet bare, her eyes swollen with weeping, and dressed in such a pickle that if she hadn't been lovely to a fault these circumstances would have made her most disagreeable. The spark that was enamoured with the music-girl said only: 'She's well enough.' But ours . . .

DAVUS, *interrupting.*   . . . Was smitten, I warrant.

GETA. Ye cannot guess how deeply! But now pray observe what came of it. The very next day he goes to the old woman, and politely begs her leave for a night's lodging; which she as politely denies him. She told him that his demand was unreasonable, the girl being a citizen's daughter, well-bred, and of a good family—that if he would take her for better or for worse, he had the law on his side. But if not, she had nothing more to tell him. This put my gentleman to a sad nonplus. Marry her he would with all his heart, but what might the old gentleman his father not say, who was now abroad?

DAVUS. Wouldn't his father have consented to the match, think ye, when he came back?

GETA. What? Give him leave to marry a girl who had neither fortune nor honour? Not while he yet lived!

DAVUS. Well, and what came of it at last?

GETA. What? Why, a certain wheedling rascal, Phormio by name, an audacious fellow, for all I care the Devil may have him!

DAVUS. What of Phormio, prithee?

GETA. He put a damned project into the young man's head that I'm just about to tell ye of. You know 'tis the law here, that every orphan-girl must be married to her next of kin, and the same law binds the next of kin to marry her. 'Now,' says he, 'I'll pretend you to be the girl's kinsman, and commence a suit against ye as, forsooth, being a friend of her father's, and bring the case to a trial. As for who was her father, who her mother, and how you came to be her kinsman, trust me to concoct the story to your best advantage. When you fail to defend your case, the verdict will go by default. As soon as your father comes home, he'll bring an action against me, there's no doubt of that. But what care I? The girl will be yours.'

DAVUS. A very pretty piece of roguery, in truth!

GETA. Antipho was persuaded, Phormio brought the suit, the case was tried, we lost, and he married.

DAVUS. What's that you tell me?

GETA. 'Tis even as I say.

DAVUS. Ah, poor Geta, what will become of thee, then?

GETA. Faith, I can't tell; only thus much I know, that which-ever way the coin falls, we must bear the consequences.

DAVUS. Now I like ye. Spoken like a philosopher.

GETA. I've no hopes but in the inventions of my own noddle.

DAVUS. I commend thee.

GETA. Should I go now and ask some friend of my old mas-ter's to plead for me, saying: 'Good Sir, pardon him this once, and if he ever does the like again, I'll have no word to speak for him'? I should be in luck if he didn't add: 'But for all I care, you can hang him like a dog.'

DAVUS. Now for this other pupil of yours—the music-wench's gentleman escort, how does he fare?

GETA. Poorly enough, Jove knows.

DAVUS. I warrant he has little ready money to bestow on her.

GETA. Not a penny-piece. Only fine words and gay prospects.

DAVUS. Is his father home again?

GETA. Not yet.

DAVUS. When d'ye expect the old gentleman?

GETA. I can't tell positively; but I hear there's a letter from him at the custom house, brought in by the packet-boat. I am just stepping along there to fetch it.

DAVUS. D'ye need anything else of me, Geta?

GETA. Nothing but goodbye to ye!

Exit DAVUS.

GETA, *alone, to them within.* Soho, Sirrah! Is nobody at home?

Enter a FOOTBOY.

GETA. Here, take this bag and carry it to Dorcio.

Gives him the money.

Exeunt severally.

End of the First Act

ACT TWO

ANTIPHO *and* PHAEDRIA

ANTIPHO, *entering.* But Phaedria, that it should ever have
come to this pass that I fear my own father, and stand in
dread of his return? And a father that loves me so! If I
had not been so rash a blockhead, I might have welcomed
him home as a dutiful son should.

PHAEDRIA. What d'ye mean by all this?

ANTIPHO. A pretty question, when you yourself were my chief
supporter in this mad prank! Well, I could wish Phormio's
tongue had been out before he had given me such counsel
and urged me to perform what has proved the foundation
of all my miseries. If I hadn't enjoyed her at all, it might
have made me melancholy for three or four days or so;
but then I shouldn't have had this perpetual burden upon
my mind . . .

PHAEDRIA. I am listening to ye.

ANTIPHO. . . . of being in hourly expectation of my father's
sudden return, who will pluck me from her embraces.

PHAEDRIA. Others are grieved for lack of pleasure, but you
for being glutted with it. The God of Love has been too
liberal to ye, Cousin. Yours is a life I'd have as soon wished
for, as any other whatsoever. Had the Gods blessed me
with so long a banquet of love as you've been blest with,
I should thank them heartily and be content to die the

next moment. Pray consider what trouble I endure by
being debarred from the woman I love, and what comfort
you might take in your plentiful enjoyment. I'll say nothing
of your having got a civil, well-bred woman without any
cost to yourself, and being married to a woman not only
of your own choice but of unspotted reputation. 'Tis manifest you're happy, and only need a friend who can assure
you of it. Had you to treat with a bawd-master as I have,
you'd feel the difference between your plight and mine.
But 'tis the nature of man never to be contented.

ANTIPHO. Nay, in my opinion, Cousin, 'tis you yourself, who is
the happy man. You still have power to consult your own
convenience: whether you had best love your girl, or leave
her. But I've brought myself into such unhappy straits that
I can neither abandon mine, nor keep her.

Enter GETA *at a distance in great haste.*

ANTIPHO, *in a surprise.* But what's the matter now? Isn't that
Geta in such haste? 'Tis he for certain. Alas! My poor heart
forebodes that he's the messenger of some bad news or
other.

GETA, *to himself.* In truth, Geta, thou art a dead man if thou
dost not find some cunning shift or other to save thyself,
and that quickly, too! So many misfortunes are ready to
seize thee, before thou art prepared for them. I can't tell
ye either how to escape them, nor how to be rid of them.
Our foolhardiness can be concealed no longer. If my wits
don't befriend us at this pinch, either I or my poor master
must smart for it.

ANTIPHO. What puts him in such a flurry?

GETA, *to himself.* Then I've scarce a minute's time for laying
my plans. My old master's home!

ANTIPHO. What ill luck has come to town now?

GETA, *to himself.* When he comes to hear of it, how am I to
pacify him? If I speak, he'll be choleric; if I say nothing,
he'll nurse suspicions. As for excusing myself, I might as
well talk to the wind . . . Poor Geta! Alas for thee! Then,
in addition to these troubles, Mr Antipho is a great load
upon my spirits; 'tis him I pity, and am even more con-

cerned for. 'Tis he who keeps me here, else I'd have made a shift for myself well enough, and been revenged on the old man for his ill temper: I'd have snatched up a thing or two, and shown him a clean pair of heels.

ANTIPHO, *partly hearing.* What is the fellow talking of?

GETA, *to himself.* But where shall I find my master Antipho? Or where shall I look for him?

PHAEDRIA, *to Antipho.* He seeks for you, Cousin.

ANTIPHO. I fear he brings news of some shrewd misfortune.

PHAEDRIA. Pho! Are ye out of your wits?

GETA, *to himself.* I'll e'en get me home; 'tis ten to one that he's there.

Going off.

PHAEDRIA, *to* ANTIPHO. Let's call him back.

ANTIPHO. You, Sir, stay.

GETA, *not knowing him.* You show much presumption, Sir, whoever you are.

ANTIPHO. Geta, I say!

GETA, *turning about.* Od's me! 'Tis the very man I wanted.

ANTIPHO. Prithee, what's the news? Give it in a word, if ye can.

GETA. So I will.

ANTIPHO. Out with it, quick.

GETA. Just now at the water-side, I saw . . .

ANTIPHO. My father!

GETA. You've hit it.

ANTIPHO. Then I'm a dead man.

PHAEDRIA. 'Sdeath!

ANTIPHO. Prithee, what shall I do?

PHAEDRIA, *to* GETA. How's this?

GETA. I tell ye I saw his father, your uncle.

ANTIPHO. What course shall I follow to lift me out in this sudden misfortune? Ah! should my unlucky stars but rend me from dear Phanie's embraces, life would be a heavy burden to bear.

GETA. Since things are as they are, Sir, you ought to be the more upon your guard; for 'Faint heart never won fair lady.'

ANTIPHO. I'm quite distracted.

GETA. But considering your present circumstances, you've every reason to seem otherwise. For once your father sees ye down in the mouth, he'll be assured of your guilt.

PHAEDRIA. And he'll be in the right there.

ANTIPHO. I can't change my nature.

GETA. Suppose you were put in even worse straits . . .

ANTIPHO. Why, not being able to meet these, I could never meet those.

GETA. Pshaw! He's good for nothing, Mr Phaedria. Self-condemned already. Why should we trifle away our time with him? I'll e'en be jogging.

PHAEDRIA. And so will I.

They are going off.

ANTIPHO. Prithee, Geta! . . . Suppose I look thus . . .

He tries to assume a pleasant look.

Will this pass my father's scrutiny?

GETA. 'Tis not worth a farthing.

ANTIPHO. Nay, look again! What d'ye think of this?

Here he makes grimaces a good while and at last composes his countenance.

GETA. No.

ANTIPHO. What say ye to this, now?

GETA. Somewhere thereabouts.

ANTIPHO. And this?

GETA. That will do. Hold it, now! And be sure you answer him word for word, and let not his huffing and hectoring put you out of countenance.

ANTIPHO. I will even do what I can.

GETA. Say you were forced to the marriage by the laws of Athens and the Court's ruling. D'ye mark me?

He looks to one corner of the stage.

But what old man's yonder, at the farther end of the street?

ANTIPHO, *peeping.* 'Tis my father! O, I find I cannot stand my ground.

Going off.

GETA. What have ye a mind to do, Sir? Whither so fast? Stay, stay, I tell ye!

ANTIPHO. I know my own faults and frailty too well. I commit Phanie and my life into your hands!

Exit ANTIPHO.

PHAEDRIA. Prithee, Geta, what shall we do now?

GETA. Why, you must expect a drubbing, but poor Geta (if my stars don't deceive me) will be trussed up and lashed without mercy. Troth, I think we must even follow the same advice we gave to Mr Antipho.

PHAEDRIA. Hang your 'must'! Whatever you'd have me do, I'm at your service.

GETA. Don't ye remember, when we first began this enterprise, how ye agreed to manage it? You would admit that their plea was just and well founded—in fine, the clearest case in the world!

PHAEDRIA. That was our reply.

GETA. Why, then you must not unsay it. If you can think of a better or a finer course to take, let me hear of it!

PHAEDRIA. I'll do what I can.

GETA. Do you make the first attack. I'll lie in ambush as a reserve if ye are obliged to give ground.

PHAEDRIA. Very well.

Enter DEMIPHO *at a distance;* PHAEDRIA *and* GETA *move to one side upon observing him.*

DEMIPHO, *to himself.* . . . Is it come to this, then? My son Antipho marries without my consent? Surely a father's authority . . . But why do I name authority? The fear of my displeasure should have created some respect. What! has he no shame in him? O, impudent wickedness! And that hang-dog Geta his tutor, too . . .

GETA, *aside to* PHAEDRIA. So I'm brought in as the culprit.

DEMIPHO, *to himself*. Suppose they pretend that it was done against his will, that the law forced him into it . . . Well, I understand that, and grant the compulsion.

GETA, *aside*. Well said, well said!

DEMIPHO, *to himself*. But to yield so willingly, and without one word in his own defence! Did the law force him to silence as well?

PHAEDRIA, *to* GETA. That's a hard question.

GETA, *to* PHAEDRIA. Leave me alone to answer it.

DEMIPHO, *to himself*. I'm at a sad nonplus, things have happened so contrary to my expectations and belief. Then my passion runs away with me, so that I can't bring my mind to the common way of thinking. But in a calm we should be always sure to provide for a storm. One who comes home from a long journey ought to consider what dangers, losses and banishment may befall him. He may find his son debauched, his wife dead, his daughter dangerously ill. These are common accidents, and should surprise no man; whereas, if things fall out better than he expected, he may regard that as clear gain.

GETA, *aside to* PHAEDRIA. Troth, Sir, you wouldn't think how much wiser I am than this old fox, my master. I've forecast all my misfortunes, such as this: that when my master comes home, I must expect to beat hemp in Bridewell all the days of my life, to be whipped and shackled, or sent to delve in the fields. All this will be no news to me. If anything happens better than I expect, i' faith I shall look upon it as clear gain . . . But, why don't you go and sweeten him a little?

PHAEDRIA *moves towards* DEMIPHO.

DEMIPHO, *seeing* PHAEDRIA. Yonder comes my nephew Phaedria to meet me.

PHAEDRIA. Dear Uncle, your humble servant!

DEMIPHO. I'm glad to see thee, lad; but where's Antipho?

PHAEDRIA. You're welcome home, Sir.

DEMIPHO. I thank ye; but pray answer my question.

PHAEDRIA. He's very well, Sir; within call . . . But your affairs, Sir, do they succeed to your desire?

DEMIPHO, *sighing*. I wish they did.

PHAEDRIA. Why, what's amiss, Sir?

DEMIPHO. Amiss, Phaedria? You've arranged a fine match between you in my absence, haven't ye?

PHAEDRIA. Oh, ho! Is it that makes you so angry with him?

GETA, *aside*. A rare actor, i' faith!

DEMIPHO. And haven't I reason to be angry? I wish in my soul he were in my presence: he would see what it is to provoke a good natured father.

PHAEDRIA. Indeed, Sir, he has done nothing to deserve your anger.

DEMIPHO, *angrily*. Look ye here! They're all of a piece, they all hang on the same string; know one, know all!

PHAEDRIA. It is not so, Sir.

DEMIPHO. Does one commit roguery? Then, whip! the other's ready to bear out his lies. And contrariwise, too. So they take turns to help one another.

GETA, *aside*. The old man is nearer to the mark than he could guess.

DEMIPHO. If there was such a bargain between ye, you wouldn't take his part so readily as you do.

PHAEDRIA. Sir, if my Cousin Antipho had committed a fault to the prejudice of either his honour or his estate, I'd sooner die than plead for him, and leave him to suffer the just demerit of his crimes. But on the other hand, if some bold cheat should lay his snares to entrap an unwary youth, and should accomplish his designs, is the fault ours? Or should the judges? Who oft through envy take from the rich their right, and for pity give it to the poor.

GETA, *aside*. Were I not privy to this whole affair, I should think what he says to be as true as an oracle.

DEMIPHO. Can any judge in the world know a man's in the right, when he stands like a post, as Antipho did?

PHAEDRIA. He acted like a modest gentleman. For when he came in the open court, fear and modesty so surprised him, that he couldn't utter a word of what he had premeditated.

GETA, *aside*. An orator, i' faith. . . . But why don't I go and salute the old fogey . . .

Goes to DEMIPHO.

Dear Master, your humble servant, welcome home with all my heart!

DEMIPHO, *jeeringly*. Ho! Mr Pedagogue! The very prop of our family! The trustee over my son in my absence! I'm your humble servant too.

GETA. I hear, Sir, that you're pleased to blame us all undeservedly, and me that deserve least of all. For what would ye have had me do in the case when, as you know, Sir, the law won't admit a slave to plead or be a witness?

DEMIPHO. Pish! I grant all this; and more than that, I own the boy was bashful, and you a slave. But let the girl be never so close a kinswoman, there was no necessity for his having her. The law obliges him only to give her a portion, and let her look out for another husband. Your reason, pray! Why did he rather choose to marry a beggar wench?

GETA. Nay, 'twasn't reason we lacked, but money!

DEMIPHO. He might have borrowed it anywhere.

GETA. Anywhere, say ye? Sooner said than done.

DEMIPHO. Rather than fail, he should have borrowed it upon interest.

GETA. Ho, bravely spoken! As though anyone would have lent him money while you are alive.

DEMIPHO. Well! It shall never go thus, it mustn't be. Shall I suffer them to live as man and wife even a day longer? No, they deserve no kindness from me. . . . But I'd fain have this paltry rascal brought before me, or else be directed to where he lives.

GETA. You mean Phormio, Sir, don't ye?

DEMIPHO. Yes, the woman's chief supporter.

GETA. I'll fetch him to ye without delay.

DEMIPHO. But where's Antipho now?

GETA. Gone out, Sir.

DEMIPHO. Good nephew, do me the service of seeking him, and bringing him hither.

PHAEDRIA. I'm going by the shortest road.

Exit PHAEDRIA.

GETA, *aside*. To his mistress, he means.

Exit GETA.

DEMIPHO, *alone*. I'll just step home and return thanks to the Household Gods for my safe arrival; from thence I'll to the Piazza, and call some friends to stand by me in this business, that I mayn't be found unready when Phormio appears.

Exit DEMIPHO.

End of the Second Act

ACT THREE

Enter PHORMIO *and* GETA

PHORMIO, *entering*. How! Mr Antipho is playing at Bo-peep for fear of his father, say ye?

GETA. Very true.

PHORMIO. So then poor Phanie, his wife, is left in the lurch?

GETA. Even so.

PHORMIO. And the old man's enraged?

GETA. Yes, indeed.

PHORMIO, *to himself*. So then, poor Phormio! The burden lies all upon thy shoulders. Thou must take what comes of it, and brew as thou hast baked. To work then, old boy!

GETA. Prithee, about it then.

PHORMIO, *not heeding* GETA. Suppose he should ask me . . .

GETA. 'Tis only in you we trust.

PHORMIO, *aside, considering*. That's right. . . . And what if he should reply? . . .

GETA. 'Twas you who planned our policy.

PHORMIO, *still considering*. . . . Ay, that will do well.

GETA, *pulling him by the sleeve*. Prithee, help us out, then.

PHORMIO, *turning quick to* GETA. Prithee, decoy the old fox hither: I've all my traps ready laid for him.

GETA. Upon what design are ye now set?

PHORMIO. What would ye have me do? Ye want Phanie to continue as Mr Antipho's wife, and Mr Antipho cleared of all guilt, and the whole stream of the old man's rage turned upon myself?

GETA. Ay, that's the matter in a nutshell! Spoken like a courageous man and a true friend. But i' faith, honest Phormio, I fear this lion's heart of yours will bring you to the pillory at the last.

PHORMIO. Pshaw! Never fear that! I am no apprentice to my trade; I know where to set my feet. How many men d'ye think I have in my time beaten and left for dead—Athenian citizens as well as strangers? The oftener I exercised my hand, the greater skill I got; and pray when did ye ever hear of an action for assault and battery brought against me, and proved?

GETA. How comes that about?

PHORMIO. Pho! Your fowlers never aim at hawks or kites or other birds of mischief; but 'tis the harmless sort they are after, for profit, with no powder and shot wasted. In the same manner, those folk who have anything to lose stand in the most danger. As for me, 'tis well known that I've nothing to lose but my skin. You'll say perhaps: 'They might distrain upon your person.' But you'd be in the wrong there. They would think twice before they'd maintain such a devouring glutton as I am. And truth, I fancy they are in the right there. Why should they do me such an excellent good turn for a bad one?

GETA. Faith, my young master will ne'er be able to repay ye for this kindness.

PHORMIO. We vassals owe the princes who favour us more than our lives are worth. Isn't it a rare thing to feast free of cost, to perfume and bathe oneself, to have no trouble upon one's spirit, while another bears the trouble and charge of all? For you to have all things to your liking, to laugh and take your pleasure, to be honoured with the first cup, and set at the upper end of the table to eat of the puzzle-banquet while he sits and frets.

GETA. What d'ye mean by a puzzle-banquet?

PHORMIO. When there's such a plenty that ye puzzle your mind which dish to choose first, ye little rogue. And, considering how delicious and costly all these blessings are, how can ye call their provider less than a God on earth?

Enter DEMIPHO *at a distance, with* HEGIO, CRATINUS *and* CRITO.

GETA. Our old gentleman's hard upon us! Mind your head: the first onset will be the bloodiest of all! If you bear the brunt of that, you may afterwards drive him all about the field.

DEMIPHO, *to his followers*. Hark ye, my friends, was ever man treated in such a contemptuous fashion as I? . . . Your opinion, Gentlemen!

GETA. The man's in wrath.

PHORMIO, *softly*. Hold your tongue! 'S't! . . . I'll give him cause for wrath, I'll warrant ye.

Very loud.

O wonderful! Dares Demipho deny Phanie to be his kinswoman? Heavens bless us! . . . What, deny his own kindred?

GETA. He does indeed!

DEMIPHO. Yonder's our antagonist, I think. . . . Keep close, neighbours.

PHORMIO, *aloud*. Doesn't he know who her father was?

GETA. No.

PHORMIO. Denies that his name was Stilpho?

GETA. Yes, that he does.

PHORMIO, *aloud*. Ay, because Stilpho left Phanie nothing, Demipho disowns him as his kinsman, and speaks only evil of her. See what it is to be a covetous old hunks.

GETA, *pretending passion*. Be hanged to ye, dog! Dare ye call my master covetous?

DEMIPHO, *overhearing*. Abominable impudence! He flies to the attack, instead of skulking away.

PHORMIO, *aloud*. Now I can't blame young Mr Antipho for not knowing Stilpho; because he was an old poor man,

who lived by his labour in the country, where he hired a
small piece of ground from my father. How often would he
complain to me how basely Demipho, his kinsman, had
slighted him! And what sort of a man was this Stilpho,
that he should be treated thus? Why, one of the honestest
men that ever wore a head!

GETA. That is a tale ye'll have to prove in black and white.

PHORMIO. You be hanged! If I hadn't found Stilpho to be so
true a man, I should never have engaged our family in
such terrible feuds upon Phanie's account—this daughter-
in-law whom your master has now so ungenteelly slighted.

GETA. What, still abuse my master behind his back? Ye foul-
mouthed varlet!

PHORMIO. 'Tis no more than he deserves.

GETA. Say ye so, gaol-bird?

Unbuttons his collar, and clenches his fist at him.

DEMIPHO, *coming nearer.* Geta!

GETA, *not heeding* DEMIPHO. Abominable thief, damnable
cheat!

PHORMIO, *softly to* GETA. Prithee, give him an answer.

GETA, *turning about.* Who's that calls? . . . Oh! Sir . . .

DEMIPHO. Don't quarrel!

GETA. This varlet has been laying such base things to your
worship's charge, as none but a scoundrel would have
been guilty of.

DEMIPHO. Well, say no more of it.

To PHORMIO.

But hark ye, young man, by your good leave I'd ask ye
one civil question, if you'd please to return me an answer.
Pray, who was this friend of yours that you spoke of? Tell
me plainly. And how nearly did he say he was related
to me?

PHORMIO. Would you pump me as though you knew nothing
of the matter?

DEMIPHO. I deny all knowledge of him! If you affirm that I
do, prove it, and rub up my memory.

PHORMIO. You don't know one of your own flesh and blood?

DEMIPHO. You make me stark mad. Can't ye tell me his name?

PHORMIO. His name? With all my heart!

Pauses.

DEMIPHO. Why don't ye out with it, then?

PHORMIO, *softly to* GETA. Pox on't, how can this be? The name's slipped out of my head, as though I never heard it.

DEMIPHO. What's that you mutter?

PHORMIO, *softly to* GETA. If you remember the name I mentioned just now—prithee, prompt me . . .

Aloud to DEMIPHO.

Ha, ha, he . . . Why should I give you the name that you know so well already? You're trying to catch me out.

Here PHORMIO *laughs and speaks as loud as he can, that* GETA *may tell him the name and* DEMIPHO *not hear it.*

DEMIPHO. I scorn your words.

GETA, *softly to* PHORMIO. Stilpho, Stilpho.

PHORMIO. The name, ha . . . ha . . . he . . . But what care I? The name's Stilpho.

DEMIPHO. What say ye?

PHORMIO. I say, Stilpho; as if you didn't know him!

DEMIPHO. I'll take my corporal oath I know no such man, nor was I ever akin to any of that name.

PHORMIO. Is it possible that you aren't ashamed to say so? Had he left you a sousing sum of money . . .

DEMIPHO. The Devil take ye!

PHORMIO. . . . you'd have been the first to claim kinship and trace your pedigree back twenty generations.

DEMIPHO. Well! But if I had done so, I must have known which way she was my kinswoman. Therefore, prithee, do you the same: tell me how she's related to me.

GETA. Faith! well argued Sir . . .

Aside to PHORMIO.

Be careful how you reply, my friend.

PHORMIO. I proved the kinship, as clear as the sun, in open court, which was the proper place for such a disclosure. If I trusted to forged evidence, why didn't your son expose it?

DEMIPHO. Do not speak to me of my son! He has behaved himself worse than a changeling.

PHORMIO. Very well, Sir, you who are so wondrous wise! Go into court, and apply for a second hearing, since you play the King here, and claim sole prerogative of having the same case tried twice over.

DEMIPHO. Very well, then. I've been much abused in this business, yet rather than be plagued with law-suits and your impertinent tongue, let her pass for my kinswoman. I'll give her a marriage portion as the law requires.

Offers him money.

Here, take half a score of those and to the Devil with her!

PHORMIO. Ha . . . ha . . . he . . . A very pleasant man, i' faith!

DEMIPHO. What would you? Don't I make a very fair offer? Can't I claim the privilege of the common law?

PHORMIO. Is that what you think, sweet Sir? When you've taken a citizen's daughter as your wife, does the law allow ye to give her a whore's fee, and send her packing? Or doesn't it rather require that she should be married to her next of kin, and keep faithful to him lest a lack of substance should lead her into a trade that would be a scandal to her quality? And you are against that view, are ye?

DEMIPHO. Ay, ay, let her be married to her next of kin. But how is she akin to us, pray?

PHORMIO. Enough, enough! We needn't plead the case again.

DEMIPHO. I don't intend to do so; but I shall push hard till I've brought this business to an end.

PHORMIO. You'd be better off catching butterflies.

DEMIPHO. I say, I will do it.

PHORMIO. Besides, Sir, this business does not concern you. 'Tis your son who received the Court's order, not you. Your marrying-days were over long ago.

DEMIPHO. Then it must be supposed that my son is saying all that I now say. And if he won't agree, I'll turn him and his trull out of doors.

GETA, *aside.* Now his back's up.

PHORMIO. You had better take a counsellor's advice first.

DEMIPHO. Unlucky dog, are ye resolved to do me all the mischief in your power?

PHORMIO, *aside, to* GETA. He's damnably afraid, though he does all he can to conceal it.

GETA, *aside, to* PHORMIO. You are doing rarely.

PHORMIO, *to* DEMIPHO. Why don't ye endure with patience what can't be cured?

Jeering.

Come, act like a gentleman, that there may be a lasting friendship between us.

DEMIPHO. Pish! Do I care a fig for your friendship? Should I desire any closer acquaintance with such a rascal?

PHORMIO. If you and your son can but agree, you'll have a fine, tender woman to comfort you in your old age. Pray consider how swiftly the afternoon of your life is speeding by.

DEMIPHO. Pox! Let her comfort thee, not me! Take her, and the Devil go with ye both!

PHORMIO, *jeering.* Good Sir, moderate your passion!

DEMIPHO. Mark this, then, without any more ado: If you don't make all the haste you can, and remove your whore from my son's bed, I'll thrust her out of doors by the head and shoulders. That's my last word, Mr Knave.

PHORMIO. If ye offer her the least affront, I'll bring a heavy action for damages against you. And that's my last word, Mr Alderman!

Aside to GETA.

Hark ye, if they want me, you'll find me at home.

GETA, *softly to* PHORMIO. Well done!

Exit PHORMIO.

DEMIPHO. What a world of care and vexation has my son brought me into, by entangling himself and me in this unlucky match! . . . Nor can I get one glimpse of him to know what he will say, or how he will act . . . Run in, Geta, and see whether he's come back or no.

GETA. I will, Sir.

Exit GETA.

DEMIPHO. You see, gentlemen, how the case stands! What had I best do?

To HEGIO.

Your advice, Mr Counsellor.

HEGIO. Meaning me, Sir? I think Mr Cratinus is the fittest man to speak first, if you please.

DEMIPHO. Come on then, Mr Cratinus!

CRATINUS. Who, I, Sir?

DEMIPHO. Yes, you, Sir.

CRATINUS. I'd willingly advise ye for the best; I am of opinion, Sir, that what your son did in your absence should, in right and reason, be *ipso facto* null and void; and the law will support me in this.

DEMIPHO. Now for you, Mr Hegio.

HEGIO. I believe Mr Cratinus speaks as he thinks right. But as the saying is: 'So many men, so many minds'; and 'Everyone to his taste.' And in my opinion, what the law has once determined shouldn't be cancelled, and 'twould be a scandal to ask for any such thing.

DEMIPHO. Now for your opinion, Mr Crito.

CRITO. I beg time to consider upon it; 'tis a weighty affair.

HEGIO. Have ye any further occasion for our advice?

DEMIPHO. You've been of great assistance to me, i' faith.

Exeunt HEGIO, CRATINUS *and* CRITO.

DEMIPHO, *alone, looking after them.* So I'm more at sea now than ever I was.

Enter GETA.

GETA. They say, Sir, he isn't come back yet.

DEMIPHO. Then I'll even wait until my brother comes home; what advice he gives in this case, that I'll follow. I'll enquire at the waterside when his ship is expected.

Exit DEMIPHO.

GETA, *alone.* And I'll go see for Mr Antipho, and let him know how things go. . . . But look yonder, he comes in pudding-time.

Enter ANTIPHO *at a distance.*

ANTIPHO, *to himself.* In good truth, faint-hearted Antipho, thou art mightily to be blamed! What, run away, and leave thy very life and soul to the care of deputies? As though, forsooth, they'd take more care of thy business than thou thyself? Let other matters have gone how they would, Phanie at least ought to have been looked after, for fear the poor soul, who has lodged all her hopes and fortunes in thy hands, should come to any mischief from trusting in thee.

GETA, *goes up to him.* Faith, Sir, we were just praying heartily for ye—ay—praying backwards, because you slunk away and left us so sadly in the lurch.

ANTIPHO. 'Tis thee I have come to seek, Geta.

GETA. But for all that, we didn't flinch a handsbreadth.

ANTIPHO. Prithee, tell me in what posture my affairs stand, and to what I must trust. Does my father know anything of the main business?

GETA. Not a bit.

ANTIPHO. Is there any hope then?

GETA. Indeed, I can't tell.

ANTIPHO. Dear heart!

GETA. But Mr Phaedria pleaded like a counsellor for ye.

ANTIPHO. He has been very obliging.

GETA. As for Phormio, he has behaved himself like a hero, as his habit is.

ANTIPHO. What did he do?

GETA. Mad as your father was, this Phormio quite outhectored him.

ANTIPHO. God be thanked, Phormio!

GETA. And I also did my best.

ANTIPHO, *hugging him.* Ah, honest rogue! Faith, I'm obliged to ye all.

GETA. The first encounter was well fought, as I tell ye; and for the present our affairs prosper. Your father, it seems, will let the matter rest till your uncle comes home.

ANTIPHO. Why till then?

GETA. He says, that he'll follow his advice to the letter.

ANTIPHO. Ah Geta! How I dread my uncle's return, if I must stand or fall by his sentence alone.

GETA. Look, yonder's your cousin Phaedria.

ANTIPHO. Where?

GETA. Look ye; he's come out still hot from his old sweating-house.

Enter PHAEDRIA *and* DORIO; ANTIPHO *and* GETA *move on one side, and observe them.*

PHAEDRIA. Nay, good Dorio, hear me!

DORIO. The Devil I will!

PHAEDRIA. But one word!

DORIO. Pox! Don't tease me so.

PHAEDRIA. But do hear what I have to say.

DORIO. I'm sick from hearing the same thing a thousand times over.

PHAEDRIA. But I have something that you'll be glad to hear of.

DORIO. Well, let's hear it then.

PHAEDRIA. Can I not possibly prevail upon ye to wait but three short days?

DORIO *is going off, but* PHAEDRIA *holds him.*
Whither so fast, pray?

DORIO. I'd have chalked it up for a wonder, if you had made me any profitable new offer.

ANTIPHO, *to* GETA. Alas, I'm much afraid this bawd-master is doing himself no good.

GETA, *to* ANTIPHO. And so am I, too.

PHAEDRIA. You won't believe me then?

DORIO. That's well guessed.

PHAEDRIA. Suppose I pledged you my word?

DORIO. Mere stuff!

PHAEDRIA. You'd say 'twas the best day's work you ever did in your life.

DORIO. Idle talk.

PHAEDRIA. Come now, put me to the test: my time isn't so long.

DORIO. Cuckoo . . . cuckoo!

PHAEDRIA. You are my kinsman, my Father, my friend, my . . .

DORIO, *interrupting.* Tattle on, tattle on.

PHAEDRIA. Are ye of such a barbarous nature that neither pity nor plea can mollify ye?

DORIO. And are you, Sir, so senseless and shameless, as to think your gay words and fine flourishes shall ever cheat me out of what's my own?

ANTIPHO, *to* GETA. Truth, I'm sorry for him.

PHAEDRIA, *aside.* Alas, I'm convinced he has right on his side.

GETA, *to* ANTIPHO. How closely to his proper character each acts!

PHAEDRIA. And must this misfortune light upon me at a time when my cousin Antipho is in the very same trouble himself?

ANTIPHO *and* GETA *approach them.*

ANTIPHO, *to* PHAEDRIA. Ha! Cousin, what's the matter?

PHAEDRIA, *turning to him.* Ah, most fortunate cousin Antipho! The happiest man alive.

ANTIPHO. Who, I?

PHAEDRIA. In having the woman you love in your own custody; not tormented, like me, with such a villain as this.

ANTIPHO. In my custody, say ye? . . . Ay, indeed I have a

wolf by the ears, as the saying is. How to part from her
I know not, and how to keep her I know even less.

DORIO. My very case, by the mackins!

ANTIPHO, *to* DORIO. Courage, man, don't play the bawd-master
so half-heartedly.

To PHAEDRIA.

But, prithee, what has he done?

PHAEDRIA. Dorio? . . . Why, like the hard-hearted wretch
he is, he has gone and sold my dearest Pamphila.

GETA. How! Sold her?

ANTIPHO. Sold her, say ye?

PHAEDRIA. So indeed he has.

DORIO. What crime is this, that a man should make money
by sale of his own wares!

PHAEDRIA. I can't prevail upon him to wait even three days,
and break off the bargain until such time as I receive the
money my friends promised to lend me . . .

To DORIO.

If I don't pay it ye then, you need not wait a minute
longer for me.

DORIO. You'll crack my brain-pan with your importunities.

ANTIPHO. He asks no unreasonable thing, Dorio. What are
three days? Prithee, be not so hard-hearted; the favour
shall be requited you double, take my word for it.

DORIO. Mere shams.

ANTIPHO, *to* PHAEDRIA. Can you suffer your mistress to be
banished from this pleasant town?

To DORIO.

And can you have the heart to part such fervent lovers?

DORIO. All this is neither my fault, nor yours.

GETA, *aside*. A plague on thee for a rascal!

DORIO. Look ye: many a month have I had patience with
you, though it went against the grain. You've brought me
nothing but court-promises, crocodile's tears, and a beggar's purse. Now, on the other hand, I've gotten a customer

who will pay me freely and with dry eyes. Therefore, Sir, *Cede Majoribus*, I say: make way for your betters!

ANTIPHO. But in good earnest, was there not a day set for my cousin to have her?

PHAEDRIA. There was so.

DORIO. Do I deny it?

ANTIPHO. Is that day past then?

DORIO. No, but another's day has come before it.

ANTIPHO. Aren't ye ashamed of your knavery?

DORIO. Not so long as it brings me good business.

GETA. Sordid villain!

PHAEDRIA. Dorio, can you so abuse your conscience?

DORIO. I am what I am; and if 'tis to your taste, then make use of me.

ANTIPHO. Why should you cheat him thus?

DORIO. I' faith, Mr Antipho, 'tis rather he who cheats me! He knew well enough what I was, but I took him for an honest gentleman; so that he has deceived me, whereas I am for all the world just as I used to be. But let that pass; thus much I'll do. Tomorrow morning the Captain says he'll bring me the money. Now, Mr Phaedria, if you'll bring it first, I'll follow my own rule: First come, first served. And so goodbye to ye.

Exit DORIO.

PHAEDRIA *walks to and fro dejectedly.* What shall I do now? Where shall poor I, who now am worse than nothing, scrape up such a sum at so short a notice? If I could but have got him to wait three days! The money was promised me by that time.

ANTIPHO, *to* GETA. What, shall we leave our friend in such a miserable case, when today, as you told me, he pleaded my cause so handsomely? Shan't we requite his kindness in time of need?

GETA. I confess 'tis but right and reason that we should.

ANTIPHO. Come on, then; you are a man who keeps his head above water.

GETA. What would ye have me do?

ANTIPHO. Find him the money.

GETA. That I would do with all my heart; but where?

ANTIPHO. My father's at home.

GETA. That I know, but what then?

ANTIPHO. Pho! A word to the wise is enough.

GETA. Is it so, Sir?

ANTIPHO. Yes, indeed.

GETA. Pretty counsel, i' faith! You may ask him yourself if you please. I shall have done handsomely if I escape with a whole skin upon your own account. Now must I needs venture my neck upon your cousin's account too?

ANTIPHO. That's what I ask of ye.

PHAEDRIA. What, Geta! Am I nobody in your eyes?

GETA. Not so, neither. But do you think it nothing, now that we've stirred up the old gentleman's anger against us all, that we should provoke him further beyond all hopes of reconciliation?

PHAEDRIA. Shall my rival carry away my dearest Pamphila, and shall I watch while he ships her oversea? Ah, Cousin, speak with me while yet you may; give me one farewell look before I depart.

ANTIPHO. Why, Sir, what new crotchet is this? Prithee, tell me.

PHAEDRIA. I'll traverse sea and land in pursuit of her, or perish in the attempt; that I'm resolved upon.

GETA. A pleasant journey to ye, Sir; but mark well where ye tread.

ANTIPHO. Prithee, Geta, see if thou canst help him a little.

GETA. Help him! Pray how?

ANTIPHO. I beseech you to find a way, lest he do what shall afterwards make us both repent, more or less.

GETA. I am in search of such a way . . .

Ponders.

Very well, I have it. He's out of danger now, unless I am

mistaken. But still I'm afraid that my poor hide will smart for it.

ANTIPHO. Don't be afraid; we'll stand or fall with thee in any event.

GETA, *to* PHAEDRIA. Well, how much money do ye want? Tell me.

PHAEDRIA. Fourscore guineas or so. That's all.

GETA. Fourscore guineas! Whoop! Whoop! She's a plaguily high-priced bit, Mr Phaedria.

PHAEDRIA. No, she's the best pennyworth ever offered for public sale.

GETA. Come! No more; you shall have the money.

PHAEDRIA, *hugging him.* Excellent rogue!

GETA. Come, let me alone.

PHAEDRIA. I need it at once.

GETA. And you shall have it at once; but Phormio must second me in the design.

PHAEDRIA, *to* GETA. Pray step to his house, and desire him to await me.

ANTIPHO. He's ready, I warrant ye. Lay what load you will upon Phormio—he'll bear it. He's the only man in a thousand who stays true to his friends.

GETA. Let's away to him in haste then.

ANTIPHO. Can I do ye any kindness in this matter?

GETA. None at all. Pray go home and comfort your poor wife. I know she's almost dead with fear. . . . Why d'ye stay Sir?

ANTIPHO. I know nothing I'd do more willingly.

Exit ANTIPHO.

PHAEDRIA. How will ye set to work in this business?

GETA. I'll unfold my design as we go along; therefore pray be moving.

Exeunt both.

End of the Third Act

ACT FOUR

Enter DEMIPHO *and* CHREMES

DEMIPHO, *entering.* Well, have ye dispatched the business that took ye to Lemnos, Brother? And have ye brought your daughter back with ye?

CHREMES. No.

DEMIPHO. Why didn't ye?

CHREMES. Because when her mother saw that I stayed longer here than ordinary, and that the girl was of a ripe age for marriage, she grew impatient of delay. She took ship with her family, and (as I'm informed) sailed hither in search after me.

DEMIPHO. When you heard of this, how came you to tarry so long behind them?

CHREMES. Alas! I was sick.

DEMIPHO. How sick? Of what disease?

CHREMES. That's an idle question! To have passed the age of threescore is disease in all conscience sufficient. But the master of the ship that brought them over has told me they all landed safe.

DEMIPHO. That is good news. But, Brother, have ye heard of the misfortune that befell my son in my absence?

CHREMES. Ay, truly; a misfortune that has broke the neck of all my designs. For, should I offer my daughter in marriage to a stranger, I must tell the whole story, how I came by her, and by whom; but you, I know, are as faithful to my interests as I could be myself. A stranger who agreed to be my son-in-law, would hold his tongue, as long as we were good friends together; but if ever he and I fell out, he'd know more by half than I'd have him know. And I should be horribly afraid that the business might come to my wife's ear; for if it does, I shall have no remedy but take to my heels and be gone. To speak the truth, I have only one friend in the whole family, and that is myself.

DEMIPHO. I'm aware of your hard case, Brother, and 'tis a great trouble to me, but I'll leave no stone unturned till I've shown myself as good as my word.

They walk aside.

Enter GETA *at a distance.*

GETA, *to himself.* Never in my life did I set eyes on a craftier whore's-bird than this Phormio! I went to the bastard, to tell him that we wanted ready money, and how we proposed to angle for it. Well, I had scarce gaped open my lips, when he caught my meaning. He was tickled at the fancy, clapped my shoulders, asked where old Mr Demipho could be found, and kneeling on his marrow-bones thanked the Gods a thousand times, that they had given him an opportunity to show himself as much Mr Phaedria's friend as he had been Mr Antipho's. I bade him wait for me at the Piazza, where I'd bring the old cully along to him.

Seeing DEMIPHO.

Look, there he is! . . . But who's that looking over his left shoulder? . . . O, the Devil! Mr Phaedria's father? Pish! What a fool am I to be afraid of that? What could be better than to catch two woodcocks in the snare, instead of one? I'm sure 'tis profitable to have two strings to one's bow. I'll try first to draw blood from Demipho, as I designed. If I succeed, well; if not, then have at the new-comer!

Enter ANTIPHO, *observing the rest from another part of the stage.*

ANTIPHO, *to himself.* I watch every minute for this Geta's return . . . Hah! yonder are my uncle and my father, laying their heads together. 'Sdeath! how I dread what they may hatch to my ruin.

GETA, *aside.* I'll go to them.

Approaches that part of the stage where DEMIPHO *and* CHREMES *are.*

Why! my master Chremes!

CHREMES. Honest Geta, how is it?

GETA. You're heartily welcome home, Sir.

CHREMES. I thank you.

GETA. How goes the world with you, Sir? Doubtless upon your return here, you find, as usual, many alterations.

CHREMES. Too many, indeed!

GETA. Yes, yes! Then you've heard of Mr Antipho's business, I suppose?

CHREMES. The whole sorry tale.

GETA, *to* DEMIPHO. Did you unfold it to him, Sir? . . . Ay, wasn't it an abominable thing to be so treated, Mr Chremes?

DEMIPHO. 'Twas upon this very point that he and I were just discoursing.

GETA. In truth, Sir, my mind has been hammering upon the same thing, and I fancy I've found an expedient.

DEMIPHO, *hastily.* How, Geta? What expedient?

GETA. Just as I parted from you, by chance whom should I meet but Phormio?

CHREMES. Who? Phormio?

GETA. Yes; he who is the young woman's . . .

CHREMES. Oh, I know him.

GETA. It came into my head to feel the weight of his purse. I took him aside: 'Prithee, Phormio,' said I, 'hadn't ye better end this quarrel by fair means, rather than foul? My master's a free-hearted gentleman, and one that hates law-suits; but i' faith, if he had listened to his legal friends, he'd have kicked his daughter-in-law to the Devil long before this time . . .'

ANTIPHO, *behind, overhearing.* What does the rogue mean? What is he at?

GETA. Says I to Phormio: 'I'll warrant that ye think the law could punish him for so doing? Pish! We've had counsellors' advice upon that business already; and, take my word for it, Phormio, if you once begin a suit with Mr Demipho, he has so ready a tongue, he'll make you smart for your trouble. And even suppose he should lose the action, 'tis no hanging matter, and a little money will put all to rights again.' This discourse of mine took him down a peg lower: 'Here's only you and myself,' I continued. 'Prithee, good boy, tell me plainly how much money you ask: that my master need not venture upon any tiresome lawsuit; that the girl be taken off our hands; and that you plague us no further . . .'

ANTIPHO, *aside.* What? Has Old Nick bewitched the fellow?

GETA. 'If you will but propose anything that's just and reasonable,' says I to him, 'I'm sure he's such a civil gentleman that scarcely two words between ye will close the matter.'

DEMIPHO. Who gave you commission to say all this?

CHREMES. Pho! He couldn't have spoken better if we had prompted him ourselves.

ANTIPHO, *aside.* All's lost.

CHREMES. On with your story!

GETA. At first he talked like a madman.

CHREMES. Why, what sum did he name?

GETA. The Devil and all! Whatever his wild fancy pleased.

CHREMES. Let's hear it, though.

GETA. He talked of two or three hundred guineas.

CHREMES. As many Devils take him! What, has he no conscience?

GETA. I asked him that very question. 'Listen, my friend,' said I, 'suppose that Mr Demipho had a daughter of his

own to marry, would he give her so large a portion as
that? He's no better off, it seems, for having none, now
that you force him to provide a portion for Phanie . . .'
To be short, omitting certain impertinencies, at last he
comes to the point. 'I had a mind,' said he, 'from the very
first, to marry my friend's daughter, which was no unreasonable design; for I foresaw the trouble that would over-
take the girl if she married into a rich family. For want
of a marriage portion to sustain her, she would be a slave,
not a wife. Now: to be plain with ye, I need a wife who
will bring me enough money to pay off my debts. Now,
therefore, if Mr Demipho will offer as large a portion with
Phanie as I'm likely to receive from the father of the
woman I'm already engaged to, why, I'll choose her before any woman alive.'

ANTIPHO, *aside.* I can't make head or tail of this—whether it
be foolery or knavery—whether the man knows what he
does, or whether not.

DEMIPHO. And suppose him to have pawned body and soul,
must we redeem them?

GETA. 'I've mortgaged,' continued Phormio, 'a piece of ground
for twenty-five pounds.'

DEMIPHO. Well, well, that is little enough. I'll pay it willingly
to be rid of the wench.

GETA. 'And an old house or two, for another twenty-five
pounds.'

DEMIPHO, *angrily.* Pox on him, that's too much by half!

CHREMES. Prithee, less noise! I'll lift those houses out of
mortgage.

GETA. 'Then,' quoth he, 'my wife must have a maid, we must
lay in more household stuff, and provide a good handsome
wedding. These things, put all together, will come to
twenty-five pounds more.'

DEMIPHO. He shall bring six hundred actions against me before I'll part with a groat! Shall the paltry rascal make a
butt of me?

Walks about in a passion.

CHREMES. Good Brother, be pacified! I'll lay down the money, if you can only get your son in the mood to marry . . . the girl we have chosen for him.

ANTIPHO, *aside.* Alas for me! Ah, Geta! Thy treacheries have undone me.

CHREMES. Since it is upon my account that Phanie must be turned out, why should I not pay the costs and charges?

GETA. 'Let me know their minds as soon as ye can,' said Phormio, 'whether they agree to let me have her or no, that I may confidently clear myself of the other marriage— for the girl's friends are fully resolved to pay down her portion this very day.'

CHREMES. He shall have it on the nail. Let him break off that match, and take Phanie instead.

DEMIPHO. And the Devil take him into the bargain!

CHREMES. I've most luckily brought with me the rent of my wife's farm on Lemnos. I'll take that, and tell her that you had occasion to borrow it.

Exeunt CHREMES *and* DEMIPHO.

ANTIPHO *comes up to* GETA.

ANTIPHO. Hark ye, Mr Rogue!

GETA. Ha, Sir!

ANTIPHO. D'ye know what you have done?

GETA. Yes; parted both the old fools from their money.

ANTIPHO. Is that enough, think ye?

GETA. Faith, Sir, I can't tell, 'twas surely what you ordered me?

ANTIPHO. Dog! Do ye dare chop logic with me?
Kicks him.

GETA. What d'ye mean, Sir?

ANTIPHO. Why, your roguery has brought matters to such a pass, that now I may go hang myself. Let Heaven, Hell and Earth confound and damn thee, as an example to all villains! My lords and ladies, if ever you want anything to be well done, and overdone and destroyed in the doing,

I'll recommend ye to this villain here. . . . What occasion had you to rip up the old sore, and bring my dear Phanie's name into question? You've inspired my father with new hopes of turning her away. And, sweet Sir, do you not understand that should Phormio accept the portion, he must marry her, and what then will become of me?

GETA. He'll be hanged before he marries her.

ANTIPHO, *scornfully.* I believe you. And when they ask him to return their money, he'll rather go to jail than betray us, I warrant ye!

GETA. There are many ways of spoiling a story: and one is omission. The best part of this you've omitted, and only mentioned the worst. Now, pray, hearken to me! If Phormio receives the portion, he's obliged to marry her, as you say . . . that I own; but then time must be allowed him for preparing the wedding, for inviting guests, for offering his oblations. In the meantime, Mr Phaedria's friends will raise the money they promised him, which Phormio may use to refund the old gentleman.

ANTIPHO. How so? Upon what pretext?

GETA. Pretext? O, he has a thousand such in his wallet! Prodigies, for an example. He'll say: 'Ah, what ill prodigies have I seen since we made this bargain! A strange black yelping dog ran into my house! A serpent swam down the water-spout from the roof. My speckled hen crowed. The priests to whom I related these horrid signs charged me to meddle with no new business till winter.' These are as good pretexts as any in the world. Phormio shall order the matter thus, believe me.

ANTIPHO. I trust he will . . .

GETA. He will indeed—take my word for it. . . . But here comes your father! Withdraw now, and tell Mr Phaedria that the money's safe in our hands.

Exit ANTIPHO.

Enter at another part of the stage DEMIPHO, *with a bag of money, and* CHREMES.

DEMIPHO, *entering.* Be content, I say! I'll take care he shan't cheat us: I'll not give him a farthing, except in the presence of witnesses. It must be perfectly understood for what this payment is made.

GETA, *aside, overhearing.* How cautious our King Solomon is when there's no need to be so!

CHREMES. Troth, I am with you there, Brother! But make haste, while the fit is upon him! If the other woman should chance to arrive before us, he may go back upon his word.

GETA. You are in the right there, Sir.

DEMIPHO. Lead me to his house, Geta.

GETA. I am ready, Sir.

CHREMES. When you've dispatched that business, pray step over to my wife, and ask her to discourse with Phanie before we pack the girl off. Let her say: 'Good child, you have no cause to be angry if we marry you to Phormio, since he's the fitter match, being more intimately acquainted with you than we are.' Let her add: 'Nor have we done contrary to our duty, but given him as good a portion as he demanded.'

DEMIPHO. Pshaw! What the deuce is all this to you?

CHREMES. O, a great deal, Brother.

DEMIPHO. Isn't it enough for a man to do his duty, without asking for the whole world's commendation?

CHREMES. I'd willingly have the girl's consent, though, to forestall any complaint that she has been turned out of doors.

DEMIPHO. I can tell her all this myself.

CHREMES. It would come better from a woman, though.

DEMIPHO. I'll call upon your wife, then.

Exit DEMIPHO *and* GETA.

CHREMES, *alone.* I'm wondering now what corner of the town to search for my daughter, her mother, and the other Lemnians with them.

Enter SOPHRONA *out of* DEMIPHO'S *house.*

SOPHRONA, *to herself.* What shall I do? . . . What friend shall I consult, poor fool that I am? To whom shall I confide a secret of such weighty importance? Or where shall I look for assistance! . . . I'm sadly afraid that my poor mistress will be ill-treated indeed for accepting my counsel, for I hear that the young gentleman's father takes it very ill.

CHREMES, *aside*. What miserable old creature is that? One from my brother's household, it would seem . . .

SOPHRONA, *to herself*. 'Twas nothing but poverty that forced me to do what I did. Though I doubted whether the match were good in law, yet I advised her to it merely to avoid starving.

CHREMES, *aside*. In good truth, unless I'm mightily out of my guess, and if my eye-sight don't deceive me, 'tis my daughter's nurse.

SOPHRONA, *to herself*. Nor can we as yet . . .

CHREMES, *aside*. What had I best do in the case?

SOPHRONA, *to herself*. . . . find out the father.

CHREMES, *aside*. Had I best speak to her, or tarry here, and pick some crumb of sense out of her rambling talk?

SOPHRONA, *to herself*. If I could find him out, my mind would be at rest.

CHREMES, *aside*. 'Tis she, for certain . . .

Aloud.

I'll go talk to her.

SOPHRONA. Whose voice is that, pray?

CHREMES. Nurse Sophrona!

SOPHRONA. And knows my name, too!

CHREMES. Take a look at me!

SOPHRONA, *turning*. Mercy o' my soul! 'Tis Mr Stilpho!

CHREMES, *winking at her*. No, not he.

SOPHRONA. What, deny your own name?

CHREMES, *softly*. Prithee, Nurse, come a little farther from that door; and not a word more of Stilpho.

SOPHRONA. No, Sir! But please your worship, aren't you he whom you always said you were?

CHREMES, *going from his own door.* 'S't! 'S't!

SOPHRONA. What? I hope, Sir, you aren't afraid of this door.

CHREMES. No; but I've a mad woman there, shut in a cage. And I once gave myself a nickname, for fear some of you should indiscreetly blab my secrets, and she might smell a rat.

SOPHRONA. And truth, that's the reason we poor souls could never hear any tidings of ye here in town.

CHREMES. Prithee, tell me what business you had at that house you came out of? And where have you left your mistresses?

SOPHRONA, *sighing.* Lack-a-day!

CHREMES. Hah! What's the matter? They aren't dead, I hope?

SOPHRONA, *weeps.* Your daughter is alive; but the poor creature her mother lately broke her heart with grief and died.

CHREMES. That's bad news, indeed!

SOPHRONA. But I, a poor forlorn old woman, married your daughter as well as I could, to the young gentleman of that house.

CHREMES. What! To Antipho?

SOPHRONA. Yes, Sir, to him.

CHREMES, *angrily.* How! Has he got two wives then?

SOPHRONA. How so, I beseech ye? He never married more than this one.

CHREMES. What's become of her that passed as his kinswoman?

SOPHRONA. Sir, your daughter is that same person.

CHREMES. How!

SOPHRONA. 'Twas only a contrivance of ours, to let him marry her without a portion, since he loved her.

CHREMES, *aside.* Bless me! How often do things fall out by chance, which we lack the heart to wish for! Upon my coming home, I've found my daughter settled with the man I chose for her: all just as I could have wished. The very thing that my brother and I aimed at, this old woman, without any hint from either, has most cunningly hit upon.

SOPHRONA. Now, Sir, you had best see what's to be done in the case. The young gentleman's father is come home, and they say that he highly resents the marriage.

CHREMES, *interrupting*. All's safe enough. . . . But in the name of goodness, I conjure ye not to let any living soul know she's my daughter.

SOPHRONA. Not from me, Sir.

CHREMES. Come along, ye shall hear all presently.

Exeunt both.

End of the Fourth Act

ACT FIVE

Enter DEMIPHO *and* GETA

DEMIPHO. If knaves thrive in their knavery, we can blame none but ourselves; for we must, forsooth, pretend to be genteel and generous. But we shouldn't have 'out-run the constable', as the saying is. Not content to be cheated by him, must we throw the rascal a good lump of money into the bargain, for him to live on till he can play us another dog's trick.

GETA. Ay, so it seems.

DEMIPHO. We managed our business with this rascal like a couple of fools!

GETA. Nay, 'tis managed well enough, provided he keeps to his word, and marries the woman.

DEMIPHO. Is there still any danger of that?

GETA. Faith, Sir, he's such a wavering sort of a fellow that I can't tell; but he may renege.

DEMIPHO. The Devil! He renege?

GETA. That I can't tell, Sir; 'tis but a supposition of mine.

DEMIPHO. I'll do as my brother would have me. I'll fetch his wife to talk with the young woman . . . Do you, Geta, go in and warn the girl of her coming.

Exit DEMIPHO.

GETA, *alone*. We've coined money for Mr Phaedria; the two

old gentlemen are as quiet as lambs. Care has been taken
that Phanie shan't stir a foot out of our house for awhile
. . . But what next, friend Geta? What's to be done now?
. . . Thou art as deep in the dirt as ever; and, like a
tinker, hast made two holes in the kettle from mending
one . . . 'Tis true; there's a sound drubbing has been put
off for a day or two longer; but i' faith thou wilt receive it,
and with interest too, if thou dost not look about thee . . .
Well, I'll go home and teach Phanie her lesson, that she
mayn't be surprised by Phormio's behaviour, or by what
Nausistrata tells her.

Exit GETA, *and as he goes off, enter* DEMIPHO, *leading in*
CHREMES'S *wife*, NAUSISTRATA.

DEMIPHO, *entering*. . . . Come on, then; and pray, Madam,
make use of your fine knack of eloquence now, that the
girl mayn't be affronted but be persuaded to do what we
wish, both freely and willingly.

NAUSISTRATA. So I will, Brother.

DEMIPHO. Let your endeavours be as helpful to me now, as
your purse was before.

NAUSISTRATA. I should be glad to please ye; but in truth,
Brother, 'tis all along of my naughty man's carelessness
that I can't do so handsomely as I otherwise might.

DEMIPHO. How so, pray?

NAUSISTRATA. Why, in truth, by his ill management he gets
scarce a farthing's worth of profit from the estate my father left me. My father used to make nigh four hundred
pounds a year of it. . . . Bless me! What a difference
there can be between man and man!

DEMIPHO. Nigh four hundred pounds a year, say ye?

NAUSISTRATA. Yes indeed, and when corn and oil sold at a
lower rate by far than now.

DEMIPHO. Very strange!

NAUSISTRATA. You wonder at it, I warrant ye?

DEMIPHO. Indeed, I can't forbear.

NAUSISTRATA. Would I had been a man! I'd have shown him . . .

DEMIPHO, *jeeringly.* Ay, ay, so you would.

NAUSISTRATA. How I would have . . .

DEMIPHO, *interrupting.* Spare yourself, good sister, lest you weary yourself ere you encounter the young woman. Perhaps she'll be too quick for ye, else, at the use of your own weapon.

NAUSISTRATA. I'll be ruled by ye . . . But here comes my good man from your house!

Enter CHREMES *and goes up to* DEMIPHO, *not observing his wife.*

CHREMES. Ho! Brother, have ye paid the money yet, or no?

DEMIPHO. I did that a little while ago.

CHREMES. I wish you hadn't . . .

Sees NAUSISTRATA *and starts, aside.*

'Sdeath, my wife! I had almost said too much.

DEMIPHO. Why d'ye wish I hadn't, Brother?

CHREMES. Nothing, all's well.

DEMIPHO. But hark ye, did ye tell Phanie upon what account your wife was coming to her?

CHREMES. The whole tale.

DEMIPHO. Well, and what says she?

CHREMES. She can't be persuaded to agree.

DEMIPHO. Soho? Why can't she?

CHREMES. Because of the love that is between her and your son.

DEMIPHO. Pish! What's that to us?

CHREMES. O, very much. . . . Besides, I've found that her tale is true. She is indeed our kinswoman.

DEMIPHO. How! are you mad too?

CHREMES. You'll find it as I say: I never speak but upon good grounds; pray recollect yourself a little.

DEMIPHO. Certainly you are mad.

NAUSISTRATA. Good Brother Demipho, you wouldn't wrong a kinswoman, would ye?

DEMIPHO. She's none of mine!

CHREMES. Don't say so; her father went by another name, and that bred your mistake.

DEMIPHO. What! Didn't she know her own father?

CHREMES. Yes, marry she did!

DEMIPHO. Why didn't he call himself by his own name?

CHREMES, *aside to* DEMIPHO. Will ye neither believe nor understand me?

DEMIPHO. How should I, if you won't tell me . . .

CHREMES, *winks imploringly.* You'll spoil all.

NAUSISTRATA. I can't imagine what this business means.

DEMIPHO. Faith, nor I.

CHREMES. Must ye needs know all? As I hope for mercy, there's none so close akin to her as you and I.

DEMIPHO. Bless my soul! Let's all go in together; I must know all or nothing.

CHREMES. Hold!

DEMIPHO. What's the matter?

CHREMES. Have I got so little credit with you, Brother?

DEMIPHO. Would ye have me credit you without searching any further into the business? . . . Well, be it so then; but to whom, in that case, will ye marry your friend's daughter?

CHREMES. She'll do well enough.

DEMIPHO. Must we send her away, then?

CHREMES. Why not?

DEMIPHO. And keep this creature here?

CHREMES. Yes.

DEMIPHO. Well, Sister, you may go home again, if you wish.

NAUSISTRATA. Truth, I think 'twould be much better to keep her, than part with her; for when I first saw this Phanie, she looked very much like a gentlewoman.

Exit NAUSISTRATA.

DEMIPHO. Now, what's all this business?

CHREMES, *looking after* NAUSISTRATA, *fearfully*. Is the door well shut?

DEMIPHO. Yes.

CHREMES. Wonderful! The best luck in the world. I find 'tis my own daughter who's married to your son.

DEMIPHO. Hah! Is it possible?

CHREMES. This is no safe place to tell ye.

DEMIPHO. Step into my house, then.

CHREMES. But hark ye, I wouldn't have even Antipho and Phaedria know anything of this.

Exeunt both.

Enter, at another part of the stage, ANTIPHO *alone.*

ANTIPHO. Let my own concerns go how they will, 'tis a comfort at least that matters go so well with my cousin. 'Tis admirable if a man can so rule his appetite, that a small matter shall please him when his fortune is at the lowest ebb. No sooner had my cousin Phaedria received the money, but his cares are over; for my part I know no way to free myself from mine. If this business be concealed, I shall always live in fear; if disclosed, infamy will be my reward. . . . I couldn't dare go home, but that I nourish some small hopes of embracing my dear Phanie once more. . . . But where shall I meet with Geta, to learn from him what will be the most convenient time for showing myself to my father?

Enter PHORMIO *at a distance.*

PHORMIO, *to himself*. I've received the cash, paid off the bawd-master, brought away the girl, and taken care that Phaedria shall now enjoy her as his own, since she's out of her slavery at last. I've one thing which must still be dispatched: that is, to get leave of absence from these two old curmudgeons. I must set aside a few days for toping and diversion.

ANTIPHO. Look, here's Phormio. . . . How goes it?

PHORMIO. What, Sir?

ANTIPHO. What's my cousin Phaedria about? Does he now think to play the epicure in love?

PHORMIO. He's going to act the part you chose.

ANTIPHO. Prithee, what part?

PHORMIO. That of keeping out of his old daddy's clutches. And he begs you'd act his former part by pleading his cause; for he and I are to sing Old Rose together. . . . I am going to tell the old gentlemen, that I am bound for Sunio Fair, to buy the little slave Geta told 'em of—so that when they see I'm not in town, they mayn't think I am making their money fly. . . . But your door opens!

ANTIPHO. Prithee, tell me who comes out?

PHORMIO. 'Tis Geta.

Enter GETA *from* DEMIPHO'S *in great haste, with a cloak in his hand.*

GETA, *to himself.* Thou blessed, blessed Goddess Fortune! How much is my master Antipho obliged to thee for this day's work.

ANTIPHO, *to* PHORMIO. What means the fellow?

GETA, *to himself.* And from how many ill winds hast thou sheltered us who are his friends? . . . But why do I loiter, and not put on my cloak? Why don't I run to seek him out, and let him know how things have gone?

Puts on his short cloak and struts about.

ANTIPHO. D'ye understand what he says?

PHORMIO. Do you, Sir?

ANTIPHO. Not a word.

PHORMIO. Nor I, neither.

GETA, *to himself, going off.* I'll go to old Dorio's, for there they are sure to be.

ANTIPHO. Soho, Geta!

GETA, *not recognizing him.* Soho, to you too! 'Tis nothing strange nor new for a man of my condition to be interrupted in the middle of his journey.

ANTIPHO. Why, Geta!

GETA. Faith, but I keep on my way for all your impertinence.

ANTIPHO. Won't ye stay, then?

GETA. Sirrah, you shall be kicked.

Aside.

Some saucy scullion or other that calls me thus.

ANTIPHO. You shall be served with the same sauce, if ye don't stay, ye dog.

GETA. This must be someone knows me very well, since he is so free of his compliments.

Turning about.

But can that truly be Mr Antipho? 'Tis he, by the Gods!

PHORMIO, *to* ANTIPHO. Go fetch him to me.

ANTIPHO *goes to* GETA. What's the news with you?

GETA. O, Sir! the happiest man this day alive! Without doubt you are the darling of the skies.

ANTIPHO. So would I gladly think myself, did ye but give me some reason to believe it.

GETA. Wait until I plunge ye head and ears into the dish of joy!

ANTIPHO. You kill me with your airs of mystery!

PHORMIO. Be damned to your preambles—say quickly what you have to say.

GETA. Oh! . . . Art thou here too, old rock?

PHORMIO. Yes; but why this fooling?

GETA, *to* PHORMIO. Observe then: Hem! hem! . . . As soon as we gave you the money at the Piazza, we went straight home.

To ANTIPHO.

And . . . on the way home my master sent me to your Lady Phanie.

ANTIPHO. For what?

GETA. Nay, that's a question needs no answer—'tis nothing pertinent to our business, Sir . . . Just as I was going into your lady's apartment, her boy Mida runs up to me, catches me fast by the cloak, and pulls me back. I turned

about, and asked him what he meant. He told me nobody
must come nigh his mistress; that Sophrona had just now
brought old Chremes, Mr Demipho's brother, to the house;
and that there they were all within together. At that word,
I stole up to the door a-tip-toe . . .

Showing how.

. . . stood close up to it, held my breath, laid my ear to
the key-hole, thus, and very attentively listened to their
discourse.

ANTIPHO. O brave Geta!

GETA. There did I hear the pleasantest things in the world
that, by George, I could hardly forbear from a huzza.

PHORMIO. For what?

GETA. For what d'ye think?

ANTIPHO. I can't guess.

GETA. And such a prodigious wonderful story, too. . . .
'Slid, your uncle is found to be your spouse's own father!

ANTIPHO. Hah! What's that?

GETA. He had formerly some private acquaintance with her
mother at Lemnos.

PHORMIO. Mere dreams! How then came she not to know her
own father?

GETA. Without doubt there was a reason for that. But d'ye
think that I who was behind the door, could understand
every word that was spoken within?

PHORMIO. Faith, now I think of it, there was some such fly-
ing report.

GETA. I'll give ye further proof. . . . While I stood listening,
out goes your uncle, and after brought your father in along
with him. They both said you might keep her and welcome. In short, they've sent me out to look for ye, and
bring ye to them.

ANTIPHO *throws his arms about* GETA's *neck.* Bless my soul!
Away I go in a moment. Lead on! Why tarry ye?

GETA. I'm your man.

ANTIPHO. Phormio, dear rogue, farewell!

PHORMIO. Adieu, adieu, Sir!

Exit GETA *carrying off* ANTIPHO.

PHORMIO, *alone.* Let me die, if this be not a lucky hit. I am glad with all my heart they've met with such good fortune, and so unexpectedly too. Faith, now, I've an excellent opportunity of cheating both the old fellows, and of taking the burden of debt off Mr Phaedria's shoulders. Now he needn't be beholden to any of his friends. The very same money I squeezed from these old gripes shall go for his use. And, egad, I've found out a way will do it effectually: I must affect a new stately tread, and a fine set countenance. Now I'll step into the next blind alley, and pop out upon them as soon as they appear; for I'm no longer bound for Sunio Fair, as I pretended.

He retires to one side of the stage.

Enter DEMIPHO *and* CHREMES.

DEMIPHO, *entering.* I bless my stars with all my heart, for this good luck. . . . But let us make what haste we can to Phormio, that we may recover our money, before he squanders every penny.

PHORMIO, *comes out from his covert, speaks to himself.* I'll go and see whether Mr Demipho be at home, that I may . . .

Meets DEMIPHO *and starts.*

DEMIPHO. We were coming to you, Mr Phormio.

PHORMIO. Upon the old business, I warrant?

DEMIPHO. Yes, truly.

PHORMIO. Yes, truly.

PHORMIO. So I thought; but what need of that? A good jest in truth. What, were ye afraid I should not stand by what I said? Hark ye, Gentlemen, though I am but a poor fellow, I have always taken care to be a man of my word.

CHREMES, *to* DEMIPHO. Isn't she a well-bred girl, as I told ye?

DEMIPHO. Yes, indeed.

PHORMIO. For that reason I'm come on purpose to tell ye, Sir, that I am ready, and you may give her away as soon as you please; for I've broken off my other engagement, as 'twas only reasonable that I should, when I found you gentlemen so eager to thrust Phanie into my arms.

DEMIPHO. But Mr Chremes here has advised me against this course. 'Brother,' urges he, 'by marrying her to Phormio you'll become the talk of the town. They will all say that when you might have sent her off without loss of credit, then you wouldn't; and it will be a fine scandal to do so now that she's married to your son.' In fine, he used almost the same arguments as you did.

PHORMIO. By our Lady, how you love to tease me!

DEMIPHO. Who, I?

PHORMIO. Ay, you, Sir! Why, now I can no longer marry the other woman. With what face, think ye, can I approach her again after so base a rejection of her hand?

CHREMES, *aside to* DEMIPHO. Tell him, you find that Antipho refuses to part with her. . . . Nay, good Phormio, pray step to the banker's, and order the money to be paid me back again.

PHORMIO. What? When I've just settled with my creditors?

DEMIPHO, *aside to* CHREMES. What shall we do now?

PHORMIO. If you'll let me have Phanie, just as you promised, all's well. But if you design to keep her person, Mr Demipho, I'll keep her portion. For there's no reason why I should be cheated of my due merely to suit your convenience. Did I not do you a great kindness by breaking off another engagement? Which would have brought me as good a portion as you offered, and better even.

DEMIPHO. Old Nick take thee with thy roguish rodomontades! I warrant, you think I don't know you or your damned tricks either.

PHORMIO. This puts me out of all patience!

DEMIPHO. Why, would you marry her if she were offered ye?

PHORMIO. Try me, try me!

DEMIPHO. So that my son might bed and board with her at your house? Was that your plot?

PHORMIO. Hah! what's that you say?

DEMIPHO. I say: give me my money!

PHORMIO. And I say: give me my wife!

DEMIPHO. Come before a Justice of Peace, Sirrah!

PHORMIO. A Justice of Peace! Nay, if you wish to pick a quarrel with me at law, I'll . . .

DEMIPHO. What will ye do?

PHORMIO. Who, I, Sir? Do ye suppose I have no moneyed women who look to me for help? I'd have ye know that I am well supplied with such.

CHREMES. What's that to us?

PHORMIO. Nothing, Sir; only I'm acquainted with a lady in this town, whose husband had . . .

CHREMES, *aside*. The Devil!

DEMIPHO. What's the matter now?

PHORMIO. . . . another wife on Lemnos.

CHREMES, *aside*. I am ruined! . . .

PHORMIO. By whom he had a daughter, whom he brought up, and nobody was ever the wiser.

CHREMES, *aside*. I am dead and buried!

PHORMIO. I'll go now and acquaint the gentlewoman with the whole story.

CHREMES, *holding him*. Pray don't!

PHORMIO. Ah ha, Sir! Are you the party concerned?

DEMIPHO, *aside*. How cruelly the rogue abuses us!

CHREMES. Come, we'll settle with you.

PHORMIO. I trust ye no longer.

CHREMES, *softly*. What? Would ye have more? I tell ye, we'll not ask for the return of our money.

PHORMIO. I hear ye. . . . What a plague is this? Do you play children's games with me? I won't, I will; I will and I won't again. Give, take; 'tis said and unsaid; done and undone again.

CHREMES, *aside to* DEMIPHO. How the deuce came he to know this?

DEMIPHO *and* CHREMES *walk on one side.*

DEMIPHO. I can't imagine; for I'm certain I never told any living soul of it.

CHREMES. There's witchcraft here, I'll stake my life upon it!

PHORMIO, *aside.* I've given them a bone to gnaw upon.

DEMIPHO, *aside to* CHREMES. 'Sblud, shall this rascal carry off so round a sum of money, and abuse us, too, to our very faces? By heavens, he shall rather have my flesh for his supper! Come, pluck up a good heart, brother, and play the man! You see that your frailties have been so noised abroad that 'tis impossible to keep them from your wife now. Since she must soon hear it from others, why won't ye earn peace and quiet by first confessing yourself to her? For then we may deal with this dirty rascal as we please.

They move nearer to PHORMIO.

PHORMIO, *aside.* O lamentable! If I don't look about me, I am lost, as sure as a gun. They swagger up, like a couple of hired bullies, to hector me.

CHREMES, *aside to* DEMIPHO. But I'm afraid my wife will never forgive my deception of her.

DEMIPHO, *aside to* CHREMES. Take heart, man! I'll manage that business for you. You may trust me, brother, now that the woman by whom you had this daughter is dead and out of the way.

PHORMIO. Is this your manner of dealing, gentlemen? You come upon me very cunningly methinks. But in truth, Mr Demipho, you've done your brother no good service by provoking me thus.

To CHREMES.

And you, Sir, after you've taken your pleasure over sea, and shown no regard to your wife, though she is a lady of quality, but offered her the most serious affronts, do ye think to expiate your fault by whining pleas? No, I'll raise such flames in her by my story that, though you dissolved into a pool of tears, they would never quench the blaze.

DEMIPHO. Plagues and furies seize the rogue, and cast him into the deepest pit of Hell! Was there ever such an impudent dog upon the face of the earth? Does he not deserve to be transported, at the public charge, to some desert island?

CHREMES. He has caught me so sadly off my balance, that I know not what course to take.

DEMIPHO. I know only one: we must hale him before a Justice.

PHORMIO. Before a Justice? Very well, then: before the She-Justice of your house.

Going towards CHREMES'S.

DEMIPHO. Follow him, catch him, hold him fast while I summon my servants!

CHREMES, *catching at* PHORMIO. I lack the strength to hold him; come, help me!

Here they both hold him.

PHORMIO. I'll bring an action for assault against you, Mr Demipho.

DEMIPHO. Do your worst!

PHORMIO. And another against you, Mr Chremes.

Enter a SERVANT *or two from* DEMIPHO'S.

DEMIPHO, *to the* SERVANTS. Here, take away this rascal!

The SERVANTS *lay hold of* PHORMIO, *he scuffles with them, throws down* DEMIPHO, *when he comes to assist them, but at last is overpowered.*

PHORMIO. Is this the sport that delights ye? Nay, then, 'tis time to cry out: 'Nausistrata, come to my aid!'

CHREMES. Gag the villain!

DEMIPHO, *panting.* What . . . a confounded strong dog he . . . is!

PHORMIO, *aloud.* Nausistrata!

CHREMES. Won't ye hold your tongue, Sirrah?

PHORMIO. I hold my tongue?

DEMIPHO, *to the* SERVANTS. If he won't go along of his own free will, give him a punch in the guts.

PHORMIO. Or scratch my eyes out. Do your worst, for I've a way to be revenged on you all.

Enter NAUSISTRATA; *the* SERVANTS *unhand* PHORMIO;
CHREMES *looks very sheepish.*

NAUSISTRATA. Who calls me?

CHREMES, *aside.* Zookers!

NAUSISTRATA. Good husband, what disturbance is this?

PHORMIO, *to* CHREMES. Hah! what, have ye lost your tongue?

NAUSISTRATA. What fellow's this? Won't ye tell me?

PHORMIO. He tell ye, Madam! I' faith, his head is so giddy he
can't tell you his own name.

CHREMES. My Duck! Don't believe one word he says.

PHORMIO. Do but go and feel him, Madam, and hang me if
you'll not find him as cold as a stone.

CHREMES. That signifies nothing.

NAUSISTRATA. But what is the fellow talking of?

PHORMIO. I'll tell ye, Madam! Pray listen to me.

CHREMES. Are ye resolved to believe him, Duck?

NAUSISTRATA. Prithee, what can I believe? He has told me
nothing yet.

PHORMIO. The poor man's fear has frighted him out of his
senses.

NAUSISTRATA. In truth, it can't be for nothing that you should
be in such a fright.

CHREMES. Who? I in a fright?

PHORMIO. Ay, for certain; for if you are not, and if what I
propose to say is of no consequence, pray tell the tale yourself, Sir.

DEMIPHO. Ye rascal, shall he tell it to oblige you?

PHORMIO. Oh, you do take your brother's part nobly.

NAUSISTRATA. What, husband, won't ye tell me then?

CHREMES, *faltering.* But . . . But, dear Duck . . .

NAUSISTRATA. But, what 'But'?

CHREMES. There's no occasion to say a word.

PHORMIO. Not for you to say it, perhaps; but for her to hear
it there is. . . . At Lemnos . . .

CHREMES. Ha! what says he?

DEMIPHO. Dog, be silent!

PHORMIO. . . . without your knowledge . . .

CHREMES, *aside.* Undone!

PHORMIO. He married a wife.

CHREMES *looks upon the ground.*

NAUSISTRATA. Who, my husband? Heavens forbid that!

PHORMIO. O my soul, 'tis all true!

NAUSISTRATA. Alas-a-day, I am utterly ruined!

PHORMIO. And there he begot a daughter upon her, a thing of which you never dreamed!

CHREMES, *aside.* What will become of me now?

NAUSISTRATA. O heavens! O base and treacherous!

Weeps.

PHORMIO. 'Tis as I say.

NAUSISTRATA. Was such an unworthy deception ever heard of? Villains like my husband, when they are with their wives, pretend they are too old to pleasure them, forsooth. . . . I address myself to you, Brother, for I'm ashamed to speak to him. Was it for this he went so oft to Lemnos and stayed so long there? Does this account for the low price of corn that has so reduced our rents?

DEMIPHO. Indeed, Sister, I own he was in some fault; yet 'tis a venial one.

PHORMIO, *aside.* He preaches to the wind.

DEMIPHO. It wasn't out of aversion to you that he did this. About fifteen years ago, he, in his drink, had commerce with this woman, and begot this daughter, but thereafter never touched her again. She who was your only grievance is now dead and out of the way. Therefore, good Sister, bear this patiently, as you do other things.

NAUSISTRATA. Take it patiently! No, I had rather part with him forever! What can I hope for now? Can I expect age to teach him wisdom? If age would have done that, he was already old enough. Or, after these same fifteen years, is my beauty likely to please him more than once it did? What reason can ye offer to make me hope for his amendment?

PHORMIO, *aside*. Ha . . . ha . . . ha . . . If anyone has a mind to come to Chremes's funeral, now is the time. And henceforth let any man dare impugn my honour and I'll serve him the same sauce, I'll warrant ye. Let Mr Chremes be friends with me now whenever he pleases, I've thrashed him sufficiently for once; and given her a stick to beat him with as long as he has an hour to live.

NAUSISTRATA, *scornfully*. I warrant ye, I deserved all this. . . . But Brother, would you have me cast accounts and reckon how faithful I've been to him in everything?

DEMIPHO. I'm as satisfied with your conduct as you are yourself.

NAUSISTRATA. D'ye really think I deserved this ill usage at his hands?

DEMIPHO. Not in the least. . . . But since your complaints can't ever undo what's already done, forget and forgive! He begs your pardon, owns his fault, and promises amends; what can ye desire more?

PHORMIO, *aside*. But i' faith, before the pardon's sealed, there must be a proviso or two made for myself and Mr Phaedria. Hark ye, Madam, let me put in a word before you answer.

NAUSISTRATA. Let's hear it then!

PHORMIO. I coaxed your husband out of threescore and fifteen pounds, which I gave your son to buy a sweetheart of his own from an old bawd-master.

CHREMES, *hastily*. Hah! How's that?

NAUSISTRATA, *interrupting*. Is it such a strange thing for your son, in his youthful days, to keep a single mistress, when you are not ashamed to have two wives? How can ye find it in your conscience to reprimand him? Answer me that, pray!

CHREMES *draws back, and looks sheepish again.*

DEMIPHO. He shall be guided by you in this matter.

NAUSISTRATA. Well, let me speak my mind plainly! I'll neither pardon him, promise him anything, nor give him any
answer till I see my son—to whose judgement I shall refer
all, and do what he orders.

PHORMIO. You've acted very discreetly, Madam.

NAUSISTRATA, *to* PHORMIO. Will that satisfy you?

PHORMIO. Yes, indeed, Madam! I have come off well, and far
beyond my hopes.

NAUSISTRATA. Pray, honest man, by what name may I call
you?

PHORMIO. Mine, Madam? 'Tis Phormio, your whole family's
humble servant, and especially Mr Phaedria's.

NAUSISTRATA. Honest Phormio; whatever kindness I can offer
thee, be it in word or deed, I'll do it.

PHORMIO. You honour me too much, Madam.

NAUSISTRATA. Truth, 'tis no more than you deserve.

PHORMIO. First then, Madam, will ye do something that will
please me and grieve your husband?

NAUSISTRATA. With all my heart.

PHORMIO. If you please, invite me to supper then!

NAUSISTRATA. Faith, come and welcome!

DEMIPHO. Let's go in, then.

NAUSISTRATA. Agreed. . . . But where's Phaedria gone, who
is to be our referee?

PHORMIO. I hope he'll be here anon . . .

To the spectators.

Gentlemen, fare ye well, and clap!

End of THE TRICKS OF PHORMIO

THE BROTHERS

A Comedy acted at the Funeral Games of L. Aemilius Paulus *when* Q. Fabius Maximus *and* P. Cornelius Africanus *were Curule Ediles by the Company of* L. Attilius Prenestae *and* Minutius Protimus.

Flaccus, *a freedman of* Claudius, *composed the music, which was performed on Tyrian flutes.*

It was taken from the Greek of Menander, *and acted under the Consulship of* L. Ancinius *and* M. Cornelius.

A.U.C.593   Before Christ 160

DRAMATIS PERSONAE

MICIO, *a rich citizen of Athens, a mild sweet-natured old gentleman, and a bachelor, extremely loving and kind to his nephews, Aeschinus and Ctesipho; the first of whom he adopts as his own son*

DEMEA, *his brother, father to Aeschinus, and Ctesipho, a violent, angry, fretful, busy, meddling country gentleman; strict and severe to his son, and a great pretender to a knowledge of education*

AESCHINUS, *Demea's eldest son, adopted by Micio, in love with Pamphila; a wild loose spark of the town, generous and free-hearted, who, by reason of Micio's indulgence, often runs into open extravagances*

CTESIPHO, *his brother, as naturally vicious as the other, but for want of encouragement very timorous and secret, concealing everything from his father, with whom he lives in the country*

HEGIO, *Sostrata's kinsman, a downright, true-hearted, honest Athenian*

SYRUS, *Aeschinus's servant, a subtle, insinuating, sly, ingenious fellow, bold and saucy, almost always bantering and imposing upon Demea*

DROMO, *another of Aeschinus's servants*

GETA, *a very honest, true, and faithful servant of Sostrata's*

SANNIO, *a foolish woman-merchant, alias a bawd*

SOSTRATA, *a decayed old gentlewoman of Athens*

PAMPHILA, *her daughter, debauched by Aeschinus*

CANTHARA, *nurse to Pamphila*

NON-SPEAKING PARTS:

PARMENO
STORAX } *servant to Micio*

OTHER SERVANTS *to Micio*

MUSIC-GIRL

RABBLE

ATTENDANTS

ACT ONE

SCENE: *The street in front of* MICIO's *door, Athens*
TIME: *Early morning*

MICIO, *speaks within.* Storax, I say!

Enter MICIO *alone.*

MICIO, *entering.* So! No news, I see, of Aeschinus since last
night's entertainment, nor of any servant who went to
bring him home. . . . Well, what they say is true. If a
man be away from his house an hour longer than he has
promised, the scolding and suspicions of a jealous wife are
no worse than a fond father's can be for his son on a like
occasion. For she, if you don't come in at your appointed
hour, takes it for granted that you have picked up a girl;
or a girl, you. Or else that you're sousing at the tavern or
some other place of diversion. 'You may be faring well,'
says she, 'but what of your poor wife languishing at home?'
But here the case is worse by far! What a world of
thoughts, and what a rabble of whimsies have I in my
head, because of my son's absence from home last night;
lest he should be starved with cold, tumbled into a cellar,
or have broken a leg or arm. . . . Lord! that a man should
so set his heart upon a person as to make him dearer than
his own self! And worse, this boy is not truly my son,
neither, but my brother's whose nature is quite different
from mine. For my part, I always chose the quiet life, to
live at ease here in Athens, and (what the wits count a
happiness) have never troubled myself with a wife. My
brother on the other hand, has always lived in the country,

pinching and taking a world of pains, committed matrimony, and become the father of two sons! The eldest I have adopted, brought up, esteemed and loved as my own; he is the only creature I dote upon. I do all I can to make him obey his own inclinations, and don't think fit to use my authority at every turn. In short, I have brought him to this, that he conceals none of the levities of his youth, which others so industriously hide from their fathers; for the boy who won't hesitate to cheat his own father, will certainly do worse with other people. It was always my opinion, that 'tis much better to keep children in order by teaching them a sense of shame and generosity, than by fear. My brother and I can't agree on this point, and my way of education won't go down with him. Ever and anon he comes open-mouthed to me: '. . . Why, Micio, what do ye mean? Will ye be the ruin of our child? Why does he wench? Why does he drink? Why do ye indulge him in all this? You let him go too far; you are extremely silly.' But I call my brother severe beyond all right and reason; and truly, in my mind, that man is very much mistaken who believes that government by pure force has more authority and a better foundation, than one accompanied by tenderness and respect. This is my logic, and I argue thus: 'He who is compelled by threats to do his duty, will do so no longer than you can keep an eye on him; whenever he sees he won't be found out, he'll follow his own inclinations. But he who is governed by love obeys most cheerfully, strives to make his due returns, and remains the same whether you are present or absent. 'Tis a father's obligation so to treat his child that his own choice, rather than outward constraint, should guide him into doing well. Here lies the difference between a father and a master; and he that acts otherwise, let him own how little he understands the management of children.'

Seeing DEMEA *at a distance.*

But isn't that the gentleman I am talking of? . . . 'Tis he for certain. He knits his brows, but I know not why. I believe he's come to rail at me, as is usual with him.

Enter DEMEA.

MICIO. Brother! You are welcome to town.

DEMEA. Oh! Well met! You're the man I want!

MICIO. What makes you look so huffish?

DEMEA. Is that a question to ask, when we are faced with such a hopeful youth as Aeschinus?

MICIO, *aside*. I said it would be so. . . . What has he done now, pray?

DEMEA. What has he done? He's ashamed of nothing, afraid of nobody, and looks upon himself as a lawless man. I care not to rake up old mischiefs, but what a prank has he just now played!

MICIO. What's that, I pray?

DEMEA. Why, he has gone and forced open a man's door, broken into his house, beaten him and all his family most barbarously, left them for dead, and by force of arms carried off a wench for whom he had a fancy. Everybody cried shame upon it. What a world of people told me the tale, as I came along! Nay, the whole town rings with it. I have only this to say: that he should take an example from his brother Ctesipho: observing how closely he attends to his business, how sparingly and soberly he lives in the country. Ctesipho wouldn't do such a thing for the world. And, Brother, in blaming Aeschinus, I blame you too; 'tis you who have spoilt him.

MICIO. There's nothing more unreasonable than a man ignorant of the world, who thinks nothing well done but what he does himself.

DEMEA. Why say you so, pray?

MICIO. Because you take things far otherwise than ye ought. Believe me, Brother, 'tis not so sad a business for a brisk young fellow to wench and drink a little. No, nor yet to break down a door. If you and I were not so extravagant in our youth, it wasn't for lack of inclination, but for lack of funds. But now you reckon as a virtue what was due only to necessity; which is not fair—for had we but possessed the money, we should have been as wild as any others. So pray, if you are blessed with common sense, give your diligent, noble son the same liberty as mine, while he's young; rather than that, when your bones are in the grave, (a time which he has often prayed for) he should debauch himself at last, and at an age when such wild courses will become him less.

DEMEA. 'Sblud! You're enough to distract one! You say there's no harm in a young man who lives at this mad rate!

MICIO. Patience, good brother! Prithee, don't deafen my ears with old stories. You made your son over to me; and by adoption he's mine. If he be extravagant, I shall bear the blame of it, and pay for it over-and-above. He stands treats, he drinks, he dresses fine! 'Tis all at my expense. He keeps a miss, too! I'll supply his pocket so long as I'm able, and when that fails, perhaps he'll be turned adrift. Has he broken any doors? They shall be repaired. Torn any clothes? They shall be mended, too. I thank my stars, I've still the money to do all this, and as yet am not uneasy about the matter. In short: either leave off complaining, or choose an arbiter to judge between us, and I warrant I'll make it appear that you're more to blame than I.

DEMEA. Mercy upon me! You should learn what it is to be a father by listening to those who are so indeed.

MICIO. You are his father by nature, but I have the care of him.

DEMEA, *scornfully*. Ay, special care!

MICIO. Nay, if you're come to make sport of me, I'll be gone.

Offers to go.

DEMEA. Will ye so?

MICIO. Should I stay only to hear the same thing a thousand times over?

DEMEA. I speak because of my concern for him.

MICIO. And I'm concerned for him too; but, good Brother, let's each concern ourselves with our own son. For you to take care of both boys looks as if you revoked that grant which made Aeschinus mine.

DEMEA. Ay! Brother . . .

Shakes his head.

MICIO. I'll have it thus.

DEMEA, *in a passion.* Will ye so? . . . Well, if that's your resolution, let him squander all, damn himself and you and everyone—'tis all the same to me. If ever I speak a syllable more . . .

MICIO. Now you grow angry again.

DEMEA. Don't ye think there's reason for it? Do I desire to take your rare son from ye? It grieves me, I must confess; for he's my own flesh and blood. If I oppose your ways still . . . But enough of this! You'd have me take care of Ctesipho, and so I will. Heavens be praised, he proves a lad after my own heart. Your profligate will feel the smart of it at last. . . . Well! But I don't want to be too hard upon him.

Exit DEMEA.

MICIO, *alone.* I believe that part of what he said is true, but not all. And truly, I'm a little moved by his speech, though I wouldn't admit myself concerned in his presence. For he's such a strange man that to pacify him you must cross, contradict and out-bluster him until he can scarce master his rage. But should I try that course, playing upon the hot coal with a bellows, I would be as mad as he is. And I must confess that my Aeschinus has been a kind of naughty boy in this business. What courtesan has he not visited? Or to what pretty face has not he presented some gift or other? In fine, not long ago (grown sick of these creatures, as I thought) he told me he would settle down to marriage. I hoped that the heats of his youth had at last abated, and was heartily glad of it; but now on a sudden, it seems, a new fire's broke out. But I'll soon discover what the matter is. I'll go see whether I can meet with my young gentleman at the 'Change.

Exit MICIO.

End of the First Act

ACT TWO

Enter AESCHINUS *with a sword drawn, leading in the* MUSIC-GIRL, *and attended by* PARMENO, *and* STORAX; *after comes* SANNIO *the bawd-master, running with the* RABBLE *at his heels*

SANNIO, *out of breath.* Help . . . good neighbours! . . . I beseech ye! Help . . . a . . . miserable, innocent . . . helpless creature.

AESCHINUS, *to the girl.* Stand your ground, my pretty rogue, and don't be afraid. Why dost thou look behind thee? There's no danger at all. And while I'm by, let any man touch thee who dare!

SANNIO. I'll have her back, in spite of the world.

AESCHINUS. Though he's a very rascal, yet he shan't provoke me to give him another beating today.

SANNIO. Hark ye, Sir, that you mightn't pretend to be ignorant of my profession, I tell ye I'm a woman-merchant.

AESCHINUS. A bawd-master, you mean.

SANNIO. And one of the greatest repute in town. And don't you fancy now that you shall get off by saying: 'I intended you no injury.' By the Lord Harry, I value your excuses not a straw. Assure yourself, I'll trounce ye to some tune; your fine words shall never make amends for the blows you gave me. I know what you will offer me. 'I'm extremely sorry for it,' you'll say, 'I'll take my oath you did not deserve this usage.' When the truth of it is, I've been used worse than a dog.

AESCHINUS, *to* PARMENO. Run quickly ahead, Sirrah, and open the door.

SANNIO. You had better stay where you are.

PARMENO *opens the door.*

AESCHINUS, *to the girl.* Step in quickly with him, my dear rogue.

SANNIO, *stepping between.* I forbid that, though.

AESCHINUS. Come hither, Parmeno! You are too far off. Keep close to that son of a whore . . . So, that's well! Take care to keep your eye full upon mine, that when I tip the wink you may be ready to give him a clout in the face.

SANNIO. I'd fain see that.

AESCHINUS *hands the* GIRL *to* PARMENO; SANNIO *runs and catches hold of her.*

AESCHINUS. Have a care, Parmeno!

PARMENO *strikes him.*

To SANNIO.

Dog! Let go your hold.

SANNIO. O, monstrous!

AESCHINUS. You shall have the second part of the same tune, if you don't take care.

PARMENO *strikes him.*

SANNIO. Murder! Murder!

AESCHINUS, *to* PARMENO. Hold, you exceed your commission. But better too much than too little . . . You may march off, Mr Sannio, now that you've got your black and blue livery.

Exit PARMENO *with the* GIRL.

SANNIO. What do you mean, Sir? Do you reign as lord and master here?

AESCHINUS. If I did, I'd reward your bawdship according to your deserts.

SANNIO. Pray what authority have you over me?

AESCHINUS. None, perhaps.

SANNIO. How! Do ye know who I am, Sir?

AESCHINUS. No, nor yet desire it.

SANNIO. Did I meddle with anything of yours, pray?

AESCHINUS. If you had, Sirrah, it should have cost you dear.

SANNIO. Then how comes it to be more lawful for you to take my goods, which I honestly bought and paid for? Answer me that, pray!

AESCHINUS. You had better not stand bawling like this before our door. If ye plague us any more, I'll have ye dragged in, and whipped as long as ye can stand.

SANNIO. Bless me! Free-born, and whipped!

AESCHINUS. That's your doom.

SANNIO. Oh the wickedness of the man! Pox on it, is this the general freedom of citizens that they talk of?

AESCHINUS. Worthy Mr Pimp! When your mad fit's over, hear me a word—if your honour is so disposed.

SANNIO. Was it I who was mad, or you?

AESCHINUS. Let that pass; now come to the point again.

SANNIO. What point of many?

AESCHINUS. Will ye give me leave to speak about your business?

SANNIO. With all my heart, provided it be just.

AESCHINUS. Heigh-toss! The bawd's turned Puritan, and would teach me the nature of justice.

SANNIO. Though I be a bawd—the common bane of youth, a forsworn wretch and a public nuisance—yet I never did you any wrong, Sir.

AESCHINUS. That's kept for later.

SANNIO. Pray, Mr Aeschinus, return to your first proposal.

AESCHINUS. The girl cost ye about fifty guineas, may it bring ye ill luck! The money shall be repaid.

SANNIO. And if I won't part with her, who in the name of plague shall force me? Will you?

AESCHINUS. No.

SANNIO. I feared you would offer that.

AESCHINUS. Truly, friend Sannio, between you and me, she's not for sale at all. For she's a gentlewoman, and so I'll prove her to be. Now, blockhead, choose whether you'll take the money, or take the case to law. Chew upon this till I come back, worthy Mr Pimpwell.

Exit AESCHINUS.

SANNIO, *alone.* Heavens! Now I don't wonder that oppression sends some men mad! This son of thunder has ravished me out of my castle, manhandled me, taken a girl from me *vi et armis,* and inflicted five hundred bastinadoes upon my poor body. After this sweet usage he'd have me surrender my right and title to the girl without interest. Faith, he shall have her indeed, since he deserves her so well, and requires nothing but what's just.

Ponders.

Well, I wish it be so, if only he pays down the ready . . . But my mind misgives me damnably; I fear that if I name a higher price, he'll presently bring witnesses to swear that fifty guineas was a direct bargain between us. Then I may go whistle for my money. He'll say: 'Come again in an hour's time.' Or: 'Come tomorrow.' That I can bear too, if I can be sure of getting it at last, though it be an inconvenience to me. . . . 'Twill be long withheld, as sure as a gun. Well, Friend Sanny, since thou hast taken up a nasty trade, thou must be content to pocket the affronts of such a hectoring gallant as this. But since nobody's here to pay me, I am counting my chickens before they are hatched.

Enter SYRUS *at a little distance.*

SYRUS, *to* AESCHINUS, *within.* Hush! Not a word more! I'll go to him myself, and make him skip at the smell of money, confessing that he's rarely well dealt by.

Goes to SANNIO.

What's the news with you, Mr Sannio? I hear my master and you have had a kind of a scuffle.

SANNIO, *shrugging.* A scuffle, do ye call it? Never that, surely?

We were both sufficiently tired: he with beating me, and I with being beaten.

SYRUS. You may thank yourself for that.

SANNIO. How could I help it?

SYRUS. You should have humoured the young gentleman a little.

SANNIO. What could I do more? I'm sure I bore all the blows that he was pleased to give me.

SYRUS. Well, do ye know what I'm going to say? To leave a debt unclaimed is sometimes the best play.

SANNIO. Hey-ho!

SYRUS. You are as timorous as a senseless sot! Now, if you had conceded a little of your right, and humoured the gentleman, you'd have got the Devil and all in the long run.

SANNIO. I don't love to buy a pig in a poke.

SYRUS. Ah, thou'lt never be worth anything. Out upon ye, as if you hadn't a snare to catch woodcocks!

SANNIO. I believe that might be the wiser course, but I never had the sense to follow it, nor to refuse ready money when I could lay my hands on it.

SYRUS. Go to, I know your generous spirit! As though you valued half a hundred guineas when you could serve my master by the loan of them. Besides, they say you are making a voyage to Cyprus?

SANNIO. Oh!

SYRUS. And have bought up several commodities to transport thither; the vessel's chartered. I know your mind's a little wavering about this fifty guineas, but when you come back I can promise you a settlement much to your advantage.

SANNIO, *aside.* I've no voyage to make. . . . Faith, I'm undone; 'tis upon this that they've built their plot.

SYRUS, *aside.* The fellow's shaken. I've put a flea in his ear.

SANNIO, *to himself.* Oh horrid! see how he has tricked me at the critical minute, when I've just laid in a stock of females, and other wares, to carry to Cyprus. If I cannot take that girl with them 'twill half break me, and if I leave this business at sixes and sevens, all will be lost. There'll be no remedy, and I shall be given a plaguey cold welcome when I sail back. 'Are you come now,' they'll say, 'to prosecute? Why did ye let the matter run so long? Where have ye been all this while?' It seems I had better lose every penny-piece, than tarry so long before I sue Aeschinus.

SYRUS, *clapping him on the shoulders.* Well, hast been reckoning up all the gains of your voyage?

SANNIO. Is this like a gentleman? Does Mr Aeschinus's conscience permit him to take away a girl by main force?

SYRUS, *aside.* He sinks! He sinks! . . . I've one thing more to propose, Mr Sannio: see if you like it. Come, settle for half, rather than run the hazard of saving or losing all; we'll scrape together about five and twenty guineas somewhere or other.

SANNIO. Oh miserable! Now I am in danger of losing part of my very principal. Is he past all shame? He has thrust my teeth down my throat, and beaten my head into an entire jelly; would he trick me of the money into the bargain? . . . I have no voyage to make.

SYRUS. That's as you please. . . . Have ye any further commands? I'm going.

SANNIO. Ay, pray good Mr Syrus, however things have been, rather than sue and quarrel, let him pay me, at least what the girl cost me. I know, ye little rogue, that you never yet had occasion to make use of me as a friend; but if you should, you'll find that I'm no forgetful or ungrateful person.

SYRUS. I'll do my best. . . . Oh, yonder comes Ctesipho i' faith, as brisk as a body-louse, in search of his mistress.

SANNIO. Well, will ye do as I desired ye?

SYRUS. Have a little patience!

Enter CTESIPHO. SANNIO *walks aside.*

CTESIPHO, *to himself.* When a man stands in need of a good turn, he's glad to receive it from any hand; but it does him a double pleasure when it is given by one from whom he has reason to expect it. Oh Brother, Brother! How do I adore thee now! This I'm sure of, that the very best words I can offer thee are short of thy deserts. And here I am, happy beyond all mortals that I've the most accomplished brother in nature.

SYRUS. Oh, Mr Ctesipho!

CTESIPHO. Dear rogue Syrus, where's my brother?

SYRUS. Look ye, he's at home waiting for you.

CTESIPHO. Oh, brave!

SYRUS. What's the matter, Sir?

CTESIPHO. The matter, old boy? I should have been cold in my grave but for his means. . . . Ah, he's an honest soul; he neglected his own interest to serve me. He has taken upon himself all the curses, scandals, love-matters, and miscarriages that belong to me. And what could he do more? . . . But who comes there? Why does the door open?

SYRUS. Stay, stay, here he comes himself!

Enter AESCHINUS.

AESCHINUS. Where's the scoundrel son of a whore?

SANNIO. Does he want me? Has he brought the money? I'm broke; the Devil a penny do I see!

AESCHINUS, *to* CTESIPHO. Hah! this is lucky, 'twas you I was wishing for . . . Well, how is it? All's well! Off with that sour look!

CTESIPHO. Now I have reason, having such a brother as you, O Aeschinus! My true brother indeed! I dare not praise ye any more before your face, lest you should think it proceeded from flattery rather than gratitude.

AESCHINUS. Leave your fooling, as though we were mere strangers to one another. But it troubles me that we didn't learn of the business sooner; for things were come to such a pass that all the world could scarce have helped you, well though they might desire it.

CTESIPHO. Modesty hindered me.

AESCHINUS. Pshaw! 'twas folly, not modesty! What, ready to

flee your country for so small a matter? Heavens forbid that!

CTESIPHO. It was not well considered, I own.

AESCHINUS, *to* SYRUS. Upon what has Sannio concluded?

SYRUS. He's grown very tame.

AESCHINUS. I'll go to the Piazza and pay him . . . But do you, Brother, go in to greet your mistress.

SANNIO, *aside to him.* Good Mr Syrus, pray push on the business.

SYRUS. Let's be quick, Sir, for the man's in haste for his voyage to Cyprus.

SANNIO. I'm in no such haste . . . I've nothing to do but wait for the money.

SYRUS. You shall have it, man, never fear that.

SANNIO. What, all?

SYRUS. Yes, all. Say no more about it, but follow us.

SANNIO. So I will.

Exeunt AESCHINUS *and* SANNIO.

CTESIPHO, *to* SYRUS, *going off.* Hark ye, Syrus! Prithee, see that this paltry rascal is dealt with as soon as possible, lest he make further provocation and the business comes to my father's ears. Then I shall be ruined, to all intents and purposes.

SYRUS. That shan't be! Take heart, Sir. Go within and while away half an hour or so with your mistress. Order the butler to lay the cloth and get things ready. So soon as the business is over, I'll march home with plenty of provisions.

CTESIPHO. Prithee, do; and since things have fallen out so luckily, let's e'en make a day of it!

Exeunt severally.

End of the Second Act

ACT THREE

SOSTRATA *and* CANTHARA

SOSTRATA. Prithee, my good Nurse, how is she likely to fare?

CANTHARA. How! Troth, I hope she'll have a good time of it. Her pains, my good mistress, are just beginning. You are as fearful now as if ye had never witnessed a labour nor ever cried out yourself.

SOSTRATA. Alas-a-day! I've nobody at home, and we are all alone. Our man Geta's out of the way too; and there's never a soul to send for the midwife, or to call Aeschinus.

CANTHARA. Without doubt, Aeschinus will be here anon. Never a day goes over his head, but we have his company.

SOSTRATA. He's the only comfort I have in my affliction.

CANTHARA. As the case stands, mistress, the business couldn't fall into better hands, since she's to be with child by such a worthy gentleman, of such a parentage, so generous, and so nobly descended.

SOSTRATA. You're much in the right! Heaven keep him ours for ever!

Enter GETA, *as if out of breath from coming a great distance.*

GETA, *to himself.* We are now brought to such a pass that if all the wise men in the world laid their heads together to remedy this mischief that overwhelms myself, my mistress, and her daughter, they could do us no good. . . . Oh, miserable! Such a flood of difficulties rush upon us that 'tis impossible to keep above water. Ravishment, poverty, oppression, desertion, infamy! . . . Is the age so debauched? Abominable villains! Cursed wretches! The devil of a man . . .

SOSTRATA. Bless me! What has put our Geta into such haste and fright?

GETA, *to himself.* . . . whom nothing can restrain or move, neither promises, oaths, nor pity, nor yet the approaching travail of the girl he has so shamefully abused.

SOSTRATA. I can't well understand what the fellow says.

CANTHARA. Pray mistress, let's go a little nearer to him.

GETA, *to himself.* Ah, poor Geta! I'm scarce *compos mentis,* my passion has so inflamed me! O, that I might disgorge my rage upon them, now that my blood's up. I'd be contented to suffer anything, if only I might have a swingeing revenge upon them. First, I'd grind underfoot that stinking snuff his father, who gave being to the vile rascal; then I'd take that dog Syrus, who persuaded him to the crime and tear him piecemeal! I'd give him such a toss, dash his skull against the stones, strew the streets with his brains! That boy Aeschinus, too! I'd tear out his eyes, and after that break his neck. . . . The rest I'd down with 'em, drive 'em, pound 'em, trample 'em under my feet. But what makes me loiter when I should be breaking this damned news to my mistress?

Going off.

SOSTRATA. Let's call him back. . . . What, Geta?

GETA. Pish! Prithee, don't trouble me, whosoever you are!

SOSTRATA. 'Tis your mistress calls.

GETA. Ay, where is she?

Turning about.

I was hunting for you, Mistress, 'twas you I looked for. You've met me as luckily as could be.

SOSTRATA. What's the matter? Why dost thou pant so?

GETA. Oh!

SOSTRATA. Why in such haste, my poor boy? Come, take breath!

GETA. We are absolutely . . .

SOSTRATA. What absolutely?

GETA. . . . Undone . . . past all recovery . . .

SOSTRATA, *in a fright.* For heaven's sake, what's the matter?

GETA. Just now . . .

SOSTRATA. What just now, Geta?

GETA. This Mr Aeschinus . . .

SOSTRATA. What of him?

GETA. . . . has quite . . . discarded and repudiated our family.

SOSTRATA. Alas! Undone indeed! But how so?

GETA. He's run mad after another face.

SOSTRATA. Wretch that I am!

GETA. He didn't do things in the dark, but forced her from a bawd-master openly and by day.

SOSTRATA. Are you sure of this?

GETA. Most sure; these very eyes saw it.

SOSTRATA, *weeping.* Oh, unfortunate Sostrata! To what canst thou trust, or in whom canst thou have reliance? Our dear Aeschinus did this? The very soul of us all, in whom we placed our hopes and happiness! How oft he swore he wouldn't live a day without his Pamphila, and that he'd lay the infant on his father's knees, and thus beg leave to marry her.

GETA. Pray, Mistress, forbear weeping, but rather consider what's fit to be done; whether we should swallow the affront, or tell it to a friend.

CANTHARA. Hold, hold, man! Hast lost thy senses? Do ye think this a business fit to be blazed abroad?

GETA. Nay, I'm for hushing it up from the world. First, the case is plain: he has left us for good and all. Now if we make the matter public, ten to one he'll disown the child; and then your reputation, and your daughter's honour will be called in question. But let us suppose that he confesses all . . . In that case it wouldn't be prudence to give him your daughter, while he keeps another miss. Therefore, take the thing whichever way you please, my vote is for concealment.

SOSTRATA. Ah, by no means! I'll not agree to it.

GETA. What will ye do then?

SOSTRATA. Divulge it.

GETA. How! Have a special care, Mistress, what you do!

SOSTRATA. The case can never be worse than it already is. For, first, Pamphila has no portion; then she's robbed of what might have served instead of one—her innocency, for now she can't pass for a virgin. I have one shift left: namely the ring he lost. If he denies the fatherhood, that will be proof enough. In fine, since my own conscience tells me that this mishap can't be charged to my covetousness, or to any base ends pursued either by my daughter or by myself, we'll e'en venture to sue him at law.

GETA. Do ye think so? Pray, think the matter over again.

SOSTRATA. Do you, Geta, run in all haste to her Cousin Hegio, and tell him the whole story. For he was a choice friend of my poor husband's, and has always shown great kindness to our family.

GETA. Ay, faith, there's nobody else regards us with favour.

SOSTRATA. Good Canthara, do you run and call the midwife, that she may be at hand when we have need of her.

Exeunt severally.

Enter DEMEA alone.

DEMEA. Undone, undone! They say my boy Ctesipho assisted his brother at the rape! That Aeschinus should be able to debauch so sober a lad as he is the only thing that could add to my misfortunes. . . . Where shall I search for my son Ctesipho? I'm afraid he'll be in some bawdy-house or other. The rake-hell his brother will have drawn him there, I'm confident. . . . But yonder comes Syrus! I'll learn from

him where to look. But i' faith the rogue is one of their
gang, and if he perceives my design, he will never tell me
anything; therefore I shall keep it hid.

Enter SYRUS *at another part of the stage, very merry.*

SYRUS, *to himself.* We've been telling the whole exploit to
Mr Micio, and how 'twas carried out. I never saw the old
man so tickled in my whole life.

DEMEA, *overhearing.* Bless me! Is my brother such a coxcomb
at that?

SYRUS, *to himself.* He commended Mr Aeschinus and thanked
me for advising him.

DEMEA, *aside.* I can't hold my wrath any longer.

SYRUS, *to himself.* He counted out the money forthwith, and
gave us a broad-piece in addition to make merry with;
and, edad, 'twas employed even as he wished it.

DEMEA, *aside.* Hah! If you'd have anything done as it should
be, commend me to this gentleman!

SYRUS, *starting.* Hah, Mr Demea, I didn't see ye! How does
your worship?

DEMEA. How? . . . I can only wonder at your fine way of
living.

SYRUS. Faith, Sir, 'tis pretty simple, and to speak the truth,
somewhat odd.

Turning to MICIO'S *house.*

You, Dromo, gut and scale the rest of the fish, but let the
great conger-eel lie in the water a little. When I come
back we'll bone him, and not before.

DEMEA. Are these scandalous villainies to be condoned?

SYRUS, *to* DEMEA. Truly, Sir, I don't like them at all, and do
often cry out in protest . . .

To a slave within.

Stephanio, see that the salt fish be well watered!

DEMEA. Oh, Heavens! Does he do this on purpose, or does
he think it a creditable matter to ruin his son? What a sad
creature am I! Methinks the day is soon at hand when this

boy will be forced by penury to flee his country, and enlist in the King of Persia's army.

SYRUS. Oh, Sir! There's wisdom now! To foresee coming events, and not merely look at what's just before your eyes.

DEMEA. Well, have ye got the girl fiddler at your house?

SYRUS. Ay, she's within.

DEMEA. The Devil! Surely she's not going to dwell there?

SYRUS. I believe they're mad enough to have it so.

DEMEA. Is it possible?

SYRUS. Ah, the soppy fondness and pernicious indulgence of a father!

DEMEA. In good truth, I'm ashamed and heartily grieved for my brother.

SYRUS. There's too much—ay, a great deal too much difference, Sir—between you two (though I shouldn't say so much before your face). You, Sir, are wisdom all over; but his mind is mere gimcrack! Would you have allowed your son to do this?

DEMEA. Allowed him? Zooks! I should have smelt him out six whole months before he had been concerned in such a business.

SYRUS. Ah, Sir, you need not tell me what a wary man you are.

DEMEA. Heaven grant my son may continue as he is!

SYRUS. Children prove to be as their fathers make them.

DEMEA, *fawningly.* But hark ye, Syrus, didst see him today?

SYRUS. Mr Ctesipho, Sir!

Aside.

I'll send the old fool packing into the country.

Aloud.

He's gone back to the farm: he'll be hard at work by this time.

DEMEA. Are you sure he's there?

SYRUS. Sure? Why I trudged out of town at his side!

DEMEA. That's well. I feared he might have loitered here-abouts still.

SYRUS. He was in a plaguey huff, too.

DEMEA. At what, prithee?

SYRUS. He fell out with his brother in the open market about the music-wench.

DEMEA. Say ye so?

SYRUS. I' faith, he spoke his mind freely! For while we were paying the money, in he comes unawares at our backs, and sets up an outcry: 'Are ye not ashamed, Brother Aeschinus, to commit such villainies? That you should so vilely dishonour our family!'

DEMEA *wipes his eyes.* Edad, he makes me weep for joy.

SYRUS. 'You don't only weaken your estate,' says he, 'but your reputation too.'

DEMEA. Heavens bless him! I hope he will never degenerate.

SYRUS. Who questions it?

DEMEA. O Syrus, the poor boy has had his head full of these noble morals!

SYRUS. And well he may, with such a father to fill it.

DEMEA. I do my best, and leave no stone unturned to exercise him in all that's good. Above all I charge him: 'Look into men's actions as one who gazes into a mirror, and take example by them. Practise this!' say I.

SYRUS. Very well said, indeed.

DEMEA. 'Shun that!' say I.

SYRUS. Shrewd.

DEMEA. 'This is commendable,' I add.

SYRUS. There you hit it again.

DEMEA. 'But that won't be allowed at all.'

SYRUS. Most admirable.

DEMEA. 'And moreover . . .'

SYRUS, *interrupting.* Your pardon, Sir, I am not at leisure to hear your 'moreovers'. I've got a toothsome dish of fish on the fire, and I must take special care that they be not spoiled. For we servants think such neglect as scandalous a business, Sir, as you would think the neglect of your son's education. Therefore, according to my abilities I give my fellow servants instructions after the self-same manner. 'This is too salt,' say I. 'That's too much, this isn't done cleanly enough; that's well done, pray remember to do so another time!' I instruct them diligently, as well as my palate will serve me. Last of all, too, I bid them look into their dishes, as one who gazes into into a mirror, and there learn their duty. I confess, these are mere trifles, but what signifies that? We must suit our moral sayings to the persons we deal with . . . Please to command me, Sir?

DEMEA. I wish you would get a little more sense into their heads.

SYRUS. Do ye intend to march into the country, Sir?

DEMEA. That I do.

SYRUS. Ay, what can you do here, Sir, where all your good morals are wasted and thrown away?

Exit SYRUS.

DEMEA, *alone.* Ay, truly, I'll go to my farm, since my son who drew me hither is gone back again. . . . That boy's all I care about. He's my true son; since my brother will have his own way, let him look to the other rake-hell. . . . But who comes yonder at a distance? Mr Hegio, one of our own city-ward? . . . If my eyes don't fail me, 'tis he indeed! Ah, we've been cronies from our cradles. By Jove, such honest citizens are very scarce nowadays: a man of the right old stamp for virtue and fidelity, and would not do the government any harm for the world. How glad I am that one at least remains of the old stock! Ay, life is a pleasure to me now. I'll wait for him here, and bid him goodmorrow, and have a little discourse with him.

Enter HEGIO *and* GETA *at a distance.*

HEGIO. Ye powers! A dishonourable action! What is it you say, Geta? Hah!

GETA. Just as I told ye.

HEGIO. That ever so noble a family should commit such an

ungenteel action! Oh, Aeschinus! You didn't learn this from your father, I'm sure!

DEMEA, *overhearing*. Yes, he has heard of this music-wench too, and it offends him, though he be no relative of ours. Yet my sweet brother takes no notice of it!

DEMEA. Oh dismal! Would he were here only a little while, that he might hear all these complaints.

HEGIO. If they won't give satisfaction, they mustn't hope to carry the matter off so brazenly.

GETA. We all rely upon you, Sir! We have none else to stand by us! You are our guardian and father too. The old gentleman upon his death-bed bequeathed us all to your care, and if you forsake us, we're utterly undone.

HEGIO. No more of that! I'll not forsake ye, nor could I do so with an easy conscience.

DEMEA. I'll speak with him . . . Honest Hegio, I'm heartily glad to see you.

HEGIO. Oh! Mr Demea, I'm your humble servant! You are the very man I wanted.

DEMEA. How so, Sir?

HEGIO. Why your eldest son Aeschinus, whom your brother has adopted, has acted neither like an honest man nor a gentleman.

DEMEA. What has he done?

HEGIO. You know one Simulus, a friend and contemporary of ours?

DEMEA. Yes, very well.

HEGIO. Why, Aeschinus has debauched Simulus's daughter.

DEMEA. Oh!

HEGIO. Hold, Sir, the worst is to come yet.

DEMEA. What, more mischief still?

HEGIO. Yes, truly; for that was in some measure excusable. He had opportunity, heat, wine, and youth to prompt him to what was but a human frailty. But when he became aware of his fault, he went forthwith to her mother, weeping, praying, entreating, promising and swearing he'd take her home and marry her. Upon this, all was pardoned, hushed, and honourably agreed upon. The young woman proved with child and has gone her forty weeks; but in the Devil's name, this sweet youth has now bought a music-wench, keeps her at his father's, and leaves the other woman to shift for herself.

DEMEA. Is all this true? Are you sure?

HEGIO. The mother is ready to prove it, the young woman's big belly speaks for itself; besides, here's Geta none of the worst, as servants are now, a painstaking fellow, who maintains the whole family himself. Take him, bind him, force the truth out of him.

GETA. Yes, verily, Sir, rack me to death, if it be not all true! Besides, Mr Aeschinus himself won't deny it. Pray, Sir, bring us face to face.

DEMEA. I'm horribly ashamed! I can't imagine what to do, or what answer to make him.

PAMPHILA, *within.* Oh, me! I'm torn in pieces . . . Help ye powers above, and ease me for Heaven's sake!

HEGIO, *to* GETA. Hah! Prithee, was that she who cried out?

GETA. Without doubt, Sir.

HEGIO. Ah, Mr Demea, she calls upon your honour now, and begs ye to do freely what the law obliges ye to do. I beg Heaven to inspire ye rightly; but if you are otherwise minded, Mr Demea, I'll maintain her and her dead father's cause, to the last penny in my purse. He was my kinsman, we were bred up children together, we served together in war abroad, and in peace at home, together we underwent the straits of poverty. Therefore I'll do my utmost and rather lose my life than desert these poor women . . . What answer will ye return?

DEMEA. I'll go talk with my brother, Sir! What advice he gives, that I'll follow.

HEGIO. But, Mr Demea, do but consider that the more comfortably you live, the more powerful, the more rich, the more happy, and the more noble you are—so much the more honest and just you two ought to be, if you'd be considered men of honour.

DEMEA. Away! No more, you shall have all right and justice done you!

HEGIO. Spoken like a worthy gentleman. . . . Geta, lead me to your mistress!

Exeunt HEGIO *and* GETA.

DEMEA, *alone.* This was no more than I foretold. I wish to my soul that this were his last mad prank; but I fear that the allowance of so much liberty will end at last in some worse disgrace. . . . Well, I'll go hunt for my brother, and fire off this news in his very face.

Exit DEMEA.

At the same time re-enter HEGIO.

HEGIO, *to* SOSTRATA *within.* Cheer up, good coz, and comfort your child's poor heart as much as you can. I'll go seek Mr Micio at the Piazza, and let him know how the case stands; if he designs to do right by us, well and good; if not, let him make a plain declaration, that I may take my measures accordingly.

Exit HEGIO.

End of the Third Act

ACT FOUR

CTESIPHO *and* SYRUS

CTESIPHO, *entering*. My father's gone into the country, say ye?

SYRUS. Above an hour ago.

CTESIPHO. Prithee, tell me true!

SYRUS. He's at his farm and slaving most horribly by this time, I'll warrant ye.

CTESIPHO. Faith, if it might not endanger his health, I could wish he might get so miserably tired as to be laid up for the next three days.

SYRUS. So say I! And longer too, if possible.

CTESIPHO. Ay, ay. For now I've begun the day merrily, I very fain would make an end of it merrily too. The only quarrel I have with our country-house is, that 'tis too nigh the town. Were it farther off, 'twould be night before he could get thither and back again. But now, when he finds no Ctesipho at home, I'm sure he'll be run back again in an instant. Then he'll be for catechizing me: 'Pray where have you been, Sir? Why can't a man have a glimpse of ye in a whole day's time?' What excuse shall I have?

SYRUS. Haven't ye got one ready?

CTESIPHO. The Devil a one.

SYRUS. So much the worse! Why, if you only had a friend, or a guest, that were better than nothing.

CTESIPHO. I have, what then?

SYRUS. Pretend you have had hasty business to dispatch.

CTESIPHO. What, when I had none? . . . It won't do.

SYRUS. It will, though.

CTESIPHO. Ay, for the day! But if I stay out all night, what excuse then, Syrus?

SYRUS. Would it were more the fashion to serve a friend by night as well as by day! . . . However, set your heart at rest; I know your father's ways to a hair. Though he rage like a lion, I can soon make him as quiet as a lamb.

CTESIPHO. And how, I prithee?

SYRUS. Oh, he's mightily tickled when any man commends you. I present ye to him as a very saint, and reckon up all your virtuous qualities.

CTESIPHO. Mine?

SYRUS. Ay, yours. Then of a sudden the good man cries for joy like a little child. . . . Look to yourself, there!

Enter DEMEA *at a distance.*

CTESIPHO, *starting.* What do ye mean?

SYRUS. Talk of the Devil, and his horns appear.

CTESIPHO. Is it my father?

SYRUS. The very same.

CTESIPHO. Prithee, Syrus, what shall we do now?

SYRUS. Run in quickly! I'll set my wits to work.

CTESIPHO. If he ask for me, say you haven't seen me, do ye hear?

SYRUS. Can't ye hold your tongue?

Exit CTESIPHO.

DEMEA, *to himself.* I'm the unluckiest creature who ever was born! In the first place, my brother is nowhere to be found. Then, as I was looking for him, whom should I see but a workman just come from my country-house; he says my boy isn't there neither. Nor can I tell, for my life, what course to steer.

CTESIPHO, *softly, appearing at the window.* Syrus!

SYRUS. What say ye?

CTESIPHO. Does he enquire for me?

SYRUS. Yes, faith.

CTESIPHO. I'm undone.

SYRUS. Come, don't be discouraged.

DEMEA, *to himself.* I'll e'en go again to see whether my brother be come back.

CTESIPHO. Prithee, good Syrus, take care he don't break in upon us unawares.

SYRUS. Peace, I say! I'll take care about it.

CTESIPHO. Faith, Sir, but I shan't trust my concerns in your hands today. I'll secure my girl and myself in some hidden closet or other. Edad, that will be the surest way by half.

CTESIPHO *retires.*

SYRUS. Away! I'll clear the coast of him in a trice.

SYRUS *moves towards* DEMEA, *shrugging his shoulders and snivelling.*

DEMEA. Oh! There's the hell-hound, Syrus.

SYRUS, *to himself.* If this manner of things continues, the house will be no longer endurable. I'd fain know how many masters I am to have! What a damnable thing this is!

DEMEA. Such a yelping this cur makes! What ails him? . . . What say, you honest fellow? Is my brother at home, hah?

SYRUS. Pox on your honest fellows! I'm a dead man.

DEMEA. What's the matter?

SYRUS. The matter, with a plague? Your sober-sided son Ctesipho has almost beaten poor me and the music-girl to death.

DEMEA. What's that you say? Hah!

SYRUS. See how he has slit my lip up to the nose!

DEMEA. How came this to pass?

SYRUS. He says I was the occasion of her being bought.

DEMEA. Didn't you just tell me that he had gone into the country, and you brought him part of the way?

SYRUS. True, Sir, but after that he came raving like a madman, sparing never a mother's son of us. He might have been ashamed to fall upon a poor old man like me, who not long since dandled him in my arms, when he was no higher than this.

Shows how high.

DEMEA. Ha . . . ha . . . he . . . God-a-mercy Ctesipho! Old Demea's right! Well! Thou art a man, every inch of thee.

SYRUS. Do ye commend him? I' faith, he had best keep his flippant fingers to himself another time, if he knows what is to his benefit!

DEMEA. 'Twas bravely done!

SYRUS. Very bravely indeed! To crow like a cock over a silly woman, and a poor servant, who daren't lift a finger against him? . . . Yes, 'twas wonderful brave, i' faith!

DEMEA. He couldn't have done better. He's of my opinion in thinking you to be the ring-leader of this roguery. . . . But is my brother within?

SYRUS. No, Sir, he's away.

DEMEA. I'm wondering where the deuce I may look for him.

SYRUS. I know where he's gone, but I shan't tell until tomorrow.

DEMEA. What's that you say, Sirrah? Hah!

SYRUS. Just so, Sir.

DEMEA. I'll crack your skull presently, ye dog.

Holds up his cane.

SYRUS, *bantering.* I know not the name of the man at whose house he is; but the place I do.

DEMEA. Then tell me the place, Sirrah!

SYRUS, *still bantering.* Do you know the great portico that overlooks the Butcher's Row, as you go down there?

DEMEA. Well, what then?

SYRUS, *still bantering.* Go straight along this street, up there . . .

Pointing with his fingers.

When you are got there, you'll find on this hand a descent, make a careful step down there. After that you'll see a little chapel on the left hand, and hard by, a little narrow lane . . .

DEMEA. Whereabouts is that?

SYRUS. 'Tis where the great wild fig-tree stands—do ye know it, Sir?

DEMEA. I do.

SYRUS. Keep directly through that lane.

DEMEA. But the lane is no thoroughfare.

SYRUS. Ud's my life, that's true! I see I'm a silly blockhead; I was out. You must come back again to the great portico. Edad, here's a nearer way, and easier to find. Do ye know my Lord Cratinus's great house?

DEMEA. Yes.

SYRUS. When you are past that, turn to the left-hand down the same street, and when you're come to the city gates hard by the horse-pond, there's a certain mill, and right over against that is a joiner's shop, and there you'll find the gentleman.

DEMEA. What business has he there?

SYRUS. To bespeak some little oaken-legged tables to set in the sun . . .

DEMEA. For your worships to drink around! Fine work, i' faith! But why do I not go to him?

Exit DEMEA.

SYRUS, *alone*. Go thy ways for a fool. I'll walk thee off thy stumps, as thou deservest, thou old doting churl . . . But Mr Aeschinus stays a bloody long while; dinner will be quite spoiled. As for Ctesipho, he's wholly taken up with his mistress; but I'll take care of my own sweet body, and pick out all the good bits I can find, drain cup after cup at my leisure, and make the day as long as I can.

Exit SYRUS.

Enter MICIO *and* HEGIO.

MICIO, *entering*. . . . Indeed, Mr Hegio, I can see nothing in what I have said that deserves such mighty commendations. I do nought but fulfil my duty and give satisfaction for the faults of my own house. Perhaps you took me to be one of those men who think they receive an injury when they strike the first blow? Now, because I didn't serve you so, have you any reason to feel obliged to me?

HEGIO. Far be it from me! I never imagined ye to be otherwise than I really find ye; but let me beg you at least to step over at my side to the girl's mother; and tell her the very same thing you told me: namely that their jealousy was ill-grounded, since he took away the music-girl for his brother, not for himself.

MICIO. If you think it convenient and necessary, let's be going.

HEGIO. You do well, Sir! For you'll lighten the heart of the poor creature who's ready to sink with grief and vexation, and you'll keep up the character of a worthy gentleman. But, Sir, if you don't think this a proper request, why, I'll tell her what you said myself.

MICIO. No, no, I'll go with ye!

HEGIO. You oblige me, Sir. For, howsoever it comes about, all who are a little down in the world become very suspicious, take everything for worse than it is, and fancy themselves slighted, because of their misfortunes. Therefore 'twill give them great satisfaction that you clear Mr Aeschinus yourself.

MICIO. You say nothing but what's true and reasonable.

HEGIO. Be pleased, Sir, to come this way.

MICIO. I will.

Exeunt HEGIO *and* MICIO *at the same time.*

Enter AESCHINUS *alone.*

AESCHINUS. I'm quite distracted, being so surprised by this unlucky misfortune, that I know not what to do or undertake! Fear enfeebles my limbs, amazement shakes my soul, and my heart's incapable of advice. Alas! How shall I wind myself out of these difficulties, since their jealousies are seemingly well grounded? Mrs Sostrata believes that I bought the music-girl for myself. Old Canthara gave me

to understand as much. For, by chance I saw her as she
was going to the midwife; I up and asked her how my
dear Pamphila fared, and whether she was near her time;
and was this errand to fetch the midwife? She at once let
fly upon me . . .

In another tone.

'Away, away, Mr Aeschinus! You've befooled us long
enough, cajoled us sufficiently with your fine promises!'
'Alack-a-day,' said I, 'prithee, what dost mean?' 'You may
go now,' continued she, 'and take up with the girl you are
so enamoured of.' I immediately perceived their jealousy;
yet kept my tongue between my teeth, that I might not
blab any of my brother's secrets to that rattling gypsy, to
have it blazed about the town in an instant. . . . But what
shall I do now? Shall I go and admit that the wench is my
brother's—a secret that ought not to be divulged for the
world . . . ? Well! Let that pass, perhaps they may not
discover it. Then I'm afraid they won't accept things as
they are, having so many probabilities to weigh against
me. 'Twas I who took her away, I who paid the money
for her, and I who furnished her with lodgings. I must
own that the blame for all this lies at my own door, for
not telling my father how matters stood between me and
Pamphila—for not begging his consent to take her home and
marry her. We've been in a dead sleep till now, but now,
Aeschinus, rouse thyself! First of all I'll go to them and
clear myself . . . I'll march up to the door straight.

Goes and stops short.

Oh, my heart! How sadly it pants whensoever I knock at
the door!

Goes and knocks.

Soho! 'Tis your friend Aeschinus; somebody open the door
quickly . . . But hah! I can't imagine who is coming out
of there? I'll step to one side.

Enter MICIO.

MICIO, *to* SOSTRATA, *within*. Do as I ordered ye, Mrs Sostrata!
I'll find Aeschinus, and acquaint him how matters are going.
. . . But where's he that knocked at the door?

AESCHINUS, *aside*. 'Sdeath! My father's voice! What can I say or do?

MICIO. Aeschinus!

AESCHINUS, *aside*. What business has he here?

MICIO. Was it you who knocked at the door?

Aside.

He's mute . . . Suppose I should banter with him a little, I believe it wouldn't be amiss, since he never trusted me with his secret . . .

MICIO, *to* AESCHINUS. What, can't you speak?

AESCHINUS. I didn't knock, so far as I recall.

MICO. Indeed! Nay, I wondered what business should bring you hither.

Aside.

He blushes; that's a good enough sign.

AESCHINUS. Good Sir, if I may be so bold, what business had you at that house?

MICIO. None of my own. A friend of mine brought me from the 'Change to be spokesman in a concern of his.

AESCHINUS. What was the concern, Sir?

MICIO. I'll tell ye: in this house dwells an ordinary woman or two—which I suppose you don't know, nay, I'm sure you don't; for they haven't been long in these parts.

AESCHINUS. Well, Sir, and what then?

MICIO. Here's an old woman and her daughter . . .

AESCHINUS. So, Sir?

MICIO. The daughter has buried her father. Now this friend of mine, being the nearest relation, is by law forced to marry her himself.

AESCHINUS, *aside*. Undone!

MICIO, *partly hearing*. What's the matter?

AESCHINUS. Nothing! Very well! . . . Proceed, Sir.

MICIO. You must know he's just now come to take her away with him; for he dwells at Miletus.

AESCHINUS, *concernedly.* How! To take the girl away with him?

MICIO. Yes.

AESCHINUS. What, as far as Miletus, pray, Sir?

MICIO. Ay.

AESCHINUS, *aside.* It stabs me to the heart.

Aloud.

. . . And the women, Sir, what say they to it?

MICIO. What should they say, think ye? Even just nothing. Only the mother pretends that her daughter has a child by another man (I can't say by whom, for she named him not), and that since he was the first comer, she tells the kinsman he must go without her.

AESCHINUS. So, Sir! And wasn't that a sufficient plea?

MICIO. No, indeed.

AESCHINUS. Why so, I beseech thee? Will he take her away in good earnest?

MICIO. Ay, why shouldn't he?

AESCHINUS. Indeed, Sir, this was extremely severe and cruel—if I might take the liberty—I might even say, ungenteelly done.

MICIO. How so?

AESCHINUS. How so! What do ye think will become of the poor young man, her first lover, who, for ought you know, loves her most desperately, when he shall see her ravished before his very eyes, and hurried away from his sight forever? Oh, it was a very dishonourable thing of you, Sir.

MICIO. Why do ye talk at this rate? Whose promise had he, or whose consent? When and how were they married? Pray who's the spark? What made him encroach upon another man's right?

AESCHINUS. Was it fit for a girl of her age to sit cross-legged at home waiting for a kinsman's coming, the Lord knows when? Indeed, dear Father, you ought in justice to have pleaded that, and defended it, too.

MICIO. Very good! Should I have pleaded against my own client? . . . But prithee boy, what's all this to us? Or what have we to do with them? . . . Come, let's be going! How now, boy! Why in tears, though?

AESCHINUS *weeps.*

AESCHINUS. Hear me one word, I beseech ye.

MICIO. Poor boy, I've heard and know all. For, loving thee, I couldn't but be concerned in whatever thou dost.

AESCHINUS. Dear Sir! I'd fain deserve your love as long as you live. This fault grieves me to the soul, and I'm quite ashamed to look you in the face.

MICIO. I believe it sincerely; for I well know thy generous temper; but I'm afraid you don't take good heed to your own concerns. What kind of government dost think thou livest under? Thou hast got a girl with child, whom by law thou oughtest not to have touched, that's a great fault; but though great, 'tis indeed a common failing; others have done it often, and men of repute too. But when that was done, tell me, did you take the least care about it? Or, did you foresee in such a case what should have been done, or how it should have been done? And if thou hadst been ashamed to tell me of it, couldn't I have been told by others? Of this you stood in doubt for ten months together. Thus you have betrayed yourself, the poor young woman, and your own child too, as much as you were able. What! Do ye think that the Gods should do your work for ye while you sleep? Must she be brought to your bed-side as if she were hardly worth the fetching? I wouldn't for the world have thee so miserably careless in other things. . . . Come, don't be cast down, however; thou shalt marry her!

AESCHINUS. How?

MICIO. Don't be cast down, I say.

AESCHINUS. Pray, Sir, are ye in earnest?

MICIO. In earnest? Why not?

AESCHINUS. That I can't tell, unless 'tis because the more passionately I desire to have it so, the more I'm afraid it won't be so.

MICIO. Get thee home and say your prayers, and then send for your wife! Go, get thee gone.

AESCHINUS. What! Send for her at once?

MICIO. Yes, at once.

AESCHINUS. What? At once?

MICIO. At once, or as soon as possible.

AESCHINUS. Let me never see daylight, Sir, if I don't love ye better than my very eyes.

MICIO. Or than your mistress too?

AESCHINUS. Full as well.

MICIO. That's much indeed.

AESCHINUS. But what's become of that Milesian kinsman?

MICIO. He's vanished, been shipped off, and already wrecked by this time. . . . But why don't you go, I say, to your prayers?

AESCHINUS. It would be better for you to do that, Sir; I'm sure your prayers will be heard sooner than mine, since you are the better man of the two.

MICIO. I'll go in, and take care of what's lacking. Do as I bid thee, if thou knowest what's best for thyself.

Exit MICIO.

AESCHINUS, *alone.* What happiness is this! Would anyone think him my father, or me his son? If he had been a friend or a brother, could he have been more obliging? Ought I not to love him, and wear him next my heart? His wonderful kindness has obliged me to be so cautious as to do nothing that may displease him; wherefore I'll now be always upon my guard. . . . But why don't I go in, and hasten my marriage?

Exit AESCHINUS.

Enter DEMEA *alone, out of breath.*

DEMEA. I'm quite foundered with trotting up and down! Plague seize thee, Syrus, for thy damned directions. . . . I've hobbled over the whole town, to the gates, to the horse-pond, and where not? The Devil a joiner's shop could I find, or any soul who had so much as seen my brother.

Going off.

. . . But now I'm resolved I won't stir a step out of his house till he comes back.

Enter MICIO.

MICIO. I'll go and tell them that, for our part, we are ready.

DEMEA. Oh, here he comes! . . . I've been looking for you these two hours.

MICIO. What's the business now?

DEMEA. I've fresh news to tell ye, horrid villainies of that fine son of yours.

MICIO. Look ye, now!

DEMEA. New villainies, damnable villainies!

MICIO. Prithee, no more!

DEMEA. Ah, you don't know what a fine blade he is.

MICIO. But I do.

DEMEA. Poor simpleton! I warrant thou dreamest I have come about the singing-wench. No, the rascal has debauched a citizen's daughter.

MICIO. That I know too.

DEMEA. Bless me! Do ye both know and pardon it?

MICIO. Ay, why shouldn't I?

DEMEA. What! Methinks you ought to bellow and run mad at the news.

MICIO. No; though I could wish it otherwise.

DEMEA. He has got a bastard, too.

MICIO. 'Heaven bless it,' say I!

DEMEA. And the woman's not worth a groat.

MICIO. So they say.

DEMEA. And shall he be married to a beggar?

MICIO. Yea, verily.

DEMEA. Well, and what's to be done next, pray?

MICIO. Why, even what should be done next; have the young woman brought home.

DEMEA. Monstrous! And will you permit it?

MICIO. How can I avoid it?

DEMEA. Avoid it! Why, if you were not really concerned at this disgrace, it would at least become you to seem so.

MICIO. I've given consent already; the business is concluded, the wedding's as good as over, everything is secure, and I think this becomes me even better.

DEMEA. The adventure pleases you wonderfully!

MICIO. It would not, if I knew how to help it. Since I can't, I must bear it patiently. Man's life is like a game at tables; if you miss the throw that you most needed, you must correct by skill what came about by chance.

DEMEA. Your servant, Mr Corrector! Your skill, as you call it, has fooled away fifty guineas upon a music-wench, who in three or four days' time must be packed off, whether or not you can recoup part of the loss.

MICIO. There's nobody to buy her, nor do I design to sell her.

DEMEA. What the deuce will ye do with her, then?

MICIO. Why, keep her at home.

DEMEA. Mercy upon my soul! A whore and a wife under the same roof?

MICIO. Why not, prithee?

DEMEA. And you are sure you aren't mad?

MICIO. Yes, indeed.

DEMEA. Let me die, if ever I saw such folly! I' faith, I believe thou hast a mind to have a merry song with her now and then.

MICIO. Why shouldn't I?

DEMEA. And the bride, won't she learn the same tunes?

MICIO. No doubt of it.

DEMEA. And thou, pretty child, wilt hobble among them out of the hay?

MICIO. Likely enough.

DEMEA. Likely enough, with a pox!

MICIO. And rather than fail, Brother, thou shalt make one of the company.

DEMEA. 'Sdeath! Are you past all shame?

MICIO. Prithee, Brother, throw off this sullen humour of thine, and be free and merry at your son's wedding like a civil person. . . . I'll just go speak a word at that house and then come back again.

Exit MICIO *to* SOSTRATA'S.

DEMEA, *alone.* Here's a sweet life! Here are fine morals! Here's mad work with a vengeance! . . . Let me see, a wife not worth a groat, a music-wench under the same roof, everything running to ruin in the house. A profligate young rogue, and a doating old sot into the bargain. Why, Providence itself, if it should go about it, could never save this family!

End of the Fourth Act

ACT FIVE

SYRUS *and* DEMEA

SYRUS, *to himself.* Faith and truth, my little rogue Sy, thou hast junketed thy pretty self deliciously. Thou hast played thy part sumptuously. Ah, thou dear wag!

Strokes himself.

Since I've stuffed my sweet body with the dainties within, 'tis my pleasure to take a turn in the fresh air.

Walks and struts.

DEMEA. There goes a rare model of their education.

SYRUS. Oh, here's our Old Stingo, i' faith . . . How is it, old gentleman? Why so down in the dumps?

DEMEA. Oh, damned rascal!

SYRUS *belches.* How now, Reverend Wisdom? Are you come to preach more morals here?

DEMEA. Would I were thy master!

SYRUS. Egad, you'd be the richest man under the sun, and your estate would be improved to a miracle.

DEMEA. I'd make an example of thee to all rogues.

SYRUS. Why so? What have I done?

DEMEA. Done, rascal! In the heat of a disturbance, in the midst of a most horrid crime, scarce yet settled, you've got drunk, ye swine, as if all were well and over!

SYRUS, *aside.* Faith, would I had stayed where I was!

Enter DROMO.

DROMO. Do ye hear, Syrus? Mr Ctesipho prays ye to come in.

SYRUS, *softly.* Away, with a pox!

Exit DROMO.

DEMEA. What's that he said of Ctesipho?

SYRUS. Nothing, Sir.

DEMEA. How, ye gaol-bird! Is Ctesipho nested there?

SYRUS. No, Sir; no.

DEMEA. Then how came the boy to name him?

SYRUS. That's another of the name, a young smell-feast; do ye know him?

DEMEA. I will know him presently.

Going off.

SYRUS, *holding him.* What do ye mean, Sir? Whither are ye going?

DEMEA. Pray, let me be.

SYRUS. That I will not, Sir.

DEMEA. Hands off, ye hell-hound; or by Heaven I'll brain ye!

He holds up his cane, and Syrus releases him.

Exit DEMEA *in a fury.*

SYRUS, *alone.* The Devil go with him! I'll be sworn he'll be no welcome reveller to any of them, especially to poor Ctesipho. . . . Zookers! Where shall I bestow myself? . . . While this plaguey story is blowing over, I'll even slink into some corner, and there sleep out this dose of tipple. I think that will be best.

Exit staggering.

Enter MICIO, *as from* SOSTRATA'S.

MICIO, *to* SOSTRATA, *within.* Everything's ready, as I said before. And the wedding shall be when you please.

Coming forward.

But who makes our doors fly open?

Enter DEMEA *from* MICIO'S, *raving in a passion.*

DEMEA, *to himself*. Hell and furies! What shall I do? . . . What will become of me? Heavens, earth, sea! Whither can I direct my complaints?

MICIO, *aside*. Here's a man for ye! He has smelt out the intrigue, and 'tis that makes him bellow so brutishly. . . . Well, then: I may expect a smart brush. But the boys must be helped.

DEMEA. Ah, here comes the bane and ruin of our two sons!

MICIO. Pray, Brother, moderate your passion, and keep cool, if you can.

DEMEA, *controlling his passion*. Nay, I am moderate; I am cool. . . . I'll not give ye an ill word. Let's reason the case calmly. . . . Wasn't it a plain bargain between us (and proposed by your own self, too) that you should have nothing to do with my son, nor I with yours? Answer me directly now.

MICIO. True. I don't deny it.

DEMEA. Why is he guzzling at your house, then? Why do ye entertain my Ctesipho? Why did ye procure him a wench, Brother? Have you not the same reason to deal fairly by me, as I by you? Since I never meddle with your son, methinks you shouldn't with mine.

MICIO. There's no reason to speak so, none at all. The old proverb holds which says: 'Among friends, all things are held in common.'

DEMEA. Very pretty, i' faith! Have you come to that belief at last?

MICIO. Good Brother, listen awhile, unless it be too great a trouble for ye. First of all, if your son's expenses are such a woeful burden to ye, pray remember that formerly you maintained both sons according as your estate would bear it, and thought it would suffice for the pair of them considering that I was likely enough to marry and have sons of my own. Why, then follow that old course still: hoard, scrape, pinch, do all you can to increase their fortunes, and take all the credit for it yourself. But at least let the poor rogues make use of my purse freely, since that is over and

above their allowance from you. It won't diminish one fur-
row of your land, and what they get from me you may
look upon as clear gain. Now, Brother, if you would weigh
all this impartially, you'd save me, yourself, and the poor
boys a world of trouble.

DEMEA. I don't talk of their money; it is their morals.

MICIO. Hold, I understand ye! That's the point to which my
discourse leads. Many observations may be made, Brother,
upon two persons doing the same thing; from which we
may conclude that this thing may be the ruin of the one,
but no great hurt to the other. There's no difference in
the thing itself, but only in the persons that do it. Truly
I'm confident, by what I observe of the boys, that they'll
satisfy our hearts' desire. I find they have wit, discretion,
and modesty enough, upon occasion. And they love each
other so entirely that 'tis easy to perceive their generous
nature and spirit. You may reclaim them when you please.
But perhaps you fear they won't prove good enough husbands? Ah, Brother, age has always this ill effect that, as
it makes us wiser, so it makes us more worldly. And age as
it steals upon them, will presently incite them to be good
citizens and husbands.

DEMEA. Have a care, Brother, that your fine reasonings and
gentle nature don't ruin us all!

MICIO. Peace, never fear that! Leave off this discourse, and
be ruled by me today. . . . Come, compose your countenance. Smile upon me!

DEMEA, *more pleasantly.* Well, since the case requires it, I
must do so; but tomorrow I'll take my son into the country
by break of day.

MICIO. At midnight, if you please, if you consent to be merry
today.

DEMEA. And I'll take that singing-wench along with me, too.

MICIO. Best of all! For thus you'll keep your son from rambling. Only take care that she don't give ye the slip.

DEMEA. I'll warrant ye. . . . And between the oven and the
mill, I'll besmear her with cinders, smoke, and flour. In

the heat of the day, too, I'll send her to rake up stubble, until she be burned black as a coal.

MICIO. That's excellent! Now, methinks you have some prudence in ye. And while she's in this cursed pickle, make your son lie with her whether she likes it or not.

DEMEA. Do ye banter me? Well, you are a happy man if you can bear all these troubles so well. For my part, I must . . .

MICIO, *interrupting.* What? Always in the same strain?

DEMEA. I have done, I have done.

MICIO. Pray walk in then, and since the day's designed for mirth, let's spend it merrily.

Exit MICIO.

DEMEA, *alone.* Never did man reckon up the business of his life so exactly, but that years of experience still brought in new particulars that he had overlooked, and showed his ignorance of what he thought he knew, and made him reject his former opinions. This is plainly my case at present; and since the sands are almost run out in my hourglass, I shall renounce this rigid life I have always led. But why so? Because I have learned at last that there's nothing like gentleness and good nature—a truth which appears plainly to all who know me and my brother. He always spent his time in ease and pleasure; always courteous, complaisant, speaking ill of no man, but caressing all, living as he pleased, spending as he thought fit. The world blesses him and loves him, too. But I, this rustic, rigid, morose, pinching, brutish, griping fellow, must needs marry; and how have I smarted for my folly! I begot children, and these were new troubles. And truly, I've worn out my life and best days in increasing their fortunes. And now that I'm just marching off the stage, the fruit of all my labour is that I am hated like a toad. Whereas my brother enjoys all the pleasures of a father, without any of the drudgery. They esteem him, and flee from me as from the plague. Him they trust with their secrets, dote upon him, live with him; me they slight. They both pray for his life, long for my death. These two lads whom I have brought up with the greatest labour, he has won over at little cost to him-

self. Thus I take all the pains, but he reaps all the pleasure.
. . . Well, well, since my brother urges me to it, for once
I'll try what can be done, whether I can speak generously
and act the gentleman. I'd willingly have my children love
and respect me, too; therefore, if gifts and compliments
effect the same, I'll not lag behind. And if my estate go
to wrack; what care I for that? I've one foot in the grave
already.

Enter SYRUS.

SYRUS. Do ye hear, Sir, my master desires that you won't
keep away.

DEMEA. Who calls there? . . . Honest Syrus, I'm glad to see
thee. How is it? How goes the world?

SYRUS, *yawning.* Very well, Sir.

DEMEA, *aside.* Excellent! This is the first time I have ever
used such expressions. 'Honest Syrus, how is it? How goes
the world?' They came out plaguily against the grain,
though . . .

To SYRUS.

Thou hast shown thyself an admirable servant, and I will
do thee a good turn with all my soul; i' faith, I will.

SYRUS. I'm very much obliged to you, Sir.

DEMEA. I'fack boy, 'tis true; and thou shalt find it so before
long.

Enter GETA, *at another part of the stage.*

GETA, *to* SOSTRATA, *within.* I'll go find them, Madam, and
see that they make haste to carry over my young mistress . . .

Coming from the door.

Oh, here's Mr Demea! Your humble servant, Sir.

DEMEA. Prithee, lad, how may I call thee?

GETA. Geta, Sir.

DEMEA. Honest Geta, why, I consider thee to be worth thy
weight in gold. I'd never desire to be better satisfied in a
servant, than that he should be as trusty to his master as
I have found thee to be, Geta. For that reason, should it

ever fall in my power, I'll do thee a good turn with all my soul, i'fack I will . . .

Aside.

I'm acting Sir Courtly, and I do it rarely, methinks.

GETA. That's more your goodness than my deserts.

DEMEA, *aside.* I shall do it by degrees. First of all I'll win these scoundrels over to me.

AESCHINUS, *entering, to himself.* These delays kill me! That they should trifle away the time with such formal ceremonies and long preparations for the wedding.

DEMEA. Aeschinus, boy, how wags the world?

AESCHINUS. Hah! Are you here, my dear father?

DEMEA. Ah, i' faith, boy, I am thy father both by inclination and by nature too, and value thee more than my eyes. . . . But why dost thou not send for thy sweet lady?

AESCHINUS. I desire nothing more; I only wait for the musicians and singing-men and torch-bearers.

DEMEA. Ho, wilt thou take an old fellow's counsel for once?

AESCHINUS. Let's hear it pray, Sir.

DEMEA. Hang your singing-men, your hubbubs, your flambeaux and fiddle-scrapers! Order the great stone wall in the garden to be pulled down immediately, and bring her home that way. Run both houses into one; fetch over the mother and her whole family to yours.

AESCHINUS. With all my heart. You are the pleasantest father in the world.

DEMEA, *aside.* Hey, this is brave! I'm called pleasant now. My brother's house will be a thoroughfare within the hour, the whole town will troop in! There'll be a great hole burned in his purse! But what's that to me if by my complaisance I can please all.

Aloud to AESCHINUS.

Go bid Babylo count out fifty guineas, quick. . . . But Syrus, why don't you do as you are bid?

SYRUS. What, Sir?

DEMEA. Break down the wall! . . . And you, Geta, pray go and fetch them hither.

GETA. Ay, God bless your worship for being so kind to our poor family.

Exeunt GETA *and* SYRUS.

DEMEA. 'Tis no less than you deserve. . . . What sayest thou boy, hah!

AESCHINUS. I'm of your opinion, Sir.

DEMEA. 'Tis forty times better than bringing a woman in her condition along the streets.

AESCHINUS. Indeed, Sir, I know nothing to better it.

DEMEA. This is my way . . . But here comes my brother!

MICIO, *to* SYRUS, *within*. My brother ordered it, say ye! Where is he? . . . Hah, Brother, was it you who ordered this?

DEMEA. Yes, that I did! And in this and all things else I'm ready to do whatever may conduce to the uniting, serving, helping, and the joining together of both families.

AESCHINUS, *to* MICIO. Pray, Sir, let it be so!

MICIO. Well, I've nothing to say against it.

DEMEA. Truth, 'tis no more than we are obliged to do. For first, she's your son's mother-in-law . . .

MICIO. What then?

DEMEA. A very virtuous and modest woman . . .

MICIO. So they say indeed.

DEMEA. Not weighed down by years . . .

MICIO. Not yet.

DEMEA. But past child-bearing: a lonesome woman whom nobody esteems . . .

MICIO, *aside*. What the Devil is he at?

DEMEA. . . . Therefore you ought to marry her; and you Aeschinus, should do what you can to bring this about.

MICIO. Who? I marry?

DEMEA. Yes, you.

MICIO. I, prithee?

DEMEA. Yes, you I say.

MICIO. Pho, you are fooling us, surely?

DEMEA, *to* AESCHINUS. If thou hast any life in thee, persuade him to it.

AESCHINUS. Dear Father . . .

MICIO, *interrupting.* Blockhead! Dost thou take in earnest what he says?

DEMEA. 'Tis in vain to refuse; it can't be avoided.

MICIO. Pho, you are in your dotage!

AESCHINUS. Good Sir, let me win this one favour.

MICIO, *angrily.* Art out of thy wits, let me alone!

DEMEA. Come, come! Hearken for once to what your son says.

MICIO. Haven't ye played the fool enough yet? Shall I at threescore and five marry an old woman who's ready to drop into the grave? This is your wise counsel, is it?

AESCHINUS. Pray, Sir, do; I've promised you shall.

MICIO. You promised, with a mischief! Promise for thyself, thou chit!

DEMEA. Fie, fie! What if he had begged a greater favour from you?

MICIO. As if there were any greater favour than this!

DEMEA. Pray grant his request.

AESCHINUS. Good Sir, be not so hard-hearted.

DEMEA. Pho, promise him for once!

MICIO. Will ye never leave baiting me?

AESCHINUS. Not till I've prevailed, Sir.

MICIO. Truth, this is downright forcing a man.

DEMEA. Come, Micio, be good-natured and consent.

MICIO. Though this be the most damned, foolish, ridiculous whim, and the most averse to my nature that could possibly be, yet since you are so extremely set upon it, I'll humour ye for once.

AESCHINUS. That is excellent; I'm obliged to ye beyond measure.

DEMEA, *aside.* Well, what's next? . . . What shall I say next? This is as I'd have it. . . . What's more to be done?

To MICIO.

Ho! There's Hegio our poor kinsman, and nearest relation; in truth, we ought in conscience to do something for him.

MICIO. What, pray?

DEMEA. There's a small plot of land in the suburbs, which you farm out—pray let's give him that to live on.

MICIO. A small one, say ye?

DEMEA. Though it were a great one, you might yet give it to him. He has been as good as a father to Pamphila; he's a very honest man, our kinsman, and you couldn't bestow it better. Besides, Brother, there's a certain proverb (none of my own, I assure you) which you so well and wisely made use of: 'That age has always this ill effect of making us more worldly, as well as wiser.' We should do well to avoid this scandal. 'Tis a true proverb, Brother, and ought to be held in mind.

MICIO. What's all this? . . . Well, so let it be, if he has need of it.

AESCHINUS. Brave Father, I vow!

DEMEA. Now you are my true brother, both in body and soul.

MICIO. I'm glad of it.

DEMEA, *aside, laughing.* I've stabbed him with his own weapons, i'fack!

Enter SYRUS, *with a pick-axe upon his shoulders.*

SYRUS, *to* DEMEA. The job is done as ye ordered, Sir.

DEMEA. Thou art an honest lad. . . . And upon my conscience I think Syrus deserves his freedom.

MICIO. He, his freedom? For what exploit?

DEMEA. O, for a thousand.

SYRUS. O dear Mr Demea, you are a rare gentleman, edad you are! You know I've looked after the young gentlemen from their cradles. I taught them, advised them, and instructed them all I possibly could.

DEMEA. Nothing more evident! Nay, more than that, he catered for them, pimped for them, and in the morning took care of a debauchee for them. These are no ordinary accomplishments, I can assure ye.

SYRUS. Your worship's very merry.

DEMEA. Besides, he was prime mover in buying this music-girl. It was he who managed the whole intrigue, and 'tis no more than justice to reward him, as an encouragement to others! In short, Aeschinus desires the same thing.

MICIO, *to* AESCHINUS. Do you desire it too?

AESCHINUS. Yes, if you please, Sir.

MICIO. Since 'tis so, come hither, Syrus! Thou art a free man.

SYRUS *kneels down,* MICIO *lays his hand on his head, and after that gives him a cuff on the ear.*

SYRUS, *rising up.* Generously done! A thousand thanks to ye all, and to you, Mr Demea.

DEMEA. I'm well satisfied.

AESCHINUS. And I too.

SYRUS. I won't question it, Sir. But I wish heartily my joy were more complete, that my poor spouse Phrygia might be made as free as I am.

DEMEA. Truth, she's a mighty good woman.

SYRUS. And your grandson's first foster-mother, too.

DEMEA. Faith, in good earnest, if for that, she deserves her freedom before any woman in the world.

MICIO. What! For that simple service?

DEMEA. Yes, indeed! In fine, I'll pay for her freedom myself.

SYRUS. God's blessing light upon your worship, and grant all your wishes.

MICIO. Syrus, thou hast made a good day's work of it.

DEMEA. Besides, Brother, it would be a deed of charity to lend him a little money to set up in business that he may face the world without fear. I undertake that he'll soon repay it.

MICIO. Not a penny-piece!

AESCHINUS. He's a very honest fellow, Sir.

SYRUS. Upon my word, I'll repay you the loan. Do but trust me!

AESCHINUS. Pray do, Sir.

MICIO. I'll consider the matter with care.

DEMEA. He shall pay ye, I'll see to that.

SYRUS, *to* DEMEA. Egad, you're the best man alive.

AESCHINUS. And the pleasantest in the world.

MICIO. What's the meaning of this, Brother? How comes this sudden change of humour? Why this gallant squandering and profusion?

DEMEA. I'll tell ye, Brother. These sons of yours don't reckon you a sweet-natured and pleasant man because you live as you should and do what is just and reasonable, but because you fawn upon them, cocker them up, and give them what they'll spend. Now, son Aeschinus, if you are dissatisfied with my course of life, because I wouldn't indulge you in all things, right or wrong, then I'll not trouble my head with you any further. Be free to squander, buy mistresses, and do what you will! But if you wish me to advise ye, and set ye up, and help ye too in matters of which your youth can give ye but little understanding—matters of which you are over-fond, and don't well consider—see, here I'm ready to stand by you.

AESCHINUS. Dear Sir, we commit ourselves wholly to your charge; for you know what's fitting to be done far better than we . . . But what will ye do for my brother Ctesipho?

DEMEA. Why, let him take the music-girl; and so bid adieu to general wenching.

AESCHINUS. That's very reasonable.

To the spectators.

Gentlemen, your favour!

Exeunt all.

End of THE BROTHERS

ANCHOR BOOKS

DOLPHIN BOOKS AND DOLPHIN MASTERS

The bold face M indicates a Dolphin Master. Dolphin Masters are Dolphin Books in the editions of greatest importance to the teacher and student. In selecting the Dolphin Masters, the editors have taken particular pains to choose copies of the most significant edition (usually the first) by obtaining original books or their facsimiles or by having reproductions made of library copies of particularly rare editions. Facsimiles of original title pages and other appropriate material from the first edition are included in many Masters.

FICTION

POETRY AND DRAMA

HISTORY AND BIOGRAPHY

PHILOSOPHY AND RELIGION

ESSAYS AND LETTERS

MYSTERY